1,001 Questions & Answers

For the SAT

Dr. Nancy L. Nolan

* The SAT is a registered trademark of the College Board, which was not involved in the production of (and does not endorse) this publication.

Electronic, paperback and CD-ROM versions published by:

Magnificent Milestones, Inc.
www.ivyleagueadmission.com

ISBN 978-1-933819-563

Disclaimers:

(1) This book was written as a guide; it does not claim to be the definitive word on SAT™ preparation. The opinions expressed are the personal observations of the author based on her own experiences. They are not intended to prejudice any party. Accordingly, the author and publisher do not accept any liability or responsibility for any loss or damage that have been caused, or allegedly caused, through the use of information in this book.

(2) The SAT is a joint collaboration between Educational Testing Services (ETS) and the College Board, two non-profit groups that sponsor the test and decide how it will be constructed, administered and used. Neither Dr. Nolan nor Magnificent Milestones, Inc. is affiliated with ETS or the College Board.

(3) Admission to college depends on several factors in addition to a candidate's SAT™ scores (including GPA, recommendations, interview and essays). The author and publisher cannot guarantee that any applicant will be admitted to any specific school or program if (s)he follows the information in this book.

Dedication

For students everywhere;
may the size of your dreams be exceeded only
by your tenacity to attain them.

Acknowledgements

I am deeply indebted to the students, professors, counselors and admissions officers who have shared their perceptions and frustrations about the SAT™. This book, which was written on your behalf, would not be nearly as powerful without your generous and insightful input.

I also want to thank my colleagues at www.ivyleagueadmission.com for providing a constant source of support, along with the best editorial help in the business.

1,001 QUESTIONS & ANSWERS FOR THE SAT

1,001 QUESTIONS & ANSWERS

FOR THE SAT

Chapter 1: Guerrilla Preparation for the SAT

To achieve a top score on the SAT, students should follow a three-step plan:

1. Learn the concepts that are on the test
2. Learn the tips, traps and strategies of the test writers
3. Learn to work faster and smarter by taking timed practice tests

We address Steps 1 and 2 in our companion publication, *Guerrilla Tactics for the SAT: Secrets and Strategies the Test Writers Don't Want You to Know.* From our experience, no one should take the SAT without mastering these techniques, which can make the difference between a great score and a mediocre one.

This publication addresses Step 3, which is to build your confidence, speed, and test-taking strategies by taking mock exams under actual testing conditions. From our experience, working with sample questions isn't enough; you need to attack the questions *exactly* as they are presented on the SAT.

By design, we have organized 1,001 SAT questions in the identical format you will see on the exam:

1. Critical Reading: The SAT presents 48 questions on Passage-Based Reading and 19 Sentence Correction questions in three sections (67 total questions in 70 minutes):

> *Two 25-minute sections; 24 questions*
> *One 20-minute section; 19 questions*

2. Writing: the SAT presents 25 Sentence Improvement Questions, 18 Sentence Error Identification questions, 6 Paragraph Improvement Questions and one original essay in three sections (49 total questions and one essay in 60 minutes).

> *One 25-minute section; 35 questions*
> *One 10-minute section; 14 questions*
> *One 25-minute section: essay*

3. Quantitative: the SAT presents 44 Multiple Choice Problems and 10 Student-Produced Responses (Grid-Ins) in three sections (54 questions in 70 minutes)

> *One 25-minute section; 20 questions*
> *One 25-minute section; 18 questions*
> *One 20-minutes section; 16 questions*

Let's be honest; the content of the SAT isn't particularly difficult. With unlimited time, many students could attain a top score on the exam. The biggest challenge is working at a fast enough pace to:

1. answer as many "easy" questions as possible
2. leave the hardest ones until the end
3. formulate an intelligent guessing strategy

From our experience, there is no way to accomplish these goals without working through hundreds of practice questions under actual testing conditions. Ultimately, it isn't only a matter of timing; it's developing a plan to maximize your own strengths on each section of the exam.

And that's the aspect of test preparation that few "experts" acknowledge; one size does NOT fit all. *No two students have the same strengths and weaknesses, which means that no two preparation plans will be the same.* Ultimately, it's up to YOU to identify the areas in which you need work, and to focus your time accordingly. The 1,001 questions and answers in this publication are a great start.

Use the information in whatever way makes sense to YOU. If you want to assess the level of difficulty of the math questions, use a few of the Quantitative sections as a general review of the math topics on the SAT. Check out the typical vocabulary words that show up in the reading passages and the sentence completion questions. Note the grammar and word choice errors that are tested over and over again on the exam. Don't stop until you have them down cold.

Then, before the day of the test, complete several sections under timed conditions. Give yourself a few minutes at the end of each section; on the paper version of the SAT, you will need this time to transfer your answers to your grid. Make sure that you can work hard enough, smart enough, and fast enough to earn the score you desire.

As you scroll through the practice sections, you may notice that we have included a disproportionate number of quantitative questions. Why? Because the SAT tests more than 20 different math concepts; they also increase the level of difficulty by presenting simple concepts as word problems, which require significant experience to master. In contrast, the reading and writing sections will test significantly fewer concepts, which require a smaller number of sample questions.

Finally, if you discover that you need additional help to prepare for the SAT, we are proud to offer the following publications:

1. *Guerrilla Tactics for the SAT: Secrets and Strategies the Test Writers Don't Want You to Know* presents the underlying math and grammar concepts that are tested, along with the tricky ways the test writers will try to confuse you.

2. For students who need additional practice for the quantitative section of the exam, *Math Word Problems for the SAT: When Plugging Numbers into Formulas Just Isn't Enough* offers a complete review of the thirty types of word problems you are likely to see. Learn how to answer these questions quickly and accurately on the day of the test.

3. Finally, for students who are comfortable with the concepts on the SAT and **really** want to challenge themselves before the big day, we are delighted to offer *The Toughest SAT Practice Test We've Ever Seen*. Use this publication – and complete the mock exam - AFTER you have completed your preparation program. See how your performance compares to those of other highly competitive students. For an exam this important, why leave your preparation to chance?

Chapter 2: 1,001 Sample Questions for the SAT

1. **Critical Reading**: The 13 Critical Reading sections are labeled Read 1 – Read 13 (their corresponding answer keys are labeled RC1 – RC13). The sections are identical to the way they are presented on the SAT:

    25-minute sections; 24 questions
    20-minute sections; 19 questions

2. **Quantitative:** The 30 Quantitative sections are labeled Quant 1 – Quant 30 (their corresponding answer keys are labeled QA1 – QA30). The sections are identical to the way they are presented on the SAT:

    25-minute sections; 20 questions
    25-minute sections; 18 questions
    20-minutes sections; 16 questions

3. **Writing:** The 7 Writing sections are labeled Writing 1 – Writing 7 (their corresponding answer keys are labeled WA1 – WA7). The sections are identical to the way they are presented on the SAT:

    25-minute sections; 35 questions
    10-minute sections; 14 questions

Use these practice questions to:

- analyze your strengths
- overcome your deficiencies
- master the tricks and traps of each section of the exam

Bottom-line: At most competitive colleges, your chances for admission are directly related to your score on the SAT. Get the result (and future) that you deserve!

Reading Comprehension 1: 25 minutes 24 questions

Directions: For each question in this section, select the best answer from the choices given and fill in the corresponding circle on the answer sheet.

1. When she realized the _____ of her mistake, Janet became humble and apologetic.

    a. insouciance
    b. gravure
    c. reticence
    d. enormity
    e. prudence

2. Claire had a tendency to be _____ with her friends, always loaning them money and buying them expensive gifts.

    a. parsimonious
    b. cogent
    c. munificent
    d. capricious
    e. mendicant

3. Mary's _____ attitude at work was particularly impressive, considering her recent painful injury.

    a. nascent
    b. assiduous
    c. indolent
    d. ethereal
    e. timorous

4. When the FBI investigated the fraud at Enron, they made a startling discovery; some of the formulas to over-inflate earnings required such _____ strategies that only the most _____ agents could decipher them.

    a. onerous…nefarious
    b. extraneous…. decorous
    c. intricate…adroit
    d. amorphous…calumniate
    e. anachronistic…extrapolate

5. Only an authority in mathematics could _____ the _____ subject matter that the Nobel Prize winner discussed.

    a. attenuate….esoteric
    b. portent….intricate
    c. condone….ambiguous
    d. reproduce….heretical
    e. debunk….fabricated

6. Although the communes of the 1960 were devoted to positive values, such as sharing and simplicity, their residents gained a reputation for being rebellious and _____.

    a. banal
    b. pedantic
    c. caustic
    d. hedonistic
    e. rudimentary

7. Despite the disapproval from the crowd, the speaker argued _____ on behalf of his cause.

   a. hypocritically
   b. ingenuously
   c. facetiously
   d. vehemently
   e. irreverently

8. Only a _____ could have anticipated the unusual combination of life-changing events that occurred that fateful day.

   a. engineer
   b. humanitarian
   c. clairvoyant
   d. philanthropist
   e. statistician

9. Liz attributed her strong sense of _____ to her parents, who encouraged her to give back to the community.

   a. spirituality
   b. perspective
   c. complacency
   d. decadence
   e. generosity

10. Brandon was a _____ writer whose works include twenty novels, four textbooks and _____ newspaper and magazine articles.

   a. prosperous - sage
   b. natural - spirited
   c. technical - sardonic
   d. verbose – opinionated
   e. prolific – numerous

11. In her ninth month of pregnancy, Rita ate large quantities of food to _____ her appetite.

   a. dissipate
   b. mitigate
   c. satisfy
   d. solicit
   e. masticate

12. Although she led a(n) _____ life, Sally had a(n) _____ understanding of the world.

   a. urbane - minimal
   b. repetitive - tantalizing
   c. sheltered - unblemished
   d. isolated - simple
   e. prodigious – courageous

13. The best plans are _____ in their simplicity.

    a.   erratic
    b.   coveted
    c.   embellished
    d.   elegant
    e.   authoritative

Directions: *The passages below are followed by questions based on their content; questions following a pair of related passages may also be based on the relationship between the paired passages. Answer the questions, based on what is* <u>stated</u> *or* <u>implied</u> *in the passage and any introductory material that may be provided.*

Passage 1

On a theoretical basis, fruits and vegetables are considered to be kindling foods, which supply certain mineral elements that are not present in sufficient proportions in the coal foods, such as meats, starches, and fats. Furthermore, the product of fruit and vegetable digestion and burning in the body helps to neutralize the waste products from meats, starches, and fats. Thirdly, fruits and vegetables have a overwhelmingly beneficial effect upon the blood, the kidneys, and the skin. In fact, their reputation for "purifying the blood" and "clearing the complexion" is really well deserved. The keenness of our liking for fruit at all times, and our special longing for greens and sour foods in the spring, after their scarcity in our diet all winter, is a true sign of their wholesomeness.

9

Not the least of their advantages is that fruits and vegetables contain a large proportion of water; and this, though diminishing their fuel value, supplies the body with a naturally filtered and often distilled supply of this necessary element of life. One of the best ways to avoid that burning summer thirst, which leads you to flood your unfortunate stomach with melted icebergs, in the form of ice water, ice cold lemonade, or soda water, is to take an abundance of fresh fruits and green vegetables.

15

Many vegetables contain small amounts of starch, but few of them enough to count upon as fuel, except potatoes, which must rightfully be classified with the coal foods. Most fruits contain a certain amount of sugar-- how much can usually be estimated from their taste, and how little can be gathered from the statement that even the sweetest of fruits, like ripe pears or ripe peaches, contain only about eight per cent sugar. They are all chiefly useful as flavors for the less interesting staple foods, particularly the starches. In fact, our instinctive use of them to help down bread and butter, or rice, or puddings of various sorts, is a natural and proper one. Like vegetables, fruits also contain various salts which are useful in neutralizing certain acid substances formed in the body.

24

Soldiers in war, or sailors upon long voyages, who are fed a diet consisting chiefly of salted or preserved meat, with bread or hard biscuit and sugar, but without either fruits or fresh vegetables, are likely to develop a disease called scurvy. Little more than a century ago, hundreds of deaths occurred every year in the British and French navies from this disease, and the crews of many a long exploring voyage--like Captain Cook's—or of searchers for the North Pole, have been completely disabled or even destroyed entirely by scurvy. It was discovered that by adding to the diet fruit, or fresh vegetables like cabbage or potatoes, scurvy could be entirely prevented, or cured.

32

But how much real fuel value do fruits and vegetables have? In order to get the nourishment contained in a pound loaf of bread, or a pound of roast beef, you would have to eat: twelve large apples or pears, four and one-half quarts of strawberries; a dozen bananas, seven pounds of onions; two dozen large cucumbers; ten pounds of cabbage; or one-half bushel of celery. Notwithstanding their slight fuel value, there are few more valuable and wholesome elements in the diet than an abundant supply of fresh fruits and green vegetables. If at all possible, all people should have a garden, if only the tiniest patch, and grow them for their own use, both because of their wholesomeness and freshness when so grown, and because of the valuable exercise in the open air, and the enjoyment and interest afforded by their care.

41

14. What is the main point of the passage?

    a.   To explain the fuel value of fruits and vegetables
    b.   To discuss the nutritional value and health benefits of fruits and vegetables
    c.   To compare the nutritional value of kindling foods to coal foods
    d.   To explain the cause and prevention of scurvy
    e.   To explain the nutritional deficiencies of fruits and vegetables

15. In Line 3, what does "*neutralize*" mean?

   a. Incite
   b. Deodorize
   c. Defuse
   d. Accelerate
   e. Putrefy

16. According to the author, all of the following are coal foods EXCEPT:

   a. Potatoes
   b. Meats
   c. Starches
   d. Kale
   e. Fats

17. According to the author, which of the following is NOT a health benefit of fruits and vegetables?

   a. They improve human vision
   b. They improve the complexion
   c. They purify the blood
   d. They supply water to the body
   e. They supply mineral elements

18. According to the author, what is the chief use of fruits?

   a. They sweeten food without adding a significant amount of sugar
   b. They provide an inexpensive source of protein, compared to meats, starches, and fats
   c. They neutralize acids in the body
   d. They enhance the complexion because they are low in fat
   e. They flavor less interesting foods, such as starches

19. According to the author, all of the following will help to prevent scurvy EXCEPT:

   a. Potatoes
   b. Cabbage
   c. Tallow
   d. Pears
   e. Celery

20. From the passage, we can infer that the author.....

   a. Believes that fruits and vegetables provide too little food value to justify their cost
   b. Believes that kindling foods are inferior to coal foods
   c. Is enthusiastic about the importance of fruits and vegetables in the human diet
   d. Believes that pesticide use destroys the benefits of fruits and vegetables
   e. Believes that a vegan diet is far superior to one that includes meats, starches, and fats

Passage 2

In 19th century England, the terms flotsam and jetsam carried important legal distinctions. According to English common law, flotsam defined the cargo or parts of a wrecked ship that float on the sea. In contrast, jetsam referred to goods that were intentionally thrown overboard, either to lighten the ship or to keep them from perishing if the ship went under.

5

Any material that was dragged ashore above the high water line was considered jetsam. By law, the owner of the ship was allowed to keep it. In contrast, all cargo found on the shore belonged to the Crown, as did the

13

abandoned wreckage at the bottom of the sea. The personal effects of the crew could be either flotsam or jetsam, depending on whether it floated and how far it traveled.

10

21. What is the objective of this passage?

    a. to document the Crown's authority over the high seas
    b. to explain the difference between flotsam and jetsam
    c. to document international rules regarding shipwrecks
    d. to establish the rule of law in 19th century England
    e. to explain the Crown's ownership rights to sunken treasure

22. According to the author, what entity had the authority to define flotsam and jetsam?

    a. the British Parliament
    b. the Geneva Convention
    c. English common law
    d. the United States government
    e. the Queen of England

23. Which of the following would NOT be considered flotsam?

    a. floating debris that was not thrown overboard
    b. floating parts of the ship
    c. floating cargo
    d. wreckage on the ocean floor
    e. material dragged ashore below the high water line

24. According to the author, the Crown would be allowed to keep which of the following items?

    a. Cargo on the shore
    b. Wreckage abandoned on the bottom of the sea
    c. Material that was dragged ashore above the high water line
    d. a and b
    e. a, b and c

25. In what publication was this passage most likely published?

    a. a memoir by John F. Kennedy
    b. an Army training manual
    c. a textbook on British maritime law
    d. a collection of short stories
    e. an entomology journal

STOP

The answers to these questions are presented in Section RC1 (page 225)

Reading Comprehension 2:   20 minutes   19 questions

Directions: For each question in this section, select the best answer from the choices given and fill in the corresponding circle on the answer sheet.

1. Although Greg is a wealthy man, he is notorious for his _____ ways.

     a.   parsimonious
     b.   influential
     c.   pragmatic
     d.   savvy
     e.   indolent

2. Josh tended to be argumentative in class; moreover, his condescending tone tended to _____ his classmates.

     a.   amplify
     b.   reciprocate
     c.   intoxicate
     d.   placate
     e.   alienate

3. Despite Victoria's ebullience in the classroom, she was often _____ in social situations.

     a.   melancholy
     b.   condescending
     c.   scintillating
     d.   innovative
     e.   philosophical

4. The _____ passengers wondered if the pilot could handle the _____ turbulence.

     a.   weary - teeming
     b.   apprehensive - unexpected
     c.   angry - copious
     d.   frantic - flagrant
     e.   belligerent – daunting

5. When the rumors of impropriety began to circulate, only the Governor's most _____ friends continued to defend him.

     a.   felonious
     b.   judicious
     c.   steadfast
     d.   gracious
     e.   effusive

6. When Jill was diagnosed with mononucleosis, she was _____ by her fearful classmates.

     a.   critiqued
     b.   celebrated
     c.   aggrandized
     d.   ostracized
     e.   exhausted

7. Their _____ meetings in the middle of the night made their spouses justifiably _____.

    a. persistent - exhausted
    b. professional - hostile
    c. insignificant - bewildered
    d. clandestine - suspicious
    e. innocuous – dubious

8. A _____ student is far more likely to be admitted to a top college than one who is _____.

    a. flamboyant – self-deprecating
    b. fortuitous - stalwart
    c. successful - deliberate
    d. diligent - mediocre
    e. zealous – duplicitous

9. Damian demonstrated great _____ when he left the security of his homeland in search of a better life.

    a. discretion
    b. wanderlust
    c. courage
    d. volatility
    e. repression

Directions: *The passages below are followed by questions based on its content. Answer the questions, based on what is* stated *or* implied *in the passage and any introductory material that may be provided.*

Passage 1

About five miles from Warwick are the ruins of Kenilworth Castle, the magnificent home of the Earl of Leicester. Geoffrey de Clinton, in the reign of Henry I, built a strong castle and founded a monastery here. It was afterwards the castle of Simon de Montfort, and his son was besieged in it for several months, ultimately surrendering, when the king bestowed it upon his youngest son, Edward, Earl of Lancaster and Leicester. Edward II, when taken prisoner in Wales, was brought to Kenilworth, and signed his abdication in the castle, being afterwards murdered in Berkeley Castle. Then it came to John of Gaunt, and in the Wars of the Roses was alternately held by the partisans of each side. Finally, Queen Elizabeth bestowed it upon her ambitious favorite, Dudley, Earl of Leicester, who made splendid additions to the buildings.

8

It was here that Leicester gave magnificent entertainment to Queen Elizabeth, including a series of pageants that lasted seventeen days and cost $5000 a day--a very large sum for those times. The queen was attended by thirty-one barons and a host of retainers, and four hundred servants, who were all lodged in the fortress. The attendants were clothed in velvet, and the party drank sixteen hogsheads of wine and forty hogsheads of beer every day, while to feed them ten oxen were killed every morning. There was a succession of plays and amusements provided, including the Coventry play of "Hock Tuesday" and the "Country Bridal," with bull-and-bear-baiting, of which the queen was very fond. The display and hospitality of the Earl of Leicester were intended to pave the way to marriage, but the wily queen was not to be thus entrapped.

17

The castle is now part of the Earl of Clarendon's estate, and he has taken great pains to preserve the famous ruins. The great hall, ninety feet long, still retains several of its Gothic windows, and some of the towers rise seventy feet high. These ivy-mantled ruins stand upon an elevated rocky site commanding a fine prospect, and their chief present use is as a picnic-ground for tourists. Not far away are the ruins of the priory, which was founded at the same time as the castle. A dismantled gate-house with some rather extensive foundations are all that remain. In a little church near by the matins and the curfew are still tolled, one of the bells used having belonged to the priory.

24

Few English ruins have more romance attached to them than those of Kenilworth, for the graphic pen of the best story-teller of Britain has interwoven them into one of his best romances, and has thus given an idea of the splendors as well as the dark deeds of the Elizabethan era that will exist as long as the language endures.

28

10. What is the main point of the passage?

   a. To discuss the romantic significance of the English ruins
   b. To discuss the ownership and use of Kenilworth Castle from ancient times until modern day
   c. To discuss Queen Elizabeth's romance with the Earl of Leicester at Kenilworth Castle
   d. To explain the Earl of Clarendon's efforts to restore Kenilworth Castle to its original beauty
   e. To document the architectural genius of Geoffrey de Clinton

11. The passage mentions all of the following about Edward II EXCEPT:

   a. Taken prisoner in Wales
   b. Signed his abdication at Kenilworth Castle
   c. Murdered in Berkeley Castle
   d. Son of the Earl of Lancaster and Leicester
   e. Besieged in Kenilworth Castle

12. In Line 6, what does "*partisans*" mean?

   a. Rulers
   b. Servants
   c. Opponents
   d. Followers
   e. Clergy

13. Which of the following is NOT true about Queen Elizabeth's pageants?

   a. The pageants were designed to convince the Queen to marry the Earl of Clarendon
   b. The pageants cost $5000 per day
   c. The Queen's attendants were clothed in velvet
   d. Ten oxen were killed every morning to feed the guests
   e. The Queen's barons, retainers, and servants were lodged in the fortress

14. According to the passage, what is currently the primary use of Kenilworth Castle?

   a. A church
   b. An historic bell tower
   c. A picnic ground for tourists
   d. The current home of the Earl of Clarendon
   e. A private residence of the British royal family

15. In Line 21, what does "*priory*" mean?

   a. Tower
   b. Ruins
   c. Estate
   d. Castle
   e. Monastery

16. According to the passage, what is the most notable feature of Kenilworth Castle?

   a. It was built during the reign of Henry I
   b. It has an impressive romantic history among all English ruins
   c. It is the only castle of its time to be sufficiently preserved
   d. It is still used as a sacred monastery
   e. It has been exhaustively researched by British historians

Passage 2

The most dangerous fault that any food can have is that it shall be tainted, or spoiled, or smell bad. Spoiling, or tainting, means that the food has become infected by some germs of putrefaction, generally bacteria or molds. It is the poisons, called ptomaines, or the toxins produced by these germs which cause the serious disturbances in the stomach, and not either the amount or the kind of food itself. Even a regular "gorge" upon early apples or watermelon or cake or ice cream will not give you half so bad, nor so dangerous, colic as one little piece of tainted meat or fish or egg, or one cupful of dirty milk, or a single helping of cabbage or tomatoes that have begun to spoil, or of jam made out of spoiled berries or other fruit.

8

This spoiling can be prevented by strict cleanliness in handling foods, especially milk, meat, and fruit; by keeping foods screened from dust and flies; and by keeping them cool with ice in summer time, thus checking the growth of these "spoiling" germs. The refrigerator in the kitchen prevents colic or diarrhea, ice in hot weather is one of the necessaries of life. Smell every piece of food to be eaten, in the kitchen before it is cooked, if possible; but if not, at the table avoid everything that has an unpleasant odor, or tastes odd, and you will avoid two-thirds of the colic, diarrhea, and bilious attacks which are so often supposed to be due to eating too much.

15

17. According to the passage, which of the following is NOT considered a source of dangerous food spoilage?

    a.   Moldy egg
    b.   Unclean milk
    c.   Rotting cabbage
    d.   Unripe fruit
    e.   Jam made from rotting berries

18. In Line 2, what does "*putrefaction*" mean?

    a.   Vile
    b.   Colitis
    c.   Contamination
    d.   Reproduction
    e.   Disintegration

19. According to the passage, which of the following is NOT an effective way to prevent food spoilage?

    a.   Avoiding food with unpleasant smells
    b.   Avoiding raw meat
    c.   Refrigerating milk, meat, and fruit
    d.   Protecting food from flies and dust
    e.   Extreme cleanliness while handling perishable foods

STOP

The answers to these questions are presented in Section RC2 (page 227)

Reading Comprehension 3: 25 minutes   24 questions

Directions: For each question in this section, select the best answer from the choices given and fill in the corresponding circle on the answer sheet.

1. The Governor's desire to impress her constituents, not her commitment to Hurricane Rita victims, was the impetus for her _____ disaster recovery referendum.

    a.   autocratic
    b.   assiduous
    c.   dogmatic
    d.   provident
    e.   effusive

2. Although she was proud of her many accomplishments, Sara remained _____ when she was offered praise.

    a.   turgid
    b.   mercurial
    c.   mendicant
    d.   impudent
    e.   demure

3. Unlike other students, who took a familiar approach to the problem, Wendy's solution was _____ and clever.

    a.   hackneyed
    b.   ingenuous
    c.   ambiguous
    d.   original
    e.   immutable

4. Olivia remained _____ for many months after her mother's funeral.

    a.   fluvial
    b.   inimical
    c.   inculcate
    d.   promontory
    e.   plaintive

5. Kate's _____ wardrobe belies her _____ nature.

    a.   paltry - lucid
    b.   garish - valorous
    c.   sophisticated - simple
    d.   practical -multifaceted
    e.   juvenile – lowly

6. Although critics praised the movie, most viewers were offended by its _____ violence, which did not advance the plot.

    a.   fortuitous
    b.   hedonistic
    c.   malodorous
    d.   mawkish
    e.   gratuitous

7. Although Zelda tried to maintain her composure, she was clearly _____ by the horrific turn of events.

     a. consumed
     b. exonerated
     c. devastated
     d. aggrandized
     e. expatriated

8. Rick's rare combination of skills _____ his _____ salary.

     a. sparked - disappointing
     b. minimized - ample
     c. induced - judicious
     d. belied - competitive
     e. justified – astronomical

9. After years of living on her own, Hillary is 100% _____.

     a. disheartened
     b. captivating
     c. self-reliant
     d. callous
     e. obstinate

10. Rebecca's _____ at her engagement party was _____ by the realization that she could not marry her boyfriend until after college.

     a. apprehension - inspired
     b. jubilation - enhanced
     c. elation - tempered
     d. distress - erased
     e. turmoil – moderated

11. Although the two countries had declared a truce, their relationship continued to be _____.

     a. sapient
     b. terpsichorean
     c. tractable
     d. turbulent
     e. convivial

Directions: *The passages below are followed by questions based on their content; questions following a pair of related passages may also be based on the relationship between the paired passages. Answer the questions, based on what is* stated *or* implied *in the passage and any introductory material that may be provided.*

Passage 1

    During the sixteenth century, the most celebrated sheep in France were those of Berri and Limousin; and of all butchers' meat, veal was reckoned the best. In fact, calves intended for the tables of the upper classes were fed in a special manner: they were allowed for six months, or even for a year, nothing but milk, which made their flesh most tender and delicate. Contrary to the present taste, kid was more appreciated than lamb, which caused the rôtisseurs frequently to attach the tail of a kid to a lamb, so as to deceive the customer and sell him a less expensive meat at the higher price. This was the origin of the axiom which described a cheat as "a dealer in goat by halves."

8

    In other places, butchers were far from acquiring the same importance which they did in France and Belgium, where much more meat was consumed than in Spain, Italy, or even in Germany. Nevertheless, in almost all countries there were certain regulations, sometimes eccentric, but almost always rigidly enforced, to ensure a supply of meat of the best quality and in a healthy state. In England, for instance, butchers were only allowed to kill bulls after they had been baited with dogs, no doubt with the view of making the flesh more tender. At Mans, it was laid down in the trade regulations that "no butcher shall be so bold as to sell meat unless it shall have been previously seen alive by two or three persons, who will testify to it on oath; and, anyhow, they shall not sell it until the persons shall have declared it wholesome."

17

To the many regulations affecting the interests of the public must be added that forbidding butchers to sell meat on days when abstinence from animal food was ordered by the Church. These regulations applied less to the vendors than to the consumers, who, by disobeying them, were liable to fine or imprisonment, or to severe corporal punishment by the whip or in the pillory. We find that Clément Marot was imprisoned and nearly burned alive for having eaten pork during Lent. In 1534, Guillaume des Moulins, the Count of Brie, asked permission for his mother, who was then eighty years of age, to cease fasting; the Bishop of Paris only granted dispensation on the condition that the old lady should take her meals in secret and out of sight of every one, and should still fast on Fridays.

26

The severity of the punishment for these transgressions increased during times of religious dissensions. Erasmus says, "He who has eaten pork instead of fish is taken to the torture like a parricide." An edict of Henry II, 1549, forbade the sale of meat during Lent to persons who should not be furnished with a doctor's certificate. Charles IX forbade the sale of meat to the Huguenots; and it was ordered that the privilege of selling meat during the time of abstinence should belong exclusively to the hospitals. Orders were given to those who retailed meat to take the address of every purchaser, although he had presented a medical certificate, so that the necessity for his eating meat might be verified. Subsequently, the medical certificate had to be endorsed by the priest, specifying what quantity of meat was required. Even in these cases, the use of butchers' meat alone was granted, pork, poultry, and game being strictly forbidden.

36

12. What is the main point of the passage?

   a. To explain the best ways to tenderize meat
   b. To explain the reasoning for attaching a kid to a lamb
   c. To explain the religious implications of meat consumption in sixteenth century Europe
   d. To discuss the regulations regarding meat consumption in Europe during the sixteenth century
   e. To explain the extreme tyranny of Charles IX regarding the consumption of food

13. According to the author, in France, what was the best way to ensure that a calf's meat was tender?

   a. They were baited by dogs before they were killed
   b. They were declared wholesome by two people before they were killed
   c. The meat was cooked slowly with moisture
   d. They were fed nothing but milk for at least six months
   e. The meat was consumed within 24 hours of the calf's slaughter

14. In Line 6, what does "*axiom*" mean?

   a. Maxim
   b. Law
   c. Irony
   d. Allegation
   e. Corollary

15. Customers who ate illegal meat were punished in all of the following ways EXCEPT:

   a. Fines
   b. Starvation
   c. Whipping
   d. Imprisonment
   e. Pillory

16. In Line 28, what does "*parricide*" mean?

    a. Death via food poisoning
    b. Death by starvation
    c. Murder of a relative
    d. Religious execution
    e. Animal sacrifice

17. What is the most likely source of the passage?

    a. A food journal
    b. A history book
    c. A cookbook
    d. A religious sermon
    e. A print ad for the beef industry

Passage 2

In addition to developing the alcohol and mercury thermometers, German physicist Gabriel Daniel Fahrenheit also developed the Fahrenheit temperature scale. Ironically, its most famous "anchor points," which are a freezing point of 32 degrees and a boiling point of 212 degrees, were not Fahrenheit's intended reference points. Instead, he chose 0 degrees to represent the temperature of an equal mixture of ice and salt. In contrast, Fahrenheit chose 100 degrees to signify the normal body temperature. Unfortunately, he miscalculated somewhat; the normal body temperature is actually 98.6 degrees. As a result, scientists scaled down Fahrenheit's original number accordingly.

8

Today, only the U.S. continues to use the Fahrenheit temperature scale. The rest of the world has adopted the metric system of measurement, including the Celsius scale for measuring heat, in which 0 degrees is the freezing point and 100 degrees is the boiling point of water. For decades, scientists on both sides of the pond debated the merits of each scale. The Fahrenheit scale, in which the boiling point and freezing point are 180 degrees apart, can better detect subtle changes in temperature than the Celsius scale, in which the two points are only 100 degrees apart. Yet the Celsius scale offers more logical references that are easier for all users, particularly non-scientists, to remember.

16

To standardize their measurements, most scientists and engineers now use the Kelvin system, in which absolute zero is the base point. To a casual reader, this number means nothing. To scientists, however, it refers to –273.15 C or –459.67 F, the temperature at which particles have a minimum, or zero-point, energy.

20

18. What is the main point of this passage?

    a. to explain why the United States continues to use the Fahrenheit temperature scale
    b. to explain how to convert temperatures among Fahrenheit, Celsius and Kelvin
    c. to explain the differences between the Fahrenheit and Celsius temperature scales
    d. to explain the differences among the Fahrenheit, Celsius and Kelvin temperature scales
    e. to justify the use of the Kelvin scale among scientists

19. According to the author, Fahrenheit had two intended reference points. What was the lower one?

    a. the freezing point of water
    b. the melting point of ice
    c. normal body temperature
    d. absolute zero
    e. the temperature of an equal mixture of ice and salt

20. What is the freezing point of water on the Celsius scale?

    a.   −459.67 F
    b.   −273.15 C
    c.   0 C
    d.   0 F
    e.   32 C

21. On Line 11, to what does the author refer by "*the pond*"?

    a.   Walden Pond, where Fahrenheit conducted his research
    b.   The 1,000 gallon laboratory tank in which Fahrenheit measured his reference points
    c.   The Atlantic Ocean, which separates the U.S. and Europe
    d.   The Indian Ocean, which separates Europe and Asia
    e.   The Pacific Ocean, which separates the U.S. and Asia

22. According to the author, what is the primary benefit of the Fahrenheit scale?

    a.   Most Americans already know it
    b.   It has more logical reference points than the Celsius scale
    c.   It is preferred by scientists and engineers
    d.   It is endorsed by the American Chemical Society
    e.   It can detect subtle changes in temperature better than the Celsius scale

23. What is the significance of absolute zero on the Kelvin scale?

    a.   It is the lowest temperature that can be recorded
    b.   it is the temperature at which water becomes ice
    c.   it is the temperature at which the Fahrenheit and Celsius scales are equivalent
    d.   it is the temperature at which particles have zero-point energy
    e.   it is the temperature at which atomic bonds are formed

24. What would be the best title for this passage?

    a.   The Origin and Use of the Fahrenheit, Celsius and Kelvin Temperature Scales
    b.   A Comparison of the Fahrenheit and Celsius Temperature Scales
    c.   Temperature Scales Across the Globe
    d.   An Argument in Favor of the Fahrenheit Scale
    e.   Fahrenheit vs. Celsius: The Dilemma Continues

STOP

The answers to these questions are presented in Section RC3 (page 228)

Directions: *For each question in this section, select the best answer from the choices given and fill the corresponding circle on the answer sheet.*

1. Because medicine is a _____ profession, many students enroll in pre-medical courses with dollar signs in their eyes.

   a.   precarious
   b.   eminent
   c.   lucrative
   d.   prestigious
   e.   rigorous

2. To _____ the irate man whose flight was cancelled, the gate agent offered a complimentary dinner and hotel room.

   a.   excoriate
   b.   mediate
   c.   acknowledge
   d.   placate
   e.   solicit

3. Like her sister, who was extremely cautious, Clarissa was a _____ young woman.

   a.   munificent
   b.   prudent
   c.   discrete
   d.   indolent
   e.   dauntless

4. Due to shyness, Melissa declined many social invitations in favor of more _____ pursuits.

   a.   spiritual
   b.   industrious
   c.   productive
   d.   lucrative
   e.   solitary

5. When the husband and wife failed to reach a compromise, a separation became _____.

   a.   depressing
   b.   unthinkable
   c.   inevitable
   d.   unprecedented
   e.   indefinite

6. The bystander was _____ for her attempt to revive the injured man, despite a lack of medical training,

   a.   investigated
   b.   commended
   c.   chastised
   d.   deplored
   e.   prosecuted

7. Marianne's _____ to alcohol _____ her chances for a promotion at work.

    a. addiction - mediated
    b. predisposition- alleviated
    c. resistance – obscured
    d. aversion – aggrandized
    e. proclivity – sabotaged

8. Ovarian cancer is a(n) _____ disease, because it cannot be diagnosed until an advanced stage, when the chance of survival is _____.

    a. insidious - minimal
    b. pervasive - infinitesimal
    c. virulent - optimistic
    d. tenacious - slim
    e. aggressive – progressive

9. The designer employed a(n) _____ style, which combined different colors, styles and periods.

    a. eccentric
    b. luxuriant
    c. eclectic
    d. whimsical
    e. flippant

Directions: *The passage below is followed by questions based on its content. Answer the questions, based on what is stated or implied in the passage and any introductory material that may be provided.*

The eleventh century, during which feudal power rose to its height, was also the period when a reaction set in among the townspeople against the nobility. The spirit of Rome revived with that of the bourgeois and infused a feeling of opposition to the system which followed the conquest of the Teutons. "But," says M. Henri Martin, "what reappeared was not the Roman municipality of the Empire, stained by servitude, although surrounded with glittering pomp and gorgeous arts, but it was something coarse and almost semi-barbarous in form, though strong and generous at its core, and which, as far as the difference of the times would allow, rather reminds us of the small republics which existed previous to the Roman Empire."

8

Two strong impulses, originating from two totally dissimilar centers of action, irresistibly propelled this great social revolution, with its various and endless aspects, affecting all of central Europe, and being more or less felt in the west, the north, and the south. On one side, the Greek and Latin partiality for ancient corporations, modified by a democratic element, and an innate feeling of opposition characteristic of barbaric tribes; and on the other, the free spirit and equality of the old Celtic tribes rising suddenly against the military hierarchy, which was the offspring of conquest. Europe was roused by the double current of ideas which simultaneously urged her on to a new state of civilization, and more particularly, to a new organization of city life.

17

Italy was naturally destined to be the country where the new trials of social regeneration were to be made, but she presented the greatest variety of customs, laws, and governments, including the Emperor, Pope, bishops, and feudal princes. In Tuscany and Liguria, the march towards liberty was continued almost without effort; whilst in Lombardy, on the contrary, the feudal resistance was most powerful. Everywhere, however, cities became more or less completely enfranchised, though some more rapidly than others. In Sicily, feudalism swayed over the countries, but in the greater part of the peninsula, the democratic spirit of the cities influenced the enfranchisement of the rural population. The feudal caste was in fact dissolved; the barons were transformed into patricians of the noble towns which gave their republican magistrates the old title of consuls.

27

The Teutonic Emperor in vain sought to seize and turn to his own interest the sovereignty of the people, who had shaken off the yokes of his vassals: the signal of war was immediately given by the newly enfranchised masses and the imperial eagle was obliged to fly before the banners of the besieged cities. Happy indeed might the cities of Italy have been had they not forgotten, in their prosperity, that union alone could give them the possibility of maintaining that liberty which they so freely risked in continual quarrels amongst one another.

34

10. What is the main point of the passage?

    a.   Despite the opposition, Italians refused to relinquish their freedom
    b.   The Italian social revolution was guided by two strong, but mutually opposing, forces
    c.   Without unity, the Italian cities were unable to maintain their liberty
    d.   The eleventh century was a period of great wealth and refinement in Italy
    e.   The democratic spirit in Italian cities eventually conquered the feudalistic tendencies in rural areas

11. According to the author, what followed the conquest of the Teutons?

    a.   Opposition to the system
    b.   The fall of the bourgeois
    c.   The rise of the nobility
    d.   Cultural refinement
    e.   A widespread commitment to education and literacy

12. According to M. Henri Martin, the entity that appeared in Italy after the fall of the Roman Empire was characterized by all of the following EXCEPT:

    a.   Coarseness
    b.   Generosity
    c.   Semi-barbaric
    d.   Stained by servitude
    e.   Strength

13. According to the author, which two impulses propelled the European social revolution?

    a.   Celtic conquests versus Greek and Latin democracy
    b.   Celtic barbarism versus Greek and Latin corporations
    c.   Celtic military versus Greek and Latin barbarism
    d.   Celtic conquest of Greek and Latin democracy
    e.   Celtic spirit of freedom and equality versus Greek and Latin opposition

14. In Line 18, what does "*regeneration*" mean?

    a.   Dedication
    b.   Revision
    c.   Renewal
    d.   Exploration
    e.   Blending

15. According to the author, Italian society in the eleventh century included all of the following EXCEPT:

    a.   Feudal princes
    b.   Sicilian priests
    c.   Bishops
    d.   Emperor
    e.   Pope

16. According to the author, in what place was feudal resistance most powerful?

    a.   Tuscany
    b.   Rome
    c.   Liguria
    d.   Lombardy
    e.   Sicily

17. In Line 22, what does "*enfranchised*" mean?

    a.   Free
    b.   Wealthy
    c.   Educated
    d.   Political
    e.   Patrician

18. In Line 29, to what does the word "*yokes*" refer?

    a.   Garments
    b.   Ideology
    c.   Weapons
    d.   Values
    e.   Oppression

19. What is the author's tone in the passage?

    a.   Superior
    b.   Ironic
    c.   Neutral
    d.   Aghast
    e.   Conciliatory

STOP

The answers to these questions are presented in Section RC4 (page 229)

Reading Comprehension 5:   25 minutes   24 questions

Directions: For each question in this section, select the best answer from the choices given and fill in the corresponding circle on the answer sheet.

1. When she took the stand, the crime victim _____ the self-serving claims of the defendant.

      a.   incensed
      b.   repudiated
      c.   acknowledged
      d.   bolstered
      e.   nettled

2. The mood at the airport became _____ when the news of the crash was announced.

      a.   pliant
      b.   laconic
      c.   plethoric
      d.   timorous
      e.   dolorous

3. Stephen King novels are known for their _____ plotlines, in which the reader never knows what will come next.

      a.   convoluted
      b.   derivative
      c.   intrepid
      d.   felonious
      e.   suspenseful

4. After hearing so many _____ reviews for the horror movie, Lily was _____ by its banal plot.

      a.   positive – elated
      b.   negative – scintillated
      c.   lackluster – enthralled
      d.   captivating - disappointed
      e.   valorous – dejected

5. Monica _____ endorsed her husband's plans to buy a house, despite her worries about their finances.

      a.   obligingly
      b.   warily
      c.   valiantly
      d.   enthusiastically
      e.   cautiously

6. Although the candidate promised to lower taxes, his audience was _____ of his sincerity.

      a.   skeptical
      b.   convinced
      c.   belligerent
      d.   tenacious
      e.   amenable

7. After an extensive search for a new Corporate Treasurer, the selection committee's choice won the immediate _____ of the managers, although a few of them had _____ about her.

      a. skepticism....apprehension
      b. acclaim....reservations
      c. ire...preconceptions
      d. disapproval...repercussions
      e. approval.....disagreements

8. Courtney was a _____ reader who _____ all genres of books.

      a. respectful - condensed
      b. voracious - deplored
      c. reluctant - eschewed
      d. latent - suggested
      e. pugnacious – epitomized

9. The _____ house was too _____ for even the largest family.

      a. luxuriant - unique
      b. miniscule - panoramic
      c. opulent - spacious
      d. penurious - perfunctory
      e. flagrant – laconic

Directions: *The passages below are followed by questions based on their content; questions following a pair of related passages may also be based on the relationship between the paired passages. Answer the questions, based on what is* stated *or* implied *in the passage and any introductory material that may be provided.*

Passage A

In and of itself, competition can be a healthy ingredient in the workplace, which produces better quality products or services at the lowest possible price. It can also stimulate the search for new technologies or better ways to satisfy customers. Pushed to extremes, however, competition can often reach an intensity that results in unethical practices and detrimental consequences.

5

Such intense competition, along with the desire to maximize profits and personal wealth, lead the formerly successful Enron Corporation down an unethical and illegal path. In the early days, Enron experienced significant growth and gained substantial credibility as a natural gas company. Later on, however, most of its successful operations were replaced by the illusion of successful initiatives. Over time, executives were no longer able to generate large profits, and, in fact, gambled away a substantial part of the company's financial resources. As a result, Enron's top executives began to borrow funds from Wall Street investors to make up the difference. The company's financial deficits, however, were hidden from the investment bankers, as well as the remainder of the financial community.

14

As a result of many unwise and unethical domestic and foreign investments, extravagant corporate expenditures by the enterprise's top executives and a series of scandals involving irregular mark-to-market accounting procedures, Enron filed the largest bankruptcy in the American history on December 2, 2001.

18

Most people don't realize that Enron, like many other American corporations, possessed its very own Code of Ethics, in which the company tried to position itself as an international employer, a creator of innovative energy solutions, as well as a global corporate citizen. It assured all of its employees that these great responsibilities were not taken lightly by the corporation's executive management, which was committed to conducting itself in a respectful manner. The Code of Ethics continued to explain that Enron felt very strongly about its core values; it demanded that its employees treat each other as they would like to be treated themselves. Further, the Code of Ethics emphasized the importance of honoring all promises to clients and corporate prospects. Finally, it listed open communication and excellence at the top of its list of core values. Most impressively, all employees, including executive managers, were held to the same standards in respect to the company's vision and values. As required by most firms, Enron also mandated a signed compliance form that verified that each employee would adhere to the stipulated corporate standards.

30

Upon the approval of the company's Board of Directors, Enron's Chairman, Kenneth Lay presented the Code of Ethics in July 2000. Ironically, on May 25th, 2006, Mr. Lay was convicted of one count of conspiracy, three counts of securities fraud, three counts of bank fraud and two wire fraud counts. In addition, Mr. Lay was found guilty of signing misleading audit representation letters and making false statements and presentations to securities analysts and rating agencies.

36

Subsequently, Jeffrey K. Skilling, Enron's former Chief Executive Officer since February 2001, was also found guilty of nineteen (out of twenty-eight) felony charges filed against him during the financial collapse of the corporation. Just to name a few, the courts found Skilling guilty of one count of conspiracy, one count of insider trading, five counts of making false statements and presentations to securities analysts and twelve counts of securities fraud.

42

Lastly, Enron's former Chief Financial Officer, Andrew S. Fastow, played a key role in hiding the corporation's massive losses through creative accounting practices. On October 31, 2002, Fastow was found guilty of seventy-eight counts of conspiracy, money laundering and fraud. In exchange for his testimony against other Enron top executives, Andrew Fastow agreed to serve a ten-year prison term. Kenneth Lay and Jeffrey Skilling faced up to 185 years in prison for their fraudulent activities and conspiracy at Enron. Lay, however, died of a heart attack before his sentence could be imposed.

49

There are many lessons to remember from the story of Enron's rise, prominence, and financial collapse. Although some people feel it is an account of justified achievement, growth, innovation, and creativity, most agree it is an unfortunate (but true) testimony of human greed, ambition, competitive deceit, and arrogance. Enron's story shows that the company's Code of Ethics didn't really mean anything because it was not applied equally to everyone in the corporation. There must be a genuine and strong commitment from top management to reinforce and support the principles and values that are set forth in a corporate Code of Ethics. Further, funds should be made available in each corporate budget to conduct ethics training (and possibly hire ethics officers) to communicate, implement, and integrate the ethical behavior into the firm's culture.

58

Passage B

Most people acknowledge the tremendous gap between a company's theoretical Code of Ethics and the actual behaviors observed in the firm. The former is based on purely theoretical principles, while the latter is handled in a different manner within the organization. Enron's story is an example of an enterprise in which the Code of Ethics was a purely theoretical document that had nothing to do with the actual conduct of its top executives. Management's behavior towards the company's employees, clients, prospects, auditors, investors, bankers, and financial community was the antithesis of the values and principles specified in the company's published Code of Ethics. No doubt, this repulsive behavior revealed the organization's true priorities and served as a warning for other business enterprises in their fields of operation.

67

In his article entitled "Lessons from Enron," Mark McCormack explains that Enron's story represents a trend that has existed in the United States over the last twenty-five years. Far too often, Western corporations rely on short-term versus long-range results in order to influence the Wall Street community. Today's investors unrealistically expect business enterprises to consistently generate large profits quarter after quarter. Enron simply exploited this rigid measurement system to its fullest capacity.

73

According to McCormack, it is unlikely that Wall Street investors will change their obsession with short-term numbers anytime soon. However, this does not mean that Enron should adhere to its questionable management tactics regarding investor expectations. By creating and spinning off quasi-owned subsidiaries, companies create opportunities for dishonest and creative accounting, which will eventually be traced back to the parent company. Even legitimate subsidiaries should be established sparingly. Far too often, enterprises that devote significant interest to their side businesses can create possible conflicts of interest.

80

Businesses also need to be able to trust their bottom-line numbers. Top executives should not encourage the company accountants to "pretty up" the numbers to deliver an artificial result. Further, executives need to be able to discuss the company's numbers with the public in an open and honest manner. Some executive officers believe that a bit of data manipulation is needed to be competitive in today's market. However, as McCormack explains, "Today, people are more than willing to assume that where there is smoke, there is fire." A firm must show that it values character, which can only be accomplished by encouraging open communication, giving the employees additional responsibility, and working hard toward the company goals without relying too heavily on favors. Companies who value performance will reveal their true profits, unlike Enron, which suffered severe consequences for putting a deceptive spin on their actual performance.

90

In 2002, Congress and the Securities Exchange Commission created the Sarbanes-Oxley Act to "force corporate executives to be proactive and accountable regarding the communication of their firm's financial position." This regulation was created to restore investors' faith in the integrity of corporate America and public markets. Kelly Financial Resources confirms that effective business communication is critical to educate the public about the problems surrounding their company. The scandals at Enron, WorldCom, and Tyco have encouraged the executives of other corporations to provide fair information about their organizations to Wall

Street, which has improved their bottom-line. Ultimately, better communication yields happier, more engaged employees, which increases productivity and profits.

99

Strong and positive ethics have also been identified as one of the most important qualities in Jack Welch and Steve Jobs, two of the most ethical and exemplary business leaders in corporate America. Without exception, ethics and integrity govern how these executives conduct all aspects of their day-to-day business. By bringing a sense of fairness, respect and credibility to their interactions, Welch and Jobs set the tone for their organizations' cultures. Further, their strong positive ethics and open business communications help to build their corporations' brand names, which draw new customers and create sustained, long-term profits.

106

Competition and profit maximization have an adverse impact on ethics and communication in business, but being ethical does not have to mean losing profits. Generating wealth is necessary to make a good and positive impact on the community, but communicating ethically is also in the best interest of corporations and their stakeholders. Furthermore, such integrity cannot be imposed by the law; it is a mindset that business leaders choose to adopt when making and communicating their everyday business decisions.

112

10. According to Passage A, all of the following are positive effects of competition EXCEPT:

    a.   more educated workforce
    b.   better ways to satisfy customers
    c.   better quality products
    d.   lowest possible price
    e.   improves the search for new technologies

11. In Line 12, what does "*deficit*" mean?

    a.   expenditure
    b.   subterfuge
    c.   impairment
    d.   deficiency
    e.   disadvantage

12. According to the author of Passage A, which of the following is NOT a reason for Enron's bankruptcy?

    a.   irregular accounting procedures
    b.   unethical foreign investments
    c.   extravagant executive expenses
    d.   tax evasion
    e.   bank fraud

13. In Line 34, what does "*audit*" mean?

    a.   government
    b.   examination
    c.   repercussion
    d.   regulatory
    e.   seizure

14. According to the author of Passage A, which of the following best conveys the value of a corporation's Code of Ethics?

    a.   It assures Wall Street investors of a firm's mission and goals
    b.   It attracts the right type of employee at all levels of the organization
    c.   It is only valuable if top managers support and reinforce its principles
    d.   It is an essential public relations tool
    e.   It has no intrinsic value

15. What is the tone of Passage A?

    a. apathetic
    b. vainglorious
    c. dejected
    d. incredulous
    e. objective

16. Which of the following is the best title for Passage A?

    a. The Criminal Consequences of Enron
    b. How Top Enron Managers Betrayed Their Corporate Code of Ethics
    c. How Enron Fell from Grace
    d. Fraud at Enron: The New Corporate Culture
    e. Enron: The Aftermath

17. In Passage B, what trend has Mark McCormack observed over the past twenty-five years?

    a. Companies rely on short-term results to deliver higher profits
    b. Companies frequently move operations offshore to avoid taxation
    c. Companies use subsidiaries for unethical purposes
    d. Companies use creative accounting practices
    e. Corporate executives earn ridiculously high salaries

18. In Line 82, what does "*pretty*" mean?

    a. minimize
    b. highlight
    c. exaggerate
    d. falsify
    e. sanitize

19. What is the implication of Mark McCormack's quote on Line 85: *"Today, people are more than willing to assume that where there is smoke, there is fire."*

    a. Thanks to Enron, investors think all corporate executives are corrupt
    b. As long as a company has good numbers, investors will remain loyal
    c. The minute the SEC announces a company is under investigation, investors flee
    d. If investors see a corporation's true financial numbers, they will assume the worst and take their money elsewhere
    e. Investors only trust financial statements that are verified by an independent third party

20. According to Passage B, implementation of the Sarbanes-Oxley Act will accomplish all of the following EXCEPT:

    a. Improve the quality and quantity of information provided to Wall Street
    b. Encourage the use of outside accounting firms
    c. Improve employee happiness
    d. Improve productivity
    e. Restore investors' faith in corporate America

21. According to Passage B, which of the following corporate directives would Kelly Financial Resources be most likely to support?

    a. Formal training in ethics for all corporate CEOs
    b. Lower salaries and fewer perks for CEOs
    c. Stronger penalties for the illegal use of subsidiaries
    d. Annual IRS audits for all Fortune 1000 companies
    e. A communication campaign to educate the public about a company's problems

22. In Passage B, which of the following does the author attribute to Jack Welch?

    a. Strong ethics and integrity
    b. Open communication
    c. Commitment to cross-cultural training
    d. A and B
    e. A, B and C

23. According to the author of Passage B, what is the impact of competition on business?

    a. Positive impact on profits
    b. Negative impact on ethics and communication
    c. Positive impact on employee morale
    d. Negative impact on investment community
    e. Savvy leadership

24. How does the objective of Passage A compare to that of Passage B?

    a. Passage A discusses Enron's failure to adhere to its Code of Ethics, while Passage B discusses ways to prevent similar scandals
    b. Passage A suggests that Enron is an anomaly, while Passage B presumes that all corporations are corrupt
    c. Their objectives are the same, but Passage B is more cynical in tone
    d. Passage B finishes the presentation that Passage A started
    e. Passage A discusses the ramifications of Enron on its executives, while Passage B discusses its impact on the investment community

STOP

The answers to these questions are presented in Section RC5 (page 230)

Reading Comprehension 6: 20 minutes   19 questions

Directions: *For each question in this section, select the best answer from the choices given and fill in the corresponding circle on the answer sheet.*

1. For patients with arthritis, few kitchen chores are as _____ as scrubbing greasy pans.

    a. perennial
    b. riveting
    c. pungent
    d. onerous
    e. itinerant

2. To succeed as a researcher, a student must display a love of reading, a knack for organization and a _____ attention to detail.

    a. rudimentary
    b. meticulous
    c. implicit
    d. bewildering
    e. habitual

3. The flower girl looked _____ in her flowing red dress and matching headband.

    a. enchanting
    b. aromatic
    c. fragile
    d. magical
    e. unblemished

4. Andrea's blind date, who arrived an hour late with no explanation, was the _____ of the sophisticated gentleman she expected.

    a. cessation
    b. antithesis
    c. personification
    d. relative
    e. regression

5. It was only at age 50, when Daniel began to take music lessons, that his _____ talent as an artist began to _____.

    a. considerable - mitigate
    b. meager - wane
    c. latent - emerge
    d. misguided - falter
    e. innate – abrogate

6. Rather than _____ to her mother's wishes, Patricia had the _____ to pursue her own path.

    a. nullify - beneficence
    b. object - audacity
    c. adhere - courage
    d. concede - propensity
    e. panegyrize – execration

7. The _____ woman actually believed that she was Joan of Arc, despite all evidence to the contrary.

    a.   innovative
    b.   delusional
    c.   provocative
    d.   vainglorious
    e.   temerarious

8. The relationship between the warring spouses was _____ at best.

    a.   contentious
    b.   dauntless
    c.   calumniate
    d.   subdued
    e.   culpable

9. Although the physician had _____ credentials, the patient was convinced he was a(n) _____.

    a.   dubious - maverick
    b.   impressive - humanitarian
    c.   contradictory - fraud
    d.   prestigious - charlatan
    e.   mediocre- advocate

Directions: The passage below is followed by questions based on its content. Answer the questions, based on what is stated or implied in the passage and any introductory material that may be provided.

In his article "Surfing the Mobile Wave," David Geer notes that business people have an insatiable appetite for technology that enables them to remain in touch on the go. This increased demand for mobility imposed by the organizations' own internal customers has motivated businesses to deploy more personal devices and mobile technologies than they initially anticipated. Consumers, along with corporations, acquire mobile and hand-held devices because they offer a variety of software applications, Internet and e-mail access, instant messaging, voice calls, and networking features that are conveniently accessible in a small, portable package.

7

The biggest reason, however, for such explosive growth in mobile technologies is the potential cost savings for the companies that use them. Advanced mobile and wireless devices allow firms to communicate independently of their physical locations. In addition, by 2012, wireless technology is forecasted to outperform wired networks due to its preferable cost, reliability, and functionality. Despite their convenience, flexibility, and cost-effectiveness, however, mobile technologies and devices pose ever-changing security challenges for a corporation's top management to ensure the integrity, privacy, confidentiality, reliability, and security of their corporate data.

15

The two main issues related to mobile devices are the storage of sensitive corporate information and the means of accessing the company's networks. Mobile devices provide remote access to a company's data, which provides tremendous flexibility to their users. This flexibility, however, leaves the company's networks and data vulnerable to security breaches and viruses. Furthermore, many companies are struggling to find ways to protect the increasing amount of sensitive information that is stored in laptops, PDAs, BlackBerries, cell phones, USB drives, and other portable devices, which can be easily stolen, lost, or carried away due to their small size. Although many companies have policies against storing sensitive company information on mobile devices, many users keep corporate data on them. Additionally, even though most devices offer password protection, most hackers can easily bypass these controls and access sensitive personal or business data.

25

Although laptops and mobile devices offer many advantages, when one is lost, the subsequent costs extend far beyond the physical replacement of the unit. In many cases, the greatest threat is the loss of sensitive or proprietary data that has been stored on the device. While studies have shown that the theft of computers containing sensitive data is associated with only a small percentage of identity theft, the possible liability associated with losing confidential information is significant. Additionally, the majority of U.S. states now require that businesses notify those who might be at risk for fraud, which brings unwanted negative publicity.

32

Preventing the loss of these devices has been much more difficult than securing traditional workstation computers. Laptops, PDA's, smart phones, and USB memory sticks are smaller and extremely portable, which enables employees to transfer sensitive information from secured networks to the device and remove it from the company premises. Although some companies may not allow CD burners at their workstation computers, laptops, PDAs, and USB drives are as commonplace as house keys. Even more troubling, when cheap USB memory devices are missing, employees may not even report it.

39

Unfortunately, the loss of these devices is all too common. Last year, about 750,000 laptops were stolen; about 97% of stolen PC's are never recovered. Every month, thousands of mobile phones are also stolen. If they are Smart phones, they may contain private information like computer files and email messages, which could spark an unwanted leak of sensitive company information. According to a survey performed by the Yankee Group in 2005, 37 percent of respondents attributed the disclosure of company information to USB drives.

46

In a survey last year, the Computer Security Institute of the Federal Bureau of Investigation reported that 75% of respondents experienced laptop and mobile device theft, which was more than any other type of attack or misuse, including denial of service attacks, telecommunications fraud, unauthorized access of information, viruses, financial fraud, insider abuse of net access, system penetration, sabotage, theft of proprietary information, abuse of a wireless network, website defacement, and misuse of a public web application.

52

According to a survey performed by the Wrigley Institute, 81 percent of information security professionals reported that their companies had experienced the loss of one or more laptops containing sensitive information. The study also reported that hand-held devices and laptops were the storage devices that posed the greatest risk of data loss, followed by USB memory sticks. Sensitive information could include customer data, employee records, vendor information, intellectual property (such as product or research data, corporate plans, and strategies), and even the secret personal correspondence of key employees, which might make them vulnerable to blackmail.

60

Currently, there are numerous products and services to recover missing or stolen devices. Companies like SmartProtec provide software that can trace stolen property and return it to its rightful owner. Mr. Sanders, an inventory manager for a company that processes medical records, recently installed SmartProtec software on more than 900 computers that are used by employees who travel between hospitals to scan patient records. If any of these computers are stolen, Mr. Sanders simply has to call a hotline; the next time that laptop is connected to the internet, it will automatically send a message to the servers at SmartProtec headquarters that identifies its location. Immediately afterwards, the same information is forwarded to the police, who can retrieve the stolen laptop.

69

SmartProtec provides a similar service for cell phones, which allows users to register their devices. This simple step makes it dangerous for thieves to possess or re-sell stolen items. SmartProtec works with the police and other authorities to recover stolen devices, and even offers rewards to those who help find them. The serial numbers of all devices are stored in a SmartProtec database, so there is no need for the owner to write it on a piece of paper and worry about losing it. The moment the device is lost or stolen, the owner must immediately change its status from "In Possession" to "Lost" or "Stolen." When the police recover a stolen item, or somebody comes across a lost device, SmartProtec allows them to contact the owner through the serial number, without disclosing any personal information. Moreover, SmartProtec collaborates with FedEx to deliver the recovered device directly to the owner's doorstep.

79

Executives must keep these security services in the proper perspective. Although SmartProtec can trace stolen property and return it safely to its rightful owner, no amount of technology can substitute completely for human behavior. Ultimately, security is only as good as each company's individual policies.

83

10. According to the author, what is the main reason for the fast growth of mobile technologies?

   a. Computer networking
   b. Voice mail applications
   c. Potential cost savings
   d. Internet access and email
   e. Instant messaging

11. By 2012, what technological change do industry experts expect?

   a. Corporations will no longer allow employees to store sensitive data on mobile devices
   b. SmartProtec will capture more than eighty-percent of the wireless security market
   c. The theft of mobile devices will spark a corresponding rise in identity theft
   d. Due to problems associated with theft, USB memory devices will be prohibited at most major corporations
   e. Wireless technology will outperform wired networks

12. According to the passage, what percentage of stolen computers is recovered?

    a.   3%
    b.   37%
    c.   75%
    d.   81%
    e.   97%

13. The passage mentions all of the following mobile devices EXCEPT:

    a.   Smart phones
    b.   USB drives
    c.   BlackBerries
    d.   Memory sticks
    e.   Portable microchips

14. In Line 43, what does "*sensitive*" mean?

    a.   Easily hurt
    b.   Classified
    c.   Clandestine
    d.   Delicate
    e.   Reactionary

15. Which organization conducted a survey to determine how sensitive company information was erroneously disclosed?

    a.   Yankee Group
    b.   Federal Bureau of Investigation
    c.   Wrigley Institute
    d.   SmartProtec
    e.   Computer Security Institute

16. In the survey conducted by the Wrigley Institute, which of the following was NOT mentioned as a type of record kept on corporate computers?

    a.   Vendor information
    b.   Corporate strategies
    c.   Secret personal correspondence
    d.   Health and medical records
    e.   Employee records

17. In which scenario would the SmartProtec system NOT be helpful?

    a.   The thief takes the laptop outside the United States
    b.   The owner forgets the hotline number
    c.   The thief does not attempt to log onto the Internet
    d.   The laptop is dropped
    e.   The laptop is sold to a pawn shop

18. In Line 72, what does "*serial*" mean?

      a.   identifying
      b.   in order
      c.   repetitive
      d.   rank
      e.   production

19. Which of the following best conveys the author's attitude about the security of mobile devices?

      a.   There is no realistic way to secure them
      b.   The risks are minimal compared to the benefits the devices offer
      c.   Portable storage devices should be banned at most companies to prevent security risks
      d.   It depends on each company's policies
      e.   A system like SmartProtec provides adequate protection for most users' needs

STOP

The answers to these questions are presented in Section RC6 (page 231)

Reading Comprehension 7:   25 minutes   24 questions

Directions: For each question in this section, select the best answer from the choices given and fill in the corresponding circle on the answer sheet.

1. To convince a jury, attorneys must present compelling _____ to support their arguments.

    a. conjectures
    b. evidence
    c. theories
    d. speculations
    e. documents

2. Given Ben's _____ nature, we are not surprised that he changes jobs so frequently.

    a. ideological
    b. vehement
    c. ingenious
    d. implacable
    e. capricious

3. To choose the optimal cancer treatment, patients must evaluate the potential risks and _____ in a clear and rational manner.

    a. benefits
    b. speculation
    c. symptoms
    d. prognosis
    e. economy

4. The prolonged recovery from Hurricane Katrina revealed a _____ of political, social, and financial problems in the ravaged areas.

    a. concoction
    b. desert
    c. plethora
    d. resentment
    e. gridlock

5. Despite the intensity of the political campaign, the candidate inspired little _____ in his constituents.

    a. apathy
    b. affluence
    c. provocation
    d. exuberance
    e. reticence

6. A dedicated student would never display such a _____ attitude toward her studies.

    a. blatant
    b. recalcitrant
    c. munificent
    d. haughty
    e. cavalier

7. The _____ citizens angrily protested the tax increase.

    a.   multifarious
    b.   forlorn
    c.   reprehensible
    d.   misguided
    e.   irate

8. Compared to the _____ of New York City, life in Kansas is downright _____.

    a.   fast pace - banal
    b.   crime rate - reserved
    c.   sophistication – mundane
    d.   vibrancy - straightforward
    e.   wealth – boring

9. Although her parents were diehard liberals, Sophia's political views tend to be quite _____.

    a.   apathetic
    b.   indifferent
    c.   tentative
    d.   conservative
    e.   independent

10. The defense attorney argued _____ that his client be shown _____.

    a.   logically - clemency
    b.   cleverly - justice
    c.   methodically - innocent
    d.   passionately - leniency
    e.   persuasively – mitigation

11. Rather than _____ the mediation, the parties _____ their adversarial positions.

    a.   participate in - mollified
    b.   dispute - disclosed
    c.   abandon– cited
    d.   challenge - castigated
    e.   support – adhered to

12. Although the insecticide was extremely effective, its _____ fumes were distasteful to consumers.

    a.   flagrant
    b.   noxious
    c.   illogical
    d.   medicinal
    e.   antioxidant

Directions: *The passages below are followed by questions based on their content; questions following a pair of related passages may also be based on the relationship between the paired passages. Answer the questions, based on what is* <u>stated</u> *or* <u>implied</u> *in the passage and any introductory material that may be provided.*

Passage 1

In 2009, scientists at Yale University were awarded a patent for "GeneTropy," a home-based DNA analysis kit. The practical implications of the kit are enormous to law enforcement groups, as GeneTropy makes a positive DNA match in just thirty minutes, compared to the minimal three-week period required by previous testing methodologies. Since GeneTropy's introduction, federal, state and local law enforcement agencies have used the test to solve over 400 rapes, 120 assaults and 6,100 burglaries. In Illinois, the test has also been used to reverse the wrongful convictions of eleven murderers, including three on Death Row.

7

The burgeoning market for home-based paternity testing offers another revenue stream for GeneTropy that its developers are eager to explore. During their initial promotional work, they discovered that traditional lab-based tests cost over $650 and offer results in three weeks. Of the five accredited labs in the United States, backlogs are usually so severe that the turnaround time can be five weeks or longer. In contrast, GeneTropy costs just $100, provides reliable results in 24 hours, and can be used in the privacy of a buyer's home. The developers' primary goal for 2012 is to get FDA approval for the over-the-counter distribution of the test. From a societal perspective, the potential financial and psychological benefits to families in America are too important to ignore.

15

13. What is the main point of the passage?

a. To convince customers of traditional DNA labs to use GeneTropy as a lower cost option
b. To encourage families to have paternity tests run on their children
c. To discuss the low cost and fast speed of GeneTropy's DNA analysis kit
d. To explain what GeneTropy can offer law enforcement groups
e. To demonstrate Yale's financial interest in GeneTropy technology

14. According to the author, what is GeneTrophy's main advantage to law enforcement?

a. small sample size
b. low cost
c. fast results
d. reliability
e. FDA approved

15. In Line 8, what does "*burgeoning*" mean?

a. unexpected
b. lucrative
c. sophisticated
d. expanding
e. consumer

16. According to the author, law enforcement agencies have used GeneTropy to solve all of the following crimes EXCEPT:

a. forgery
b. rape
c. murder
d. burglary
e. assault

17. For paternity tests, which of the following is NOT a benefit provided by GeneTrophy?

a. reliable
b. low cost
c. privacy
d. over-the-counter access
e. fast results

18. The author's attitude toward GeneTrophy can be best described as?

    a.   neutral
    b.   cynical
    c.   envious
    d.   enthusiastic
    e.   laconic

Passage 2

The coffee tree, scientifically known as Coffea arabica, is native to Abyssinia and Ethiopia, but grows well in Java, Sumatra, and other islands of the Dutch East Indies; in India, Arabia, equatorial Africa, the islands of the Pacific, in Mexico, Central and South America, and the West Indies. The plant belongs to the large sub-kingdom of plants known scientifically as the Angiosperms, which means that the plant reproduces by seeds which are enclosed in a box-like compartment, known as the ovary, at the base of the flower. The word Angiosperm is derived from two Greek words, sperma, a seed, and aggeion, a box or ovary.

7

This large sub-kingdom is subdivided into two classes. The basis for this division is the number of leaves in the little plant which develops from the seed. The coffee plant, as it develops from the seed, has two little leaves, and therefore belongs to the class Dicotyledoneæ. This word dicotyledoneæ is made up of the two Greek words, di(s), two, and kotyledon, cavity or socket. It is not necessary to see the young plant that develops from the seed in order to know that it had two seed leaves; because the mature plant always shows certain characteristics that accompany this condition of the seed.

14

In every plant having two seed leaves, the mature leaves are netted-veined, which is a condition easily recognized even by the layman; also the parts of the flowers are in circles containing two or five parts, but never in threes or sixes. The stems of plants of this class always increase in thickness by means of a layer of cells known as a cambium, which is a tissue that continues to divide throughout its whole existence. The fact that this cambium divides as long as it lives, gives rise to a peculiar appearance in woody stems by which we can, on looking at the stem of a tree of this type when it has been sawed across, tell the age of the tree.

22

In the spring the cambium produces large open cells through which large quantities of sap can run; in the fall it produces very thick-walled cells, as there is not so much sap to be carried. Because these thin-walled open cells of one spring are next to the thick-walled cells of the last autumn, it is very easy to distinguish one year's growth from the next; the marks so produced are called annual rings.

27

The flower of the coffee plant is separated into sub-classes according to whether the flower's corolla is all in one piece, or is divided into a number of parts. The coffee flower is arranged with its corolla all in one piece, forming a tube-shaped arrangement, and accordingly the coffee plant belongs to the sub-class Sympetalæ, or Metachlamydeæ, which means that its petals are united.

32

Within the Dicotyledoneæ classification, plants are separated into orders according to their varied characteristics. The coffee plant belongs to an order known as Rubiales. These orders are again divided into families. Coffee is placed in the family Rubiaceæ, or Madder Family, in which we find herbs, shrubs or trees, represented by a few American plants, such as bluets, or Quaker ladies, small blue spring flowers, common to open meadows in northern United States; and partridge berries (Mitchella repens).

38

The Madder Family has more foreign representatives than native genera, among which are Coffea, Cinchona, and Ipecacuanha (Uragoga), all of which are of economic importance. The members of this family are noted for their action on the nervous system. Coffea, as is well known, contains an active principle known as caffeine which acts as a stimulant to the nervous system and in small quantities is very beneficial. Cinchona supplies us with quinine, while Ipecacuanha produces ipecac, which is an emetic and purgative.

44

All botanists do not yet agree in their classification of the species and varieties of the Coffea genus. M.E. de Wildman, curator of the Royal Botanical Gardens at Brussels, in his Les Plantes Tropicales de Grande Culture, says the systematic division of this interesting genus is far from finished; in fact, it has only yet begun.

49

19. What is the main point of the passage?

    a.   To explain the economic value of the Madder Family
    b.   To explain the botanical classification of the coffee plant
    c.   To explain the origin of Dicotyledoneæ
    d.   To explain the significance of annual rings
    e.   To differentiate between Dicotyledoneæs and Rubiales

20. Coffee grows naturally in all of the following locations EXCEPT:

    a.   Africa
    b.   Slovakia
    c.   India
    d.   Mexico
    e.   West Indies

21. According to the author, where is the aggeion?

    a.   Within the seed
    b.   On a netted-veined leaf
    c.   At the base of the flower
    d.   Within the woody stem
    e.   In a one-piece tube

22. What is the purpose of the cambium?

    a.   It holds the ovary
    b.   It stimulates the nervous system
    c.   It allows us to classify plants by their number of leaves
    d.   It allows us to determine the age of a tree
    e.   It supplies the seeds for reproduction

23. In Line 29, what is a "*corolla*"?

    a.   Stem
    b.   Leaf
    c.   Petal
    d.   Root
    e.   Seed

24. All of the following are Rubiaceæ EXCEPT:

    a.   Cacao
    b.   Bluets
    c.   Partridge berries
    d.   Shrubs
    e.   Herbs

STOP

The answers to these questions are presented in Section RC7 (page 232)

Reading Comprehension 8: 20 minutes 19 questions

Directions: *For each question in this section, select the best answer from the choices given and fill in the corresponding circle on the answer sheet.*

1. Despite his claims of innocence, John's alibi for the night of the crime was _____ at best.

    a.   recalcitrant
    b.   tentative
    c.   logical
    d.   plausible
    e.   infinitesimal

2. Alex's anger with his wife was _____ by their financial problems.

    a.   palliated
    b.   propitiated
    c.   mitigated
    d.   decimated
    e.   exacerbated

3. Considering the dire warnings by meteorologists, it was _____ that so few residents sought refuge at the shelters.

    a.   untoward
    b.   awkward
    c.   surprising
    d.   stalwart
    e.   impudent

4. Zachary, who was painfully shy as a child, surprised everyone by becoming such a _____ adult.

    a.   magnanimous
    b.   garrulous
    c.   wayward
    d.   bounteous
    e.   intransigent

5. Maria's efforts to sound sophisticated, including her tendency to adopt a British accent, merely made her seem _____.

    a.   disingenuous
    b.   parsimonious
    c.   multifarious
    d.   fastidious
    e.   plebian

6. Despite his pressure to withdraw U.S troops from Iraq, President Bush remained _____ in his commitment to the war.

    a.   vainglorious
    b.   arrogant
    c.   authoritarian
    d.   immutable
    e.   tractable

7. After years of dealing with a(n) _____ boss, who favored rumor and innuendo to direct conversation, Adrienne found her new boss's _____ to be downright refreshing.

    a. non-communicative - ego
    b. evasive - candor
    c. dishonest - ardor
    d. talkative - timidity
    e. flippant – altruistic

Directions: The passages below are followed by questions based on their content; questions following a pair of related passages may also be based on the relationship between the paired passages. Answer the questions, based on what is stated *or* implied *in the passage and any introductory material that may be provided.*

Passage 1

Until the thirteenth century, the juggling profession was a lucrative one in most European cities. There was no public or private feast of any importance without the profession being represented. Jugglers were the principal attraction at the Cours Plénières, and, according to the testimony of one of their members, they frequently retired from business loaded with presents, such as riding-horses, carriage-horses, jewels, cloaks, fur robes, clothing of violet or scarlet cloth, and, above all, with large sums of money.

6

Jugglers are also the subject of many noble stories, both veracious and fanciful. Before the battle of Hastings, Norman Taillefer was said to have advanced alone on horseback between the two armies about to commence the engagement, and drew off the attention of the English by singing them the Song of Roland. He then began juggling, and taking his lance by the hilt, he threw it into the air and caught it by the point as it fell; then, drawing his sword, he spun it several times over his head, and caught it in a similar way as it fell. After these skilful exercises, during which the enemy were gaping in mute astonishment, he forced his charger through the English ranks, and caused great havoc before he fell, positively riddled with wounds.

14

Notwithstanding this noble instance, not to belie the old proverb, jugglers were never received into the order of knighthood. They were, after a time, as much abused as they had before been extolled. Their licentious lives reflected itself in their obscene language. Their pantomimes, like their songs, showed that they were the votaries of the lowest vices. The lower orders laughed at their coarseness, and were amused at their juggleries; but the nobility were disgusted with them, and they were absolutely excluded from the presence of ladies and girls in the châteaux and houses of the bourgeoisie. The clergy, and St. Bernard especially, denounced them in one of his sermons written in the middle of the twelfth century: "A man fond of jugglers will soon enough possess a wife whose name is Poverty. If it happens that the tricks of jugglers are forced upon your notice, endeavor to avoid them, and think of other things. The tricks of jugglers never please God."

24

Thus, throughout this period, jugglers wandered about the country with their trained animals nearly starved; they were half naked, and were often without anything on their heads, without coats, without shoes, and always without money. The lower orders welcomed them, and continued to admire and idolize them for their clever tricks, but the bourgeois class, following the example of the nobility, turned their backs upon them. In 1345 Guillaume de Gourmont, Provost of Paris, forbade their singing or relating obscene stories, under penalty of fine and imprisonment. Thus, by 1350, the lucrative days of juggling in France were all but forgotten.

30

8. Which of the following is the main point of the passage?

    a. Jugglers were the most highly compensated street entertainers in thirteenth century Europe
    b. Jugglers, although talented, were not expert swordsmen
    c. The clergy took a dim view of jugglers in thirteenth century Europe
    d. Jugglers were never respected by the bourgeois class
    e. In the thirteenth century, jugglers descended from an exalted social position to one of mockery and contempt

9. In Line 7, what does "*veracious*" mean?

    a. Dull
    b. Audacious
    c. Fallacious
    d. Truthful
    e. Objective

10. Norman Taillefer did all of the following EXCEPT:

    a. Riddled the English army with wounds
    b. Forced his charger through the English ranks
    c. Diverted the English by singing the Song of Roland
    d. Threw his lance in the air and caught it by the point as it fell
    e. Rode alone on horseback between the two armies

11. In Line 15, what does "*belie*" mean?

    a. Affirm
    b. Contradict
    c. Justify
    d. Exacerbate
    e. Extol

12. Which of the following best conveys St. Bernard's impression of the jugglers?

    a. Audacious
    b. Baneful
    c. Amusing
    d. Melodious
    e. Debauched

13. According to the author, which of the following groups always admired the jugglers?

    a. The French army
    b. The bourgeois class
    c. The lower orders
    d. The ladies and girls in the châteaux
    e. The nobility

Passage 2

Although Benjamin Franklin is credited with discovering electricity, several scientific pioneers have contributed to its subsequent evolution. Initially, all electricity was direct current (DC), which flows in only one direction. Thomas Edison was a great proponent of DC, because he had a large financial stake in the technology. In the early days, DC was adequate, because the generators were close to the lights that used the electricity. In tight-knit cities, DC offered a simple, but elegant, solution to people's power needs.

6

As demand for electricity increased, however, DC's limitations became paralyzing. Electric current maintains its energy when it travels at high voltages. At the time, it was not economical to transform direct currents into the high voltages that were required for long distance transmission. Although Edison lobbied for the construction of power generating stations every three or four miles, the plan was not feasible for a nation that was growing as rapidly as the United States.

12

In the 1880's, an unknown inventor named Nikola Tesla obtained a patent for alternating current (AC) technology. Acknowledging its potential for widespread use, George Westinghouse bought the rights to Tesla's invention and championed its implementation. Alternating current could transmit higher voltages at a significantly lower price than direct current. Additionally, with a simple switch of one transformer, the voltages could be raised or lowered. With these unprecedented advantages, AC quickly became the standard in the United States, which it remains to this day.

19

14. What is the main point of the passage?

    a.   To discuss Benjamin Franklin's limitations
    b.   To explain how George Westinghouse became rich and famous
    c.   To explain the limitations of AC current
    d.   To explain how electricity evolved after its initial discovery
    e.   To discuss the difference between AC and DC current

15. In Line 5, what does the word "*elegant*" mean?

    a.   short-sighted
    b.   slow
    c.   graceful
    d.   expensive
    e.   refined

16. According to the author, in what technology did Thomas Edison have a financial interest?

    a.   electrical transformers
    b.   power generating stations
    c.   DC current
    d.   AC current
    e.   AC and DC current

17. What decreased the demand for DC current?

    a.   It could not transform current to higher voltages
    b.   It could not transform current to higher voltages at a reasonable cost
    c.   Benjamin Franklin refused to license the rights to it
    d.   People stayed in large cities, which already had electricity
    e.   It was prone to safety and fire issues

18. Which of the following is NOT a benefit of AC current?

    a.   Can transmit higher voltages at a lower price
    b.   Offers flexibility of raising and lowering voltages
    c.   Only one transformer is needed to change voltage
    d.   Reduced safety issues
    e.   Allowed widespread use of electricity across the U.S.

19. In Line 15, what does the word "*championed*" mean?

    a.   advocated
    b.   mitigated
    c.   financed
    d.   negotiated
    e.   circumvented

STOP

The answers to these questions are presented in Section RC8 (page 233)

Reading Comprehension 9:   25 minutes   24 questions

Directions: For each question in this section, select the best answer from the choices given and fill in the corresponding circle on the answer sheet.

1. Although Elaine disliked the subcompact car, it was a more_____ choice than the sports car she originally selected.

    a. economical
    b. myriad
    c. environmental
    d. malleable
    e. provocative

2. After missing three car payments, Jeffrey knew that repossession was _____.

    a. contraindicated
    b. diffident
    c. unavoidable
    d. disdainful
    e. imminent

3. The bride's designer wedding dress was far too _____ for my simple taste.

    a. subdued
    b. lugubrious
    c. ornate
    d. bombastic
    e. austere

4. If Katie were a true friend, she would not make _____ remarks about you behind your back.

    a. querulous
    b. superfluous
    c. disparaging
    d. unctuous
    e. facetious

5. Despite her best efforts, Lisa was too _____ to engage in the party scene.

    a. introverted
    b. urbane
    c. prolific
    d. fulminating
    e. quaint

Directions: The passages below are followed by questions based on their content; questions following a pair of related passages may also be based on the relationship between the paired passages. Answer the questions, based on what is stated or implied in the passage and any introductory material that may be provided.

Passage 1

"Cat or dog. Chocolate or vanilla. Yin or yang. At some point, you just have to *decide*...." Barbara Walters

2

People, for the most part, can be divided into two groups: dog people or cat people. You may find an occasional fish- or rodent-lover, but they are rare and, for the most part, insane. I am, without a doubt, a cat person. If offered a chance to spend an evening with Barbara Walters, the President of the United States or Garfield the cat, I'll pick Garfield every time.

7

I inherited this passion from my mother, who suffers from a lifelong obsession with all things feline. My father is quite the opposite; his loyalties lie with his canine pals who roam our three hundred acre ranch. Although my cat lover's gene is dominant, my passion for my fair-weathered Siamese, Burmese and Persians is not solely a result of my genealogy. My mother has always been a source of encouragement regarding the pursuit of my interests, and raising championship cats was no exception.

13

Although my mother always worked during the day, she took the time to establish a cattery in one of our abandoned barns. Her motivation, as always, was not just to breed the perfect Calico, but to rescue as many homeless animals from the shelter as possible. By age six, I had mastered all aspects of cat care, from brushing and bathing the adult cats to bottle-feeding the newborn kittens that had been rejected by their mothers. According to my father, it provided my mother with a productive outlet for her maternal instincts, which had remained dormant in the years after my birth. Whatever the reason, breeding championship cats became a joint passion that my mother and I have been blessed to share.

21

Yet, thankfully, my father's genes infused my bloodline with enough canine lust to keep my perspective well grounded. While my mother bred her seal point Siamese in the south barn, my father had his pack of champion weimaraners in the north barn. I didn't immediately warm to the German hunting dogs that saw my kittens as prey, yet the gentleness of the "gray ghost" eventually won me over. Every year, I accompanied my father and Sir Lancelot to the annual Westminster Dog Show, where we never won the big prize, but usually placed respectably in the hunting group.

28

While waiting for our turn in the ring, I glanced across the crowd of dog lovers and noted how different they were from my mother's cat-loving friends. Immediately, I mused about the common stereotypes that each passion evokes; dog lovers are loyal, intelligent and hard working, while cat lovers are sensitive, introverted and finicky. Even the names they selected for their progeny (Duke, King and Rover versus Fluffy, Muffin and Precious) suggest that cat-lovers and dog-lovers are as different as night and day. In this sea of differences, I am a true anomaly: someone who loves both cats and dogs in equal, yet different ways.

35

Cat or dog. Chocolate or vanilla. Yin or yang. I am living proof that it is not only possible to love two extremely different things, but to pursue them with enthusiasm. In the case of choosing a dessert or a house pet, the answer is usually as simple as indulging different desires at different times. Just as cats and dogs are satisfying in dramatically different ways, so are many other choices in life. Although few experiences can measure up to the Westminster Dog Show, I am excited about exploring their possibilities.

41

6. What is the objective of this essay?

    a. to dispute the opinion of a famous newscaster
    b. to discuss the author's passion for both cats and dogs
    c. to provide background information about the trainer of a championship dog
    d. to explain the author's indecisiveness
    e. to explain this family's love of animals

7. What is the author's tone?

    a. ironic
    b. succinct
    c. jubilant
    d. light-hearted
    e. vainglorious

8. Why does the author open the essay with the quote by Barbara Walters?

    a.   to name drop
    b.   to make herself sound more important
    c.   to dispute Ms. Walter's assertion
    d.   to compare and contrast
    e.   the assignment required a quotation

9. The passage mentions all of the following breeds of cats EXCEPT:

    a.   Siamese
    b.   Calico
    c.   Birman
    d.   Persian
    e.   Burmese

10. In Line 25, to what does the expression "*gray ghost*" refer?

    a.   The author's father
    b.   The author's grandfather
    c.   The weimaraner breed
    d.   The ghost of the dog that used to live in the barn
    e.   A breed of horse

11. From the passage, we can infer that cat lovers are most likely to be:

    a.   fashionable
    b.   rude
    c.   rugged
    d.   boisterous
    e.   gentle

12. What is the most likely title for this passage?

    a.   Who Says I Have to Choose?
    b.   Who Says Dogs are Better?
    c.   Cats vs. Dogs: A House Divided
    d.   Life at the Zoo
    e.   Why I Love the Gray Ghost

Passage 2A

My mother kept hers to preserve history, as did my grandmother. Even as a young girl, I thought it was a wonderful idea.   I have subsequently kept my own journal since the fifth grade, taking a moment each day to recount events, discussions and meaningful issues.   My father's attic contains a box that is filled with every journal I've kept during the past fifteen years. Each Christmas, I randomly select a volume and read through several entries. By doing so, I become immersed in the details of my past, miraculously transported back to my high school days and the seemingly insurmountable problems of adolescence. As much as I prefer to think that I've evolved beyond my childhood feelings, a quick review of my own words confirms the consistency of my emotions. Even then, I had a passion for writing and teaching. I was always a sensitive girl who loved to be surrounded by friends. My journal provides more than just memories; it is a creative expression of who I am and who I hope to become.

11

My journal is as helpful today as it was during my high school years. In my daily life, I often encounter confusing events that initially seem overwhelming.   By keeping daily notes, I confirm the importance of specific issues and reinforce important life lessons. My journal reveals areas where I need to develop, feelings I need to resolve, and thoughts that I have never shared with another human being.   My journal is my own private haven for releasing emotions in a therapeutic manner.   On an intrinsic level, my journal shapes the woman I am today, both professionally and personally. Whenever I feel off-track, I read my past entries about similar events.

My heartfelt thoughts in my journal reinforce my career path, my personal values and my commitment to my family and friends.

20

Passage 2B

My most valued possession is a small, black rocking chair, clad with a thick set of velvet cushions that were hand-sewn in the late 1950's. The chair was a fixture in my grandmother's living room, where I spent many happy days as a child. As a toddler, my parents had to lift me into the chair, as my tiny legs were not long enough to reach the floor. Later, as an adolescent, I dragged the chair onto my grandmother's large wrap-around porch, where I quietly rocked as I threw peanuts to the seagulls and inhaled the salty ocean air.

26

When I visited my grandmother during college, I always sat in my favorite rocking chair. By this time, however, the chair was in her bedroom, where she slept after receiving chemotherapy. Some days she never awakened during my visits, and the only sound in her quiet room was the creaking of the old black rocker.

30

When my grandmother died last year, my mother sold her rambling Victorian that had been filled with furniture and antiques from the 1800's. My parents meticulously detailed which grandchildren took which items, determined to keep the financial disbursement as equitable as possible. My only request seemed odd, because I didn't want the Tiffany lamps, the original artwork or the priceless china and crystal. I wanted the one piece that would always remind me of my grandmother and the magic of her home: her small, black rocking chair, clad with the hand-sewn velvet cushions. It now sits in my living room, a lovely reminder of the woman who played such a kind, supportive role in my childhood and adolescence.

38

13. Passages A and B were both written in response to which topic?

   a. Describe your most sacred childhood memory
   b. Tell us about your family
   c. What is your most valued possession?
   d. What influence did your grandparents have on your life?
   e. What is your family's legacy?

14. In Passage A, why does the author re-read her journals each year?

   a. To explore past feelings
   b. To put new experiences into perspective
   c. To remember her childhood
   d. To regain a sense of stability
   e. All of the above

15. In recounting her childhood, the author of Passage A mentions all of the following EXCEPT:

   a. Being a good teacher
   b. Being sensitive
   c. Having many friends
   d. Benefiting from therapy
   e. Suffering angst in adolescence

16. Which adjective best describes the author of Passage A:

   a. introspective
   b. lethargic
   c. whimsical
   d. melancholy
   e. effervescent

17. In Line 16, what does *"therapeutic"* mean?

    a.   emotional
    b.   self-serving
    c.   medical
    d.   relaxing
    e.   healthy

18. In Passage B, in what locale did the author's grandmother live?

    a.   in the mountains
    b.   by the ocean
    c.   in a small rural town
    d.   in a retirement community
    e.   she does not indicate

19. In Passage B, we learn that the rocking chair has been in all of the following places EXCEPT:

    a.   grandmother's porch
    b.   author's living room
    c.   grandmother's living room
    d.   grandmother's sewing room
    e.   grandmother's bedroom

20. In Passage B, what does the author suggest about the velvet cushions on the rocking chair?

    a.   they were expensive
    b.   they were impossible to reproduce
    c.   her grandmother sewed them by hand
    d.   her siblings thought they were ugly
    e.   they would need to be updated

21. By choosing to keep the rocking chair, rather than another item of her grandmother's, the author of Passage B reveals:

    a.   That she dislikes antiques
    b.   That she had room in her apartment for it
    c.   That it held the most precious memories for her
    d.   That she does not care about money
    e.   That no one else wanted it

22. In Line 31, what does *"rambling"* mean?

    a.   spacious
    b.   disjointed
    c.   old
    d.   unorganized
    e.   historic

23. In Passage B, which of the following was NOT mentioned in the description of grandmother's home?

    a.   Tiffany lamp
    b.   Mahogany furniture
    c.   Original artwork
    d.   Priceless china and crystal
    e.   Antiques from the 1800's

24. Which of the following best describes the attitude of BOTH authors?

    a.   Tangible reminders of the past provide hope for a better future
    b.   Our loved ones will always be in our hearts
    c.   Each stage of life is special in its own right
    d.   Family is forever
    e.   Pain in temporary, but love lasts forever

STOP

The answers to these questions are presented in Section RC9 (page 234)

Directions: For each question in this section, select the best answer from the choices given and fill in the corresponding circle on the answer sheet.

1. There was not enough evidence to _____ the accuser's claims.

    a. surmount
    b. supersede
    c. substantiate
    d. stipulate
    e. slander

2. If left unresolved, small issues can eventually cause a permanent _____ between marital partners.

    a. rumination
    b. sanguinary
    c. rebuttal
    d. schism
    e. respite

3. According to Strunk and White, good writing requires clear focus and a _____ writing style, which makes the most of every word.

    a. creative
    b. provisional
    c. precise
    d. original
    e. enigmatic

4. The _____ disease left Charles a wasted man who could barely move his legs.

    a. myocardial
    b. hereditary
    c. infectious
    d. debilitating
    e. inflammatory

5. If used incorrectly, statistics can _____ the truth and lead researchers to _____ conclusions.

    a. enhance - critical
    b. summarize - concise
    c. twist - negligent
    d. distort - erroneous
    e. encapsulate – spurious

Directions: The passages below are followed by questions based on their content; questions following a pair of related passages may also be based on the relationship between the paired passages. Answer the questions, based on what is stated or implied in the passage and any introductory material that may be provided.

Passage 1

Nature is filled with smart and industrious creatures that gather food in the most efficient way possible. Few are as visible and annoying as "pavement ants," which nest on sidewalks and other hard surfaces, where humans tend to drop small food particles. When ants claim the food, they release pheromones, an odor trail that is easy for other ants to detect and follow. Within a matter of minutes, a single piece of food, such as a discarded hamburger, will attract the eager eye of hundreds of ants that have picked up the scent from the "early birds" before them.

7

The sidewalk provides an ambient environment for ants to thrive; it absorbs heat, which keeps the ants warm. Its cracks are ideal for building homes and colonies. And, from a practical perspective, sidewalks are less likely than grassy areas to be treated with toxic pesticides. Once established in their urban concrete home, an ant colony may reside there indefinitely, feasting on the discarded remnants of those who litter.

12

6. What is the primary objective of the passage?

   a. to discuss the practical implications of pheromones
   b. to explain the proliferation of pavement ants
   c. to complain about insect infestation
   d. to cite the dangers of littering
   e. to justify pesticide use in urban areas

7. In Line 5, to whom does the term *"early birds"* refer?

   a. the birds who capture the ants as prey
   b. the people who drop food onto the pavement for the ants to eat
   c. the insects who leave their scent behind for other ants to follow
   d. the first insects that are killed when pesticide is applied
   e. the rare strain of ants that is pesticide-resistant

8. According to the author, an ambient environment for ants includes all of the following traits EXCEPT:

   a. warmth
   b. cracks
   c. grass
   d. source of food
   e. hard surface

9. According to the passage, which of the following places would be most conducive to the survival of pavement ants?

   a. an inner city street corner
   b. a ski slope
   c. a desert
   d. a riverbed
   e. a wheat field

Passage 2

The most prominent error in conversation is not saying too little that amounts to much, but too much that amounts to little. Talkativeness is a characteristic more common of the ignorant than of the wise. Shenstone says, "The common fluency of speech in many men and women is due to a scarcity of matter and a scarcity of words; for whoever is master of a language and has a mind full of ideas, will be apt, in speaking, to hesitate upon the choice of both; but common speakers have only one set of ideas and one set of words to clothe them in— and these are always ready at the mouth. Just so people can come faster out of a church when it is almost empty, than when a crowd is at the door!" But although, according to the old proverb, "a still tongue denotes a wise head," the faculty of speech should not be neglected, merely because it may be misused.

10

Conversation is not a gift bestowed only upon those whom genius favors; on the contrary, many men eminent for their fluency of style in writing have been noted for habitual taciturnity in their intercourse with society. Hazlitt remarked, that "authors should be read, not heard!" Charles II of England, not only the wittiest of monarchs, but one of the liveliest of men, is said to have been so charmed in reading the humor of Butler's "Hudibras," that he disguised himself as a private gentleman and was introduced to the author, whom, to his astonishment, he found to be one of the dullest of companions. On the other hand, some of the humblest men with whom one falls into company, possessed of but little variety, and less extent of information, are highly entertaining talkers. The particular topic of remark does not form so essential a part of an interesting conversation, as the words and manner of those who engage in it. Robert Burns, sitting down on one occasion to write a poem, said: "Which way the subject theme may gang, let time or chance determine; perhaps it may turn out a song or probably a sermon."

22

In the same manner, the subject of a conversation need not be made a matter of study or special preparation. Men may talk of things momentous or trivial, and in either strain be attractive and agreeable. But quitting the consideration of the thought, to refer to the mode of its expression, it must be remarked and insisted that to "murder the king's English" is hardly less a crime than to design against one of the king's subjects. If committed from ignorance, the fault is at least deplorable; but if from carelessness, it is inexcusable. The greatest of sciences is that of language; the greatest of human arts is that of using words. No "cunning hand" of the artificer can contrive a work of mechanism that is to be compared, for a moment, with those wonderful masterpieces of ingenuity, which may be wrought by him who can skillfully mould a beautiful thought into a form that shall preserve, yet radiate its beauty.

32

A mosaic of words may be fairer than inlaid precious stones. The scholar who comes forth from his study a master of the English language is a workman who has at his command hardly less than a hundred thousand finely-tempered instruments, with which he may fashion the most cunning device. This is a trade which all should learn, for it is one that every individual is called to practice. The greatest support of virtue in a community is intelligence; intelligence is the outgrowth of knowledge; and the almoner of all knowledge is language. The possession, therefore, of the resources, and a command over the appliances of language, is of the utmost importance to every individual. Words are current coins of the realm, and they who do not have them in their treasury, suffer a more pitiable poverty than others who have not a penny of baser specie in their pocket; and the multitude of those who have an unfailing supply, but which is of the wrong stamp, are possessed only of counterfeit cash, that will not pass in circles of respectability.

44

10. What is the main point of the passage?

    a.   Language is a universal tool that unites us all
    b.   The most intelligent among us are linguists
    c.   Language is a precious gift that should be cultivated and used with care
    d.   Conversational flow should not be restricted by the participants
    e.   Writing requires time and effort to master

11. Which of the following most accurately expresses Shenstone's sentiments?

    a.   Those who speak the best know the most
    b.   Those with the least to say tend to speak the most
    c.   Words allow the common man to speak with mastery
    d.   Speaking in church is boorish and ill-advised
    e.   Words are common, but language is an art

12. In Line 9, what does "*faculty*" mean?

    a.   Teacher
    b.   Hyperbole
    c.   Example
    d.   Staff
    e.   Power

13. In Line 12, what does "*taciturnity*" mean?

    a. Flowery
    b. Reluctance
    c. Boastful
    d. Circumspect
    e. Humility

14. According to the author, which of the following best describes the reaction of Charles II of England to Butler?

    a.   He found Butler charming and witty
    b.   He found both the man and his work to be woefully overrated
    c.   He enjoyed Butler's work but found him dull in person
    d.   They became close companions upon their first meeting
    e.   They shared a love of intelligent discourse

15. According to the author, what is inexcusable?

    a.   Disrespecting the King of England
    b.   Making careless grammatical mistakes
    c.   Speaking too much
    d.   A lack of education
    e.   Using a cunning hand

16. According to the author, what is the relationship between language and words?

    a.   Language is a virtue of intelligence, while words are an outgrowth of knowledge
    b.   Words are a virtue of intelligence, while language is the almoner of knowledge
    c.   Language is the greatest of sciences and using words is the greatest human art
    d.   Language is the greatest art, which relies upon the science of words
    e.   Language supports the virtue of a community through the mosaic of words

17. In Line 35, what does "*instruments*" mean?

    a.   Words
    b.   Letters
    c.   Books
    d.   Thoughts
    e.   Tools

18. In Line 37, what does "*almoner*" mean"?

    a.   Virtue
    b.   Goodness
    c.   Source
    d.   Antipathy
    e.   Benevolence

19. According to the author, which of the following is the best example of "counterfeit cash"?

    a.   Illiteracy
    b.   Apathy
    c.   Slang
    d.   Education
    e.   Verbosity

STOP

The answers to these questions are presented in Section RC10 (page 235)

Reading Comprehension 11: 20 minutes 19 questions

Directions: For each question in this section, select the best answer from the choices given and fill in the corresponding circle on the answer sheet.

1. Ironically, Amanda's efforts to make people like her only served to _____ them.

    a. ridicule
    b. coddle
    c. pacify
    d. repel
    e. confuse

2. Although the Professor was a brilliant man, he appeared to be _____ of common sense.

    a. cautious
    b. full
    c. devoid
    d. appreciative
    e. disdain

3. Clarissa was too vibrant and athletic to settle for a _____ lifestyle.

    a. humanitarian
    b. traditional
    c. spiritual
    d. sedentary
    e. chaotic

Directions: The passages below are followed by questions based on their content; questions following a pair of related passages may also be based on the relationship between the paired passages. Answer the questions, based on what is <u>stated</u> or <u>implied</u> in the passage and any introductory material that may be provided.

Passage 1

While helping a friend in 1995, Yan Lee unwittingly triggered a national phenomenon. At the time, Internet technology was still in its infancy in China, a far cry from its current role in global communication. Without textbooks or expert advice, Lee used his innate curiosity to explore the un-chartered waters of the "information superhighway." At his friend's request, he sent several urgent online messages to help a young woman who suffered from dire medical symptoms. To Lee's surprise, he received more than three thousand responses in a week, including relevant diagnostic advice. With the help of this information, doctors diagnosed and treated the young woman for Thallium poisoning, a rare (but curable) affliction.

8

For many Chinese people, the headlines about Lee's rescue story marked their first encounter with the Internet. The accompanying publicity changed Lee's life. After much work, he established one of the first web servers and news servers in China, becoming one of a handful of Chinese experts in the field. He soon received invitations to lecture to government officials, university professors, businessmen and foreign officials in the United Nations who wanted to explore the use of the Internet in their home countries. While still a full-time graduate student at Peking University, he accepted an offer to join an Internet company as technical director. Several months later, he started his own firm with several partners. After his poignant experience helping his friend, Lee was committed to help others use the Internet to improve their own lives. He wrote and researched three books on the topic between 1996 and 1998.

18

During the past ten years, the Internet has assumed a powerful role in the lives of everyday people. At the same time, Yan Lee's once meteoric rise to the top of the white-hot technology field took an unexpected turn. In 2004, when the demand for IT professionals began to slide, Lee shifted his attention to a more lucrative sideline: the creation of spy ware and the exclusive sales rights to his one-of-a-kind spy ware removal tool. Now, for the millions of users whose computers have been infected, and in many cases immobilized, by his "product," the name Yan Lee is a painful remainder of talent and skill gone awry.

25

As Albert Einstein once warned, "Our technology may one day exceed our humanity." The implications are particularly acute in Lee's case, because there is little legal regulation of intellectual property in China, and the profits from his sales of the "spy ware removal tool" cannot be seized. So, for now, Lee remains a notorious outlaw in the world of cyberspace, where he continues to leap a step ahead of the agencies that once revered him.

31

4. What is the main idea of this passage?

    a. Cyberspace is a dangerous place
    b. Spy ware is a profitable business
    c. The Internet can be used for both good and evil, depending on a person's motivation and character
    d. Technology is inherently evil
    e. China has little control over its white collar criminals

5. In what type of publication would this passage most likely have been published?

    a. A book review
    b. An autobiography
    c. A business plan for a computer company
    d. A novel
    e. A computer magazine

6. According to the author, which of the following was NOT one of Lee's accomplishments between 1995 and 1998?

    a. Attended graduate school at Peking University
    b. Helped international agencies fight cyber crime
    c. Established web servers and news servers in China
    d. Lectured to government and foreign officials
    e. Wrote and researched three books

7. According to the author, why did Yan Lee begin to market spy ware?

    a. It is a lucrative field
    b. His profits could not be seized
    c. Fewer opportunities in IT
    d. a and c
    e. a, b and c

8. Why does the author include the quotation by Albert Einstein in Line 26?

    a. To support his contention that the Internet is evil
    b. To anger the audience
    c. To indicate his support for Yan Lee's actions
    d. Because he believed that Yan Lee had fulfilled Einstein's dire prophesy
    e. To add credibility to the passage

9. According to the author, why has Yan Lee eluded the authorities?

    a. he lives in the Bahamas, which has no extradition treaty with China
    b. intellectual property is not well-regulated in China
    c. he has hidden his assets in a Swiss bank account
    d. they cannot trace the spy ware back to him
    e. his colleagues are not cooperating with the ongoing investigation

10. What is the author's tone in the passage?

    a.   authoritative
    b.   disrespectful
    c.   factual
    d.   haughty
    e.   cynical

11. In Lines 28 and 29, the author refers to Lee as "a notorious outlaw in the world of cyberspace." What type of reference is this?

    a.   illustration
    b.   metaphor
    c.   allegory
    d.   anagram
    e.   simile

Passage 2A

When I graduated from high school, my father was between jobs in the aerospace industry. Consequently, he didn't have the money to buy me an expensive gift or to send me on a summer vacation with my friends. Instead, his graduation gift to me was an antique watch that was passed down to him from his paternal grandfather. Although it kept accurate time, the watch was never aesthetically pleasing; the gold had tarnished and the hands were extremely ornamental and difficult to read. Yet I cherished the watch as a family heirloom and as a symbolic acknowledgment of my adulthood.

7

At the time, I hoped that the gift was just the first of many from my father as I began a long and happy life. Sadly, he was killed in a car crash during my freshman year in college. As a result, the gold watch he presented to me at my high school graduation was the last gift I ever received from my father. It now symbolizes much more than my impending adulthood; it represents all the missing gifts that I will never receive from a loving man who died far too soon.

13

Passage 2B

My most treasured possession is my mother's wedding ring, which I received as a gift on my eighth birthday. I don't remember my mother, as she and my father were killed in a car accident just before I turned three. Yet I grew up surrounded by love, hearing wonderful stories about my parents and their devotion to us. My older sister told me that my parents' marriage was perfect and I hoped to someday achieve the same happiness.

18

Our home was destroyed by a hurricane when I was a teenager, leaving us with just the clothes on our backs. Fortunately, my mother's ring was on my finger that day and remained in my possession. I always wear the ring, either on my right hand or on a chain around my neck. Although I have not yet found marital happiness, I still view my mother's ring as evidence of its infinite possibility. It also represents a permanent connection to my mother, a tangible piece of her life that I know far too little about.

24

12. Passages A and B share a common theme, which is:

    a.   Remembering deceased parents
    b.   Jewelry with sentimental meaning
    c.   Cherished birthday gifts from deceased parents
    d.   Parents killed in car crashes
    e.   Reminders of grief

13. In Passage A, which of the following is NOT true of the gold watch?

    a.   it kept proper time
    b.   it was gold
    c.   it was a family heirloom
    d.   it originally belonged to the author's maternal grandfather
    e.   it was the last gift the author received from his father

14. In Line 4, what does "*aesthetically*" mean?

    a.   valuable
    b.   visually
    c.   emotionally
    d.   plain
    e.   classically

15. In Line 11, what does "*impending*" mean?

    a.   eminent
    b.   eventual
    c.   immediate
    d.   imminent
    e.   illustrious

16. In Passage B, who gave the author her mother's wedding ring?

    a.   her maternal grandfather
    b.   it was part of her parents' estate
    c.   her maternal grandmother
    d.   her older sister
    e.   the author does not say

17. Which of the following is true of the ring in Passage B?

    a.   author received it on her ninth birthday
    b.   author wore it for her own wedding
    c.   author wears it on her left hand
    d.   it symbolizes her parents' happy marriage
    e.   it was lost in a hurricane

18. In Line 22, what does "*infinite*" mean?

    a.   unlimited
    b.   forever
    c.   magical
    d.   spiritual
    e.   magnificent

19. Which of the following is NOT true about the jewelry inherited by the authors of Passage A and Passage B?

    a.   It holds great sentimental value
    b.   It is symbolic to them of the parents they lost
    c.   They received the pieces as gifts
    d.   It makes them feel closer to their deceased parents
    e.   It is simple and tasteful

STOP

The answers to these questions are presented in Section RC11 (page 236)

Reading Comprehension 12:   20 minutes 19 questions

Directions: For each question in this section, select the best answer from the choices given and fill in the corresponding circle on the answer sheet.

1. In a less _____ part of town, such _____ is a rarity.

    a.   chaotic - tranquility
    b.   prestigious - chicanery
    c.   sophisticated - notoriety
    d.   gregarious - duplicity
    e.   affluent - decadence

2. Barbara was so _____ that she could not try on clothes in most tiny dressing rooms.

    a.   agoraphobic
    b.   bashful
    c.   claustrophobic
    d.   modest
    e.   conservative

3. Bank robbers are _____ for wearing clever disguises, which prevent them from being identified.

    a.   notorious
    b.   criticized
    c.   unseemly
    d.   sadistic
    e.   pliant

4. His sterling reputation as a New York theatre actress was _____ by the publication of her photos on the society page.

    a.   compromised
    b.   obliterated
    c.   enhanced
    d.   disregarded
    e.   mitigated

5. Long after Christina suffered huge losses in the stock market crash, she continued to spend _____ amounts of money.

    a.   innocuous
    b.   prudent
    c.   pragmatic
    d.   exorbitant
    e.   parsimonious

6. Denise, the office gossip, repeated personal details about her boss's life with little or no _____.

    a.   innuendo
    b.   candor
    c.   discretion
    d.   conviviality
    e.   conservation

Passage 1

Of all bakery ingredients, sugar is the least prone to microbiological contamination. Its low moisture content, generally below 2%, dehydrates the microorganisms that cause mold and prevents other chemical changes that can cause spoilage.

4

When exposed to water, however, sugar is an excellent environment for the proliferation of yeasts and molds. Hence, in humid conditions, food scientists advise consumers to store sugar in an airtight container that will retard the absorption of moisture. Research suggests that sugar has an unlimited shelf life if stored at 2% moisture or less, with a relative humidity below 60%.

9

7. What is the main point of the passage?

    a.   To explain the factors that encourage microbial growth in sugar
    b.   To explain the stability of bakery ingredients
    c.   To help housewives store sugar safely
    d.   To promote the sale of airtight food containers
    e.   To explain an outbreak of Salmonella, which was due to sugar contamination

8. According to the author, what chemical changes in sugar cause it to spoil?

    a.   High moisture content
    b.   High humidity
    c.   Insect infestation
    d.   a and b
    e.   a, b and c

9. In Line 7, what is the meaning of the word "retard"?

    a.   encourage
    b.   exacerbate
    c.   prohibit
    d.   encapsulate
    e.   crystallize

10. According to the author, which of the following sugar samples would have an unlimited shelf life?

    a.   Moisture level of 2.1%, relative humidity of 59%
    b.   Moisture level of 1.9%, relative humidity of 62%
    c.   Moisture level of 3%, relative humidity of 20%
    d.   Moisture level of 2.1%, relative humidity of 48%
    e.   Moisture level of 1.9%, relative humidity of 59%

11. In what publication was this passage most likely published?

    a.   a woman's magazine
    b.   a physics textbook
    c.   a nutrition journal
    d.   a food science journal
    e.   an advertisement for sugar

Passage 2

Civilization in its onward march has produced only three important non-alcoholic beverages--the extract of the tea plant, the extract of the cocoa bean, and the extract of the coffee bean. Of these three, coffee is universal in its appeal. In fact, for millions of people, coffee is no longer a luxury or an indulgence; it is a corollary of human energy and human efficiency. People love coffee because of its two-fold effect--the pleasurable sensation and the increased efficiency that it produces.

6

On a socioeconomic basis, coffee is a surprisingly democratic beverage. Not only is it the drink of fashionable society, but it is also a favorite beverage of the men and women who do the world's work, whether they toil with brain or brawn. It has been acclaimed "the most grateful lubricant known to the human machine," and "the most delightful taste in all nature." Yet, ironically, no "food drink" has ever encountered so much opposition as coffee. Given to the world by the church and dignified by the medical profession, nevertheless, it has also suffered from religious superstition and medical prejudice. During the thousand years of its development, coffee has experienced fierce political opposition, nonsensical fiscal restrictions, unjust taxes, irksome duties; but, surviving all of these, it has triumphantly moved on to a foremost place in the catalog of popular beverages.

16

But coffee is something more than a beverage. It is one of the world's greatest adjuvant foods whose unique flavor and aroma give it unique palatability and comforting effects. Men and women drink coffee because it adds to their sense of well-being. It not only smells good and tastes good to all mankind, heathen or civilized, but all respond to its wonderful stimulating properties. The chief factors in coffee goodness are the caffeine content and the caffeol. Caffeine supplies the principal stimulant, which increases the capacity for muscular and mental work without a harmful reaction. In contrast, the caffeol supplies the indescribable Oriental fragrance that entices us through the nostrils, forming one of the principal elements that make up the lure of coffee. There are several other constituents, including certain innocuous so-called caffetannic acids, which, in combination with the caffeol, give the beverage its rare gustatory appeal.

26

The year 1919 awarded coffee one of its brightest honors. An American general said that coffee shared with bread and bacon the distinction of being one of the three nutritive essentials that helped win the World War for the Allies. So this symbol of human brotherhood has played a not inconspicuous part in "making the world safe for democracy." Yet, like all good things in life, the drinking of coffee may be abused. Indeed, those having an idiosyncratic susceptibility to alkaloids should be temperate in the use of tea, coffee, or cocoa. In every high-tensioned country there is likely to be a small number of people who, because of certain individual characteristics, cannot drink coffee. To suit these people who are caffeine-sensitive, coffee makers have developed a curious collection of so-called coffee substitutes, which are "neither fish nor flesh, nor good red herring." Most of them have been shown by official government analyses to be sadly deficient in food value-- their only alleged virtue. One contemporary attacker of the national beverage bewails the fact that no palatable hot drink has been found to take the place of coffee. The reason is not hard to find. There can be no substitute for coffee. Dr. Harvey W. Wiley has ably summed up the matter by saying, "A substitute should be able to perform the functions of its principal. A substitute to a war must be able to fight. Sadly, a coffee substitute will never be the nectar of the Gods that I lovingly call coffee."

41

12. What is the main point of the passage?

    a. To explain the botanical origin of coffee
    b. To explain why the church and the medical profession oppose excessive consumption of coffee
    c. To explain the practical role of caffeine and caffeol
    d. To explain the pitfall of caffeine-sensitivity
    e. To explain why coffee is the most popular beverage in the world

13. In Line 3, what does "*corollary*" mean?

    a. Inkling
    b. Essence
    c. Opponent
    d. Factor
    e. Source

14. According to the author, coffee has experienced all of the following EXCEPT:

    a. Political opposition
    b. Fiscal restrictions
    c. Unjust taxes
    d. Legal prejudice
    e. Religious superstition

15. In Line 17, what does "*adjuvant*" mean?

    a. Supportive
    b. Universal
    c. Affordable
    d. Aromatic
    e. International

16. According to the author, what is the role of caffeine in coffee?

    a. It gives coffee its gustatory appeal
    b. It makes coffee a medical nuisance
    c. It increases the drinker's mental and physical capacity
    d. It is one of the principal elements that make up the lure of coffee
    e. It can easily be replaced by a synthetic compound in coffee substitutes

17. According to Dr. Harvey W. Wiley, which of the following words or expressions best describes coffee substitutes?

    a. Clever and sophisticated
    b. Woefully inadequate
    c. A necessary evil
    d. Somewhat undesirable
    e. Medically superior

18. From this passage, we can infer that the author.......

    a. Works for a coffee manufacturer
    b. Acknowledges the political opposition to coffee
    c. Is sensitive to high doses of alkaloids such as caffeine
    d. Is enthusiastic about coffee
    e. Believes that caffeine-sensitivity is just a myth

19. In which of the following was this passage most likely published?

    a. A history book about the World Wars
    b. A cookbook
    c. An article in a food magazine
    d. A medical journal
    e. A psychology textbook

STOP

The answers to these questions are presented in Section RC12 (page 237)

Reading Comprehension 13: 20 minutes 19 questions

Directions: For each question in this section, select the best answer from the choices given and fill in the corresponding circle on the answer sheet.

1. Rather than participate in a fight, Linda preferred to assume a position of _____.

   a. mediator
   b. neutrality
   c. arbiter
   d. clarity
   e. despot

2. In a less _____ society, liability insurance would be less of a necessity.

   a. decadent
   b. disreputable
   c. precarious
   d. litigious
   e. colloquial

3. True scholars are not _____ by money or fame, but by their devotion to their fields of study.

   a. distracted
   b. inveighed
   c. consoled
   d. motivated
   e. tempted

4. Hiram's _____ past, including several arrests for fraud, _____ his chances at a management job.

   a. humiliating - perpetrated
   b. criminal - ruined
   c. duplicitous - mitigated
   d. lackluster - torpedoed
   e. narcissistic – minimized

5. By failing to keep his word, Matthew _____ the trust his parents had placed in him.

   a. augmented
   b. exacerbated
   c. eroded
   d. dispatched
   e. recapitulated

Directions: The passages below are followed by questions based on their content; questions following a pair of related passages may also be based on the relationship between the paired passages. Answer the questions, based on what is stated or implied in the passage and any introductory material that may be provided.

Passage 1

Jealousy is an accidental passion, for which the faculty indeed is unborn. In its nobler form and in its nobler motives it arises from love, and in its lower form it arises from the deepest and darkest Pit of Satan. Jealousy arises either from weakness, which from a sense of its own want of lovable qualities is not convinced of being sure of its cause, or from distrust, which thinks the beloved person capable of infidelity. Sometimes all these motives may act together.

6

The noblest jealousy, if the term noble is appropriate, is a sort of ambition or pride of the loving person who feels it is an insult that another one should assume it is possible to supplant his love, or it is the highest degree of devotion which sees a declaration of its object in the foreign invasion, as it were, of his own altar. Jealousy is always a sign that a little more wisdom might adorn the individual without harm.

11

The lowest species of jealousy is a sort of avarice of envy which, without being capable of love, at least wishes to possess the object of its jealousy alone by the one party assuming a sort of property right over the other. This jealousy, which might be called the Satanic, is generally to be found with old withered "husbands," who the devil has prompted to marry young women and who forthwith dream night and day of cuckold's horns. These Argus-eyed keepers are no longer capable of any feeling that could be called love, they are rather as a rule heartless house-tyrants, and are in constant dread that someone may admire or appreciate his unfortunate slave.

19

The general conclusion will be that jealousy is more the result of wrong conditions which cause uncongenial unions, and which through moral corruption artificially create distrust than a necessary accompaniment of love. Jealousy is a passion with which those are most afflicted who are the least worthy of love. An innocent maiden who enters marriage will not dream of getting jealous; but all her innocence cannot secure her against the jealousy of her husband if he has been a libertine. Those are wont to be the most jealous who have the consciousness that they themselves are most deserving of jealousy. Most men in consequence of their present education and corruption have so poor an opinion not only of the male, but even of the female sex, that they believe every woman at every moment capable of what they themselves have looked for among all and have found among the most unfortunate, the prostitutes. No libertine can believe in the purity of woman; it is contrary to nature. A libertine therefore cannot believe in the loyalty of a faithful wife.

30

There may be occasions where jealousy is justifiable. If a woman's confidence has been shaken in her husband, or a husband's confidence has been shaken in his wife by certain signs or conduct, which have no other meaning but that of infidelity, then there is just cause for jealousy. There must, however, be certain proof as evidence of the wife's or husband's immoral conduct. Imaginations or any foolish absurdities should have no consideration whatever, and let everyone have confidence until his or her faith has been shaken by the revelation of absolute facts.

37

No couple should allow their associations to develop into an engagement and marriage if either one has any inclination to jealousy. It shows invariably a want of sufficient confidence, and that want of confidence, instead of being diminished after marriage, is liable to increase, until by the aid of the imagination and wrong interpretation the home is made a hell and divorce a necessity. Let it be remembered, there can be no true love without perfect and absolute confidence, jealousy is always the sign of weakness or madness. Avoid a jealous disposition, for it is an open acknowledgment of a lack of faith.

44

6. What is the main point of the passage?

   a. Jealousy is a sign of weakness or madness
   b. Jealousy is justifiable when infidelity has occurred
   c. Jealousy is a misguided form of personal pride
   d. Jealous people believe that others are jealous as well
   e. Jealous people are incapable of honest communication

7. In Line 8, what does "*supplant*" mean?

   a. Mollify
   b. Repudiate
   c. Diminish
   d. Prove
   e. Supersede

8. In Lines 15 - 16, to whom does the author refer as "Argus-eyed keepers?

    a.   People who suffer from unrequited love
    b.   Old husbands who do not trust their younger wives around other men
    c.   Unfaithful spouses who flaunt their extramarital affairs
    d.   Unfaithful spouses who presume their spouses are also cheating
    e.   Spouses who lack confidence in their romantic appeal

9. In Line 24, what does "*libertine*" mean?

    a.   Withholding affection
    b.   Sociopath
    c.   Self-involved
    d.   Morally depraved
    e.   Morally superior

10. The author states all of the following about jealousy EXCEPT:

    a.   Those who are most jealous are least worthy of love
    b.   Those who are most jealous believe that they are also deserving of jealousy
    c.   Most men who seek the company of prostitutes believe that women will also seek the same type of immoral companionship
    d.   Jealous is a necessary accompaniment of love
    e.   Moral corruption artificially created distrust

11. What is the likely source of the passage?

    a.   A religious sermon
    b.   A newspaper article about marriage
    c.   A documentary about sexually transmitted diseases
    d.   A psychology textbook
    e.   An argument in a college debate

Passage 2

The origin of the corset is lost in remote antiquity. The figures of the early Egyptian women show clearly an artificial shape of the waist produced by some style of corset. A similar style of dress must also have prevailed among the ancient Jewish maidens; for Isaiah, in calling upon the women to put away their personal adornments, says: "Instead of a girdle there shall be a rent, and instead of a stomacher (corset) a girdle of sackcloth."   Homer also tells us of the cestus of Venus, which was borrowed by the haughty Juno with a view to increasing her personal attractions, that Jupiter might be a more tractable and orderly husband. Coming down to the later times, we find the corset was used in France and England as early as the 12th century.

9

The most extensive and extreme use of the corset occurred in the 16th century, during the reign of Catherine de Medici of France and Queen Elizabeth of England. With Catherine de Medici a thirteen-inch waist measurement was considered the standard of fashion, while a thick waist was an abomination. No lady could consider her figure of proper shape unless she could span her waist with her two hands. To produce this result a strong rigid corset was worn night and day until the waist was laced down to the required size. Then over this corset was placed a steel apparatus called a corset-cover, which reached from the hip to the throat, and produced a rigid figure over which the dress would fit with perfect smoothness.

17

During the 18th century corsets were largely made from a species of leather known as "Bend," which was not unlike that used for shoe soles, and measured nearly a quarter of an inch in thickness. About the time of the French Revolution, a reaction set in against tight lacing, and for a time there was a return to the early classical Greek costume. This style of dress prevailed, with various modifications, until about 1810 when corsets and tight lacing again returned with threefold fury. Buchan, a prominent writer of this period, says that it was by no means uncommon to see "a mother lay her daughter down upon the carpet, and, placing her foot upon her back, break half a dozen laces in tightening her stays."

25

It is reserved to our own time to demonstrate that corsets and tight lacing do not necessarily go hand in hand. Distortion and feebleness are not beauty. A proper proportion should exist between the size of the waist and the

68

breadth of the shoulders and hips, and if the waist is diminished below this proportion, it suggests disproportion and invalidism rather than grace and beauty.

30

The perfect corset is one which possesses just that degree of rigidity which will prevent it from wrinkling, but will at the same time allow freedom in the bending and twisting of the body. Corsets boned with whalebone, horn or steel are necessarily stiff, rigid and uncomfortable. After a few days wear, the bones or steels become bent and set in position, or, as more frequently happens, they break and cause injury or discomfort to the wearer.

36

About seven years ago, an article was discovered for the stiffening of corsets, which has revolutionized the corset industry of the world. This article is manufactured from the natural fibers of the Mexican Ixtle plant, and is known as Coraline. It consists of straight, stiff fibers like bristles bound together into a cord by being wound with two strands of thread passing in opposite directions. This produces an elastic fiber intermediate in stiffness between twine and whalebone. It cannot break, but it possesses all the stiffness and flexibility necessary to hold the corset in shape and prevent its wrinkling.

43

We congratulate the ladies of today upon the advantages they enjoy over their sisters of two centuries ago, in the forms and the graceful and easy curves of the corsets now made as compared with those of former times.

47

12. What is the main point of the passage?

    a.   To argue against the use of corsets for medical reasons
    b.   To justify the use of Coraline in the manufacture of corsets
    c.   To explain the historical preference for an artificially small waistline
    d.   To mock the ancient standard of beauty in European culture
    e.   To discuss the historical evolution of the corset in women's fashion

13. In Line 5, what is a "*cestus*"?

    a.   Dress
    b.   Wig
    c.   Girdle
    d.   Stocking
    e.   Wardrobe

14. The author mentions the use of corsets in all countries EXCEPT:

    a.   Egypt
    b.   Greece
    c.   France
    d.   Italy
    e.   England

15. In Line 12, what does "*abomination*" mean?

    a.   Disgrace
    b.   Obesity
    c.   Distress
    d.   Menacing
    e.   Uncouth

16. From Lines 10 - 16 in the passage, what we can conclude about Catherine de Medici?

    a.   She was a fashion icon in her native France
    b.   She used a corset-cover to attain a thirteen-inch waist
    c.   She abolished the use of corsets due to their extreme discomfort
    d.   She imported special leather called Bend to make her corsets
    e.   She was a strong enthusiast of classic Greek costume

17. According to the author, all of the following are true EXCEPT:

    a. Corsets boned with whalebone are stiff, but comfortable
    b. Distortion and feebleness are not beauty
    c. The perfect corset prevents wrinkling, but allows the body to twist and bend
    d. Corsets and tight lacing do not necessarily go hand in hand
    e. An artificially small waist suggests disproportion and invalidism

18. Which of the following is NOT true about Coraline?

    a. Coraline is manufactured from the natural fibers of the Ixtle plant
    b. Coraline cannot break
    c. Coraline is an elastic fiber that is stiffer than whalebone
    d. Coraline revolutionized the corset industry
    e. Coraline possesses the required stiffness and flexibility to hold a corset in shape.

19. What is the tone of the passage?

    a. Ambivalent
    b. Aghast
    c. Lackadaisical
    d. Factual
    e. Incredulous

STOP

The answers to these questions are presented in Section RC13 (page 238)

Quantitative 1:   25 Minutes   20 Questions

Directions: You have 25 minutes to answer the following 20 questions. Choose the best answer from the options given.

- The use of a calculator is permitted.
- All numbers used are real numbers.
- Figures that accompany problems are intended to provide valuable information useful in solving the problems. They are drawn as accurately as possible EXCEPT when it is stated in a specific problem that the figure is not drawn to scale. All figures lie in a plane unless otherwise indicated.
- Unless otherwise specified, the domain of any function f is assumed to be the set of all real numbers x for which f (x) is a real number.

Reference Information:

- Circles. Area $= \pi r^2$, Circumference $= 2 \pi r$
- Rectangles: Area = Length X Width
- Right Triangles: Area = ½ (Base) (Height)
- Cubes: Volume = Length x Width x Height
- Cylinders: Volume $= \pi r^2 h$
- Pythagorean Theorem: for right triangles $c^2 = a^2 + b^2$

1. Pamela rode her motorcycle from Ames Street to Alvin Circle at an average speed of 35 miles per hour. On the way back, Pamela was delayed by hazardous road conditions, which forced her to slow down to an average speed of 18 miles per hour. What was Pamela's average speed for the trip, in miles per hour?

    a.   20
    b.   21
    c.   24
    d.   27
    e.   30

2. For marketing purposes Ace Hamburgers is recording the number of customers who order hot dogs during the lunch rush. During the first half of January, they collected the following daily values: 43, 56, 42, 56, 47, 28, 36, 65, 67, 89, 81, 45, 54, 44, 34. What is the mode of the data set?

    a.   47
    b.   52.5
    c.   54
    d.   56
    e.   65

3. Liz is 42 years old and Amelia is 24. How many years ago was Liz three times as old as Amelia?

    a.   9
    b.   10
    c.   15
    d.   18
    e.   20

4. Gina and Hillary have a small web design business. Gina can design a web site for Client A in 2 hours. Hillary can design the same site in 3 hours. How long will it take them in minutes to design the site if they both work at the same time?

    a.   60
    b.   66
    c.   72
    d.   90
    e.   100

5. If M I-pods cost U dollars, what do N I-Pods cost?

    a.   MU/N
    b.   UN/M
    c.   MUN
    d.   1/MUN
    e.   MN/U

6. Doug has looked everywhere for the right carpet for his living room, which measures 18 feet x 36 feet. Finally, at Designer Carpet Surplus, he finds the perfect carpet, which costs $25 per square yard. How much will it cost Doug to purchase enough of this carpet to cover his entire living room?

    a. $480
    b. $1,440
    c. $1,800
    d. $4,800
    e. $14,400

7. The sum of two numbers is 48. Their difference is 12. What is the smaller number?

    a.   18
    b.   22
    c.   26
    d.   30
    e.   36

8. What is the area of a right triangle whose legs are both equal to 12?

    a.   6
    b.   12
    c.   24
    d.   72
    e.   144

9. Find the area of a sector of a circle with a radius of 8 and a 24 degree arc (use π = 3.1416).

    a.   13.4
    b.   16.0
    c.   24.0
    d.   26.4
    e.   32.0

10. Square G has a side of 14, while square H has a side of 12. How much greater is the area of square G than square H?

    a.   4
    b.   52
    c.   72
    d.   96
    e.   144

11. $(3/6 + 4/2)^3 =$

    a. 6.25
    b. 8
    c. 15.625
    d. 16.525
    e. 48

12. Which of the following is a multiple of 10, 15 and 35?

    a. 70
    b. 150
    c. 350
    d. 525
    e. 1050

13. What is the sum of the following fractions: 1/15, 2/10, 2/5, 1/3, 3/30

    a. 11/10
    b. 29/30
    c. 14/15
    d. 31/30
    e. 32/30

14. What positive integer is 40% less than 15,600?

    a. 4,680
    b. 6,240
    c. 6,864
    d. 8,680
    e. 9,360

15. Three hundred entertainers will perform at a talent show. The group contains only singers and dancers. If the ratio of singers to dancers is 2:1, how many dancers are there?

    a. 50
    b. 100
    c. 150
    d. 175
    e. 200

16. If $x^2 - y^2 = 16$ and $x - y = 2$, what is the value of $x + y$?

    a. 1
    b. 2
    c. 4
    d. 8
    e. 12

17. For the following systems of equations, what is the value of x? $y = 10 + 2x$ $y = 5x$

    a. 1/3
    b. 1/2
    c. 10/3
    d. 11/3
    e. 50/3

18. The difference between (X + Y) and (X – Y) is 6. Find the smaller of the two numbers if XY is 30.

      a.   2
      b.   3
      c.   5
      d.   6
      e.   10

19. Simplify the following expression: $(x^4y^7/x^5y^6)^4$

      a. y^3x^2
      b. y^4/x^4
      c. $(y/x)^{12}$
      d. y^{28}/x^{20}
      e.   none of the above

20. What is the probability that a card chosen at random from a standard deck of 52 cards is a King?

      a.   1/52
      b.   1/26
      c.   1/13
      d.   1/12
      e.   4/12

STOP

The answers to these questions are presented in Section QA1 (page 239)

Quantitative 2:   25 Minutes   18 Questions

1. Throughout the hurricane season, meteorologists record the number of rip currents on the northern coast of Africa, which are most likely to form tropical storms. For the first two weeks in July, the meteorologists recorded the following values: 12, 44, 62, 56, 34, 21, 34, 90, 78, 66, 44, 18, 98, and 23. What is the range of the data set?

    a. 38
    b. 44
    c. 56
    d. 86
    e. 98

2. What is the sum of the integers between 11 and 39, inclusive?

    a. 525
    b. 625
    c. 725
    d. 1,400
    e. 1,500

3. If the area of a rectangle is 625, what is its perimeter?

    a. 5
    b. 25
    c. 125
    d. 1250
    e. It cannot be determined from the information given

4. The graph of $y = 4x^2 – 12$ is:

    a. A straight line
    b. A parabola opening upward
    c. A parabola opening downward
    d. A circle
    e. None of the above

5. Carla owed her university $585 in tuition. When she receives her paycheck of $116, she pays it all to the university, along with $219 that she has borrowed from a friend. Later in the day, Carla wins $947 in the lottery, and immediately pays off the rest of her tuition bill and her friend. How much money does Carla have left?

        a. $246
        b. $250
        c. $478
        d. $697
        e. $728

6. To make enough brownies for a Girl Scout troop, Mrs. Wilson must mix 30 pounds of batter. Her tiny mixer at home, however, can only handle batches of 24 ounces. How many times will Mrs. Wilson have to run her mixer to produce the entire 30 pounds of brownie batter?

        a.   6
        b.   15
        c.   16
        d.   20
        e.   24

7. A home improvement store bought 300 generators before a major hurricane and sold 240 of them in a single day. What fraction of the 300 generators did not sell?

        a.   1/6
        b.   1/5
        c.   1/4
        d.   1/3
        e.   2/5

8. If x + 2 = 11, then what is $(x - 7)^3$?

        a.   1
        b.   8
        c.   9
        d.   16
        e.   81

9. Nancy is three years younger than her brother Cane, who is eight years older than Jake, who is 35 years old. How old is Nancy?

10. A right triangle has side lengths of 4 and 8. What is the length of the hypotenuse?

11. If the prime numbers between 40 and 50 are added together, what is their sum?

12. A Laundromat emptied its vending machines at the end of the night and found 312 quarters, 234 dimes, 443 nickels and 444 pennies. If the owner holds back $50.00 of this amount for petty cash and deposits the rest at the bank, how much will the bank deposit be?

13. What is the product of 14/31 x 93/76 (to three decimal places) ?

14. In the past year, Karen's book collection increased from 114 to 328. What percentage increase does this number represent?

15. If three workers can clean eighteen hotel rooms in one day, how many rooms can eleven workers clean in one day?

16. When an accountant requested her client's sales records for tax season, she received a stack of invoices numbered 00236 through 00435. How many invoices were in the stack?

17. For a line with the equation $8y - 24x = 16$, what is the slope?

18. If $p = 1$ and q is 2, what is $(9^p)/(3^q) =$

STOP

The answers to these questions are presented in Section QA2 (page 241)

Quantitative 3:   20 Minutes   16 Questions

Directions: You have 20 minutes to answer the following 16 questions. Choose the best answer from the options given.

- The use of a calculator is permitted.
- All numbers used are real numbers.
- Figures that accompany problems in this test are intended to provide valuable information useful in solving the problems. They are drawn as accurately as possible EXCEPT when it is stated in a specific problem that the figure is not drawn to scale. All figures lie in a plane unless otherwise indicated.
- Unless otherwise specified, the domain of any function f is assumed to be the set of all real numbers x for which f (x) is a real number.

Reference Information:

- Circles. Area $= \pi r^2$, Circumference $= 2 \pi r$
- Rectangles: Area = Length X Width
- Right Triangles: Area = ½ (Base) (Height)
- Cubes: Volume = Length x Width x Height
- Cylinders: Volume $= \pi r^2 h$
- Pythagorean Theorem: for right triangles $c^2 = a^2 + b^2$

1. The distance between Annapolis and Charlotte is 150 miles. A car travels from Annapolis to Charlotte at 75 miles per hour and returns from Charlotte to Annapolis along the same route at 50 miles per hour. What is the average speed for the round trip?

    a. 60
    b. 62.5
    c. 65
    d. 67.5
    e. 70

2. Kathy is buying a notebook computer on an installment plan. She can pay for it over a period of 6 months or 15 months. If the notebook costs $1850, how many additional dollars would she have to pay each month to pay for it over 6 months rather than 15 months (assuming there are no finance charges)?

    a. $103
    b. $123
    c. $185
    d. $203
    e. $308

3. A financial manager buys two types of bonds for his client. He buys $4,000 worth of Bond A and $12,000 worth of Bond B, which pays an annual interest rate 3% higher than Bond A. If the total return on the client's bonds is $1600, what was the interest rate for Bond B?

    a. 6.75%
    b. 7.75%
    c. 8.75%
    d. 9.75%
    e. 10.75%

4. Jake found a great deal on discontinued paint at Home Depot. When he brought the paint home, he discovered that the four cans he purchased were enough to paint three quarters of his bedroom. How many additional cans of paint will Jake need to buy to complete his bedroom and to paint three additional rooms that are the same size as his bedroom?

    a.   13
    b.   16.7
    c.   17.3
    d.   19
    e.   19.3

5. The angles of a triangle are in the ratio of 4:5:6. What is the degree measure of the smallest angle?

    a.   18
    b.   30
    c.   36
    d.   45
    e.   48

6. Rectangle ABCD has a length of 10 and a diagonal of 26. What is its area?

    a.   72
    b.   240
    c.   260
    d.   420
    e.   480

7. If $f(v) = 5v^2 - 1/8v - 3$, what is $f(v^3)$?

    a. $5v^5 - 1/8v^4 - 3v^3$
    b. $5v^5 - 1/8v^4 - 3$
    c. $15v^5 - 3/8v^4 - 9$
    d. $(5v^2 - 1/8v - 3)^3$
    e. $(5v^5 - 1/8v^4 - 3)^{-3}$

8. What is the slope of the line that contains points (2,3) and (8, 10)?

    a.   5/4
    b.   6/7
    c.   7/6
    d.   4/5
    e.   1

9. Sara is completely broke when she receives a $74 parking ticket. When Sara's brother gives her $125 for her birthday, she pays the ticket and buys $26 in gas. How much money does Sara have left?

    a. $25
    b. $26
    c. $51
    d. $99
    e. $101

10. How many divisors of 60 are prime numbers?

    a. 2
    b. 3
    c. 4
    d. 5
    e. 6

11. For the following fractions, what is the least common denominator?

        2/3, 3/5, 4/6, 9/10, 1/3

    a. 10
    b. 15
    c. 30
    d. 36
    e. 60

12. If the 6% hotel tax on a room is $4.32, what was the total price of the room (including tax)?

    a. $70.32
    b. $72.32
    c. $76.00
    d. $76.32
    e. $78.00

13. If you roll a 6-sided die, which sides are numbered 1 through 6, what is the probability that you will roll a 3?

    a. 1/6
    b. 1/5
    c. 1/4
    d. 1/3
    e. ½

14. If $x = 0.1$, what is the value of $(10x)^2 + 100x^2$?

    a. 0.1
    b. 1
    c. 2
    d. 10
    e. 11

15. What is the area (in cubic centimeters) of a trapezoid with a height of 12 cm and parallel side lengths of 16 cm and 18 cm?

    a. 84
    b. 96
    c. 192
    d. 204
    e. 216

16. If there are 285 men and 15 women employed at a local insurance office, what is the probability that one employee picked at random will be a woman?

   a. 1/30
   b. 1/25
   c. 1/20
   d. 1/15
   e. 1/3

STOP

The answers to these questions are presented in Section QA3 (page 242)

Quantitative 4:   **25 Minutes**   **20 Questions**

Directions: You have 25 minutes to answer the following 20 questions. Choose the best answer from the options given.

- The use of a calculator is permitted.
- All numbers used are real numbers.
- Figures that accompany problems in this test are intended to provide valuable information useful in solving the problems. They are drawn as accurately as possible EXCEPT when it is stated in a specific problem that the figure is not drawn to scale. All figures lie in a plane unless otherwise indicated.
- Unless otherwise specified, the domain of any function f is assumed to be the set of all real numbers x for which f (x) is a real number.

Reference Information:

- Circles. Area $= \pi r^2$, Circumference $= 2 \pi r$
- Rectangles: Area = Length X Width
- Right Triangles: Area = ½ (Base) (Height)
- Cubes: Volume = Length x Width x Height
- Cylinders: Volume $= \pi r^2 h$
- Pythagorean Theorem: for right triangles $c^2 = a^2 + b^2$

1. Every diner at a local restaurant either ordered soup, salad or both. 35% of the diners ordered both soup and salad, while 45% ordered only salad. What percentage ordered only soup?

    a.   10%
    b.   15%
    c.   20%
    d.   25%
    e.   30%

2. The product of two consecutive even integers is 16 less than eight times the larger integer. Find the larger integer.

    a.   8
    b.   10
    c.   12
    d.   14
    e.   16

3. A restaurant depletes its supply of mustard every 25 days. If its use increases by 75%, how many days would the same amount of mustard last?

    a.   6.25
    b.   12.5
    c.   14.3
    d.   43.75
    e.   75

4. A backyard swimming pool that is rectangular in shape holds 180,000 cubic feet of water. If the pool is 80 feet long and 120 feet wide, how deep will the water be if the pool is 75% full (to the nearest foot)?

    a.   10
    b.   12
    c.   14
    d.   15
    e.   18

5. Each of the equal sides of an isosceles triangle is four less than three times its base. If the perimeter is 90, what is the base of the triangle?

    a.   12
    b.   14
    c.   15
    d.   18
    e.   28

6. A tour bus at Disney World holds 124 people. If the park requires one adult for every five children on the tour bus, how many children can ride on the bus at any given time?

    a.   20
    b.   22
    c.   24
    d.   30
    e.   32

7. The perimeter of triangle LMN is 105. If LM = 35 and MN = 40, what is the length of LN?

    a.   30
    b.   35
    c.   40
    d.   45
    e.   105

8. A pizza is divided into slices of equal size, each with a side length of 7. Assuming that each slice meets at the center of the pizza, what is the pizza's circumference?

    a.   7
    b.   49
    c. 7π
    d. 14π
    e. 49π

9. If a Ψ b = $(1 + b)^{1/2}$ what is aΨ 15?

    a.   1/2
    b.   2
    c.   4
    d.   8
    e.   16

10. If the following series continues in the same pattern, what will the next term be?

          3, 5, 4, 7, 5, 9, 6, 11.........

    a.   3
    b.   5
    c.   6
    d.   7
    e.   13

11. If the average of nine consecutive odd integers is 113, what is the smallest of the nine integers?

  a. 99
  b. 101
  c. 103
  d. 105
  e. 107

12. 2.05 x 8.99 x 54.22 =

  a. 99.25
  b. 487.43
  c. 974.87
  d. 999.25
  e. 1949.75

13. How many positive integers less than 100 are evenly divisible by 10, 6 and 5?

  a. 0
  b. 1
  c. 2
  d. 3
  e. 4

14. If 1/32 of the daily dose of a medication is 3g, what is the total weekly dose of the medication?

  a. 32 g
  b. 64 g
  c. 96 g
  d. 336 g
  e. 672 g

15. The average (mean) of eight numbers is 8. If 2 is subtracted from each of four of the numbers, what is the new average?

  a. 5.5
  b. 6
  c. 6.5
  d. 7
  e. 7.5

16. What is 0.005% expressed as a fraction?

  a. 5/100
  b. 5/250
  c. 5/200
  d. 1/250
  e. 1/200

17. Simply $\sqrt{7}$ $\sqrt{8}$ $\sqrt{9}$

  a. 6.90
  b. 18.75
  c. 20.75
  d. 22.05
  e. 22.45

18. If $x = 10$, what is the value of $x^2 + 1/x^2$?

    a.   100.001
    b.   100.01
    c.   101.1
    d.   101.01
    e.   110.01

19. What is the absolute value of twice the difference of the roots of the equation $5y^2 - 20y + 15 = 0$?

    a.   0
    b.   1
    c.   2
    d.   3
    e.   4

20. What is the set of all values of x for which $x^2 - x = 12$?

    a.   (2, 6)
    b.   (-3, 4)
    c.   (3, -4)
    d.   (-2, 6)
    e.   (2, -6)

STOP

The answers to these questions are presented in Section QA4 (page 243)

Quantitative 5:   25 Minutes   18 Questions

Directions: This section contains two types of questions. You have 25 minutes to complete both types. For questions 1 – 8, solve each problem and select the best answer choice. Fill in the corresponding circle on the answer sheet. You may use any available space for scratch work. For Student-Produced Response questions 9 – 18, use the grids at the bottom of the answer sheet to record your answers.

- The use of a calculator is permitted.
- All numbers used are real numbers.
- Figures that accompany problems in this test are intended to provide valuable information useful in solving the problems. They are drawn as accurately as possible EXCEPT when it is stated in a specific problem that the figure is not drawn to scale. All figures lie in a plane unless otherwise indicated.
- Unless otherwise specified, the domain of any function f is assumed to be the set of all real numbers x for which f (x) is a real number.

Reference Information:

- Circles. Area = πr^2, Circumference = $2\pi r$
- Rectangles: Area = Length X Width
- Right Triangles: Area = ½ (Base) (Height)
- Cubes: Volume = Length x Width x Height
- Cylinders: Volume = $\pi r^2 h$
- Pythagorean Theorem: for right triangles $c^2 = a^2 + b^2$

1. If three less than eleven times a whole number is equal to 140, what is the number?

    a.   11
    b.   13
    c.   14
    d.   17
    e.   19

2. A landscaper wishes to cover a plot with colorful ceramic tiles, which each measure 1/2 inch by 3 inches. If the plot is a rectangle that measures 10 feet by 12 feet, how many ceramic tiles will the landscaper need to complete the job?

    a.   1,152
    b.   1,728
    c.   11,520
    d.   17,280
    e.   25,290

3. For a rectangular box with a width of 6 inches, a length of 14 inches and a height of 33 inches, what is the total volume (in cubic inches)?

    a.   53
    b.   84
    c.   94
    d.   462
    e.   2772

4. Find the equation of the line with a y-intercept of 8 and an x-intercept of 2.

    a.   y = 2x + 4
    b.   y = -2 x - 4
    c.   y = 4x - 2
    d.   y = -4x + 8
    e.   y = -4x – 8

5. Diane has 18 errands to run, which take 14 minutes each, before she can go home. If Diane needs to be home by 5:00 pm, what is the latest she can start the errands?

    a.   11:48 am
    b.   11:52 am
    c.   12:48 pm
    d.   12:52 pm
    e.   1:48 pm

Use the following information to answer questions 6 – 8

F = {1, 2, 4, 5, 8}   G = {4, 5, 6, 9,}   H = {2, 6, 7, 10}

6. What is $(F \cup G) \cap H$?

    a.   {2}
    b.   {2, 6}
    c.   {2, 4, 5}
    d.   {2, 5}
    e.   {9, 10}

7. What is $(F \cup G) \cup H$?

    a.   {2}
    b.   {2, 6}
    c.   {1, 2, 4, 5, 6, 7, 10, 11, 12}
    d.   {2, 3, 4, 5, 6, 7, 8, 9, 10, 12}
    e.   {1, 2, 4, 5, 6, 7, 8, 9, 10}

8. $(F \cup G) \cup H$ has the following number of subsets:

    a.   256
    b.   512
    c.   1024
    d.   2048
    e.   4096

9. The sum of five consecutive integers is 235. What is the middle integer?

10. An octagon has seven interior angles that measure 80, 90, 105, 120, 125, 130 and 135. What is the measure of the eighth internal angle?

11. What is the largest integer that will divide evenly into 51 and 187?

12. If the value of P quarters is equal to the value of P + 45 dimes, what is the value of P?

13. If g = 2 and k = 3, what is the value of $4g^3 - 2k^2 + 9gk - 6$?

14. What is 1.5% of 3,567?

15. In a hospital with 39 patients, the average (mean) temperature of the male patients was 101.7 F. If the average (mean) temperature of the 23 female patients was 98.5 F, what was the average temperature of all 39 patients (in degrees F)?

16. $84/7 \ (0.95 - 0.55)^2 =$
17. What is the slope of the line that contains points (4,5) and (6,15)?

18. Eighty students are attending summer school courses at Beaver Falls High School. Fifty have registered for Spanish, 20 have registered for Math, and 15 have registered for both Spanish and Math. How many have signed up for NEITHER Spanish nor Math?

STOP

The answers to these questions are presented in Section QA5 (page 244)

Quantitative 6:   20 Minutes   16 Questions

Directions: You have 20 minutes to answer the following 16 questions. Choose the best answer from the options given.

- The use of a calculator is permitted.
- All numbers used are real numbers.
- Figures that accompany problems in this test are intended to provide valuable information useful in solving the problems. They are drawn as accurately as possible EXCEPT when it is stated in a specific problem that the figure is not drawn to scale. All figures lie in a plane unless otherwise indicated.
- Unless otherwise specified, the domain of any function f is assumed to be the set of all real numbers x for which f (x) is a real number.

Reference Information:

- Circles. Area $= \pi r^2$, Circumference $= 2 \pi r$
- Rectangles: Area = Length X Width
- Right Triangles: Area = ½ (Base) (Height)
- Cubes: Volume = Length x Width x Height
- Cylinders: Volume $= \pi r^2 h$
- Pythagorean Theorem: for right triangles $c^2 = a^2 + b^2$

1. If one cubic foot of water equals 7.8 gallon, how long will it take for a faucet that flows at a rate of 12 gallons/minute to fill a cube that is 30 feet on each side (in hours)?

    a.   146.25 hours
    b.   292.5 hours
    c.   585.0 hours
    d.   15,550 hours
    e.   17,550 hours

2. Grace and Edna own a small business that earned $48,000 in profits last year. If they agreed to split the profits in a 9:4 ratio, with Grace getting the larger share, how much did Edna earn from the business?

    a. $10,453.67
    b. $11,896.23
    c. $14,769.23
    d. $21,453.23
    e. $33,230.70

3. Theresa is 10 years older than Cindy. However, 5 years ago Theresa was twice as old as Cindy. How old is Cindy?

    a.   5
    b.   10
    c.   12
    d.   15
    e.   20

4. Scientists recorded the daily temperature in a research aquarium. During a six-day period, the temperatures recorded (in °F) were 67, 73, 72, 56, 68, and 78. What was the median temperature (in °F)?

    a.   68.5
    b.   69
    c.   70
    d.   72.5
    e.   73

5. What is the equation of the line that contains the points (4, 5) and (7, 11)?

    a.   y = 2x – 1
    b.   y = 3x - 2
    c.   y = 2x + 3
    d.   y = -2x - 3
    e.   y = 2x – 3

6. If the base of a parallelogram increases by 12% and the height decreases by 18%, by what percent does the area change?

    a.   9% decrease
    b.   6% decrease
    c.   6% increase
    d.   10% increase
    e.   32% increase

7. If the diameter of a circle increases by 50%, by what percent will the area of the circle increase?

    a.   50%
    b.   75%
    c.   100%
    d.   125%
    e.   150%

8. A vending machine contains 300 jelly beans in four different colors, which are dispensed in the following order: red first, blue second, white third and green fourth. Assuming that they are dispensed in this same order every time, what will be the color of the last jelly bean in the vending machine?

    a.   red
    b.   blue
    c.   white
    d.   green
    e.   it cannot be determined from the information given

9. What is the average of the following numbers: 11/5, 33/42, 4/9, 8/7, 1/11

    a.   0.567
    b.   0.786
    c.   0.932
    d.   1.091
    e.   1.140

10. On her way to the Post Office, Claire spent 10 minutes in her car, 11 minutes at the drugstore and another 11 minutes talking on her cell phone to her boyfriend. If she arrived at the Post Office at exactly 11:04 am, what time did Claire leave for the Post Office?

    a.   10:22 am
    b.   10:32 am
    c.   10:33 am
    d.   10:34 am
    e.   10:35 am

11. Two years ago, Jane saw the bridal gown of her dreams at a boutique for $1,000. The following year, the price increased by 18%. This year, a few months before Jane buys it, the gown will increase an additional 28% in price. What will Jane have to pay for the gown?

    a. $1333
    b. $1381
    c. $1460
    d. $1511
    e. $1588

12. A software company discounts its old version of web design software to 50% of its original price. Two months later, when the software has still not sold, the company lists it on eBay at a price that has been reduced by an additional 20%. By what overall percentage has the price been reduced?

    a.   55%
    b.   60%
    c.   70%
    d.   75%
    e.   80%

13. $3^5 \times 9^3 =$

    a. 3^5
    b. 3^9
    c. 3^{11}
    d. 9^5
    e. 9^6

14. If $(x - 6)^2 / 2 = (6 - 3)^2 / 2$, what does x equal?

    a.   2
    b.   3
    c.   6
    d.   9
    e.   12

15. Which of the following are the solutions to the following equation? $x^3 - x = 0$

    a.   0
    b.   0, -1
    c.   0, 1, -1
    d.   0, 1
    e.   All positive integers

16. Which of the following expressions is equivalent to $(a + b - 1)(a - b)$?

    a. $a^2 - a - b^2 + b$
    b. $a^2 + a - b^2 + b$
    c. $a^2 + a + b^2 - b$
    d. $a^2 - 2a - b^2 + 2b$
    e. $a^2 - a - b^2 + b - 1$

STOP

The answers to these questions are presented in Section QA6 (page 245)

Quantitative 7:   25 Minutes   20 Questions

Directions: You have 25 minutes to answer the following 20 questions. Choose the best answer from the choices given.

- The use of a calculator is permitted.
- All numbers used are real numbers.
- Figures that accompany problems in this test are intended to provide valuable information useful in solving the problems. They are drawn as accurately as possible EXCEPT when it is stated in a specific problem that the figure is not drawn to scale. All figures lie in a plane unless otherwise indicated.
- Unless otherwise specified, the domain of any function f is assumed to be the set of all real numbers x for which f (x) is a real number.

Reference Information:

- Circles. Area = πr^2, Circumference = $2\pi r$
- Rectangles: Area = Length X Width
- Right Triangles: Area = ½ (Base) (Height)
- Cubes: Volume = Length x Width x Height
- Cylinders: Volume = $\pi r^2 h$
- Pythagorean Theorem: for right triangles $c^2 = a^2 + b^2$

1. At a business school in Europe with 300 full-time students, 100 are studying marketing, while the rest are studying finance. If 175 of the students are male, and 40% of the students studying finance are female, how many of the students are females who are studying marketing?

    a.   30
    b.   40
    c.   45
    d.   55
    e.   80

2. After a devastating fire, a city's population decreased by 38%. If the current population is 1.37 million, what was the original population?

    a.   931,600
    b.   1,890,600
    c.   2,209,677
    d.   2,876,900
    e.   3,605,263

3. Heidi decided to invest her $750,000 lottery winnings in a financial product. Her first choice was Annuity A, which paid 8.45% simple annual interest. Heidi's second choice was Annuity B, which paid 8.65% annual interest. If Heidi leaves the money in Annuity B for one year (and makes no withdrawals), how much more will she earn than if she put the money into Annuity A?

    a. $500
    b. $750
    c. $1,500
    d. $1,750
    e. $2,750

4. The Bluebird baseball team scored the following number of runs in their first eight games: 12, 9, 8, 15, 6, 9, 17, and 7. How many runs do they need to score in game 9 to have an average of 12 runs per game for the entire 9-game season?

    a.   21
    b.   22
    c.   23
    d.   24
    e.   25

5. If f (d) = (d + 6)(d – 4), what is f (9)?

    a. 36
    b. 45
    c. 54
    d. 60
    e. 75

6. Robin's wedding anniversary is 100 days after her birthday. If her birthday is on a Wednesday this year, on what day of the week will Robin's anniversary fall?

    a. Monday
    b. Tuesday
    c. Wednesday
    d. Thursday
    e. Friday

7. What is the next term in the series? 5, 8, 7, 10, 9, 12…….

    a. 6
    b. 10
    c. 11
    d. 13
    e. 15

8. A mail order company uses a rectangular shipping carton, which has a volume of 512 cubic centimeters. If the length of the box is twice the height, and the width of the box is twice the length, what is the height of the box (in centimeters)?

    a. 2
    b. 4
    c. 8
    d. 12
    e. 16

9. A hexagon has five interior angles that measure 79, 80, 95, 147 and 152. What is the measure of the sixth internal angle?

    a. 47
    b. 67
    c. 97
    d. 147
    e. 167

10. What is the circumference of a circle that has a radius of 4444 (use π = 3.1416)?

    a. 2.22×10^3
    b. 2.79×10^4
    c. 2.22×10^7
    d. 4.44×10^7
    e. 8.88×10^7

11. The mean of two numbers is 8x – 24. If one of the numbers is x, what is the other number?

        a.   8x + 24
        b.   3x + 8
        c. $(2x - 4)^2$
        d.   15x - 48
        e.   it cannot be determined from the information given

12. A seamstress bought a beautiful bolt of silk material to use to make wedding dresses. If the bolt contains 55 yards of material and each dress requires 6-1/5 yards, how many dresses can the seamstress make from a single bolt of the material?

        a.   7
        b.   8
        c.   9
        d.   10
        e.   11

13. Reduce the following fraction to its simplest form: 2,000 / 2 million

        a.   1/1000
        b.   2/1000
        c.   1/100
        d.   2/100
        e.   1/10

14. (75% x 800) + (1/6 x 600) =

        a.   660
        b.   700
        c.   1060
        d.   1200
        e.   1400

15. Arrange the following fractions in descending order:

        11/13, 12/15, 21/27, 32/41, 48/63

        a.   11/13, 32/41, 21/27, 12/15, 48/63
        b.   48/63, 12/15, 11/13, 32/41, 21/17
        c.   11/13, 12/15, 21/27, 32/41, 48/63
        d.   11/13, 12/15, 32/41, 21/27, 48/63
        e.   11/13, 21/27, 12/15, 32/41, 48/63

16. For the following system of equations, what is the value of y? 2x + 6y = 10, 2x + 10y = 6

        a.   -3
        b.   -2
        c.   -1
        d.   −1/2
        e.   −1/3

17. Which of the following quantities is *greater than* 8.9×10^{-11}?

    a. 89×10^{-12}
    b. 0.89×10^{-12}
    c.   0.000000000089
    d. $0.0000000000445 \times 10^{-11} \times 2$
    e. 89000×10^{-6}

18. At the company picnic, each of the firm's 20 employees placed a raffle ticket into a bowl. At the end of the night, the company president picked one ticket randomly from the bowl and awarded the first prize to Greg. He then picked another ticket randomly from the bowl and awarded the second prize to Pete. Finally, after awarding two more prizes in the same manner, the president picked a fifth random ticket from the bowl and awarded the fifth prize to Jim. Assuming that the first four tickets were not placed back into the bowl after the first four prizes were awarded, what was the probability of Jim winning the fifth prize?

    a.   1.25%
    b.   2.50%
    c.   5.00%
    d.   5.25%
    e.   6.25%

19. $(15 - 11)^3 =$

    a.   4
    b.   16
    c.   64
    d.   121
    e.   225

20. Which of the following is the correct factorization of $12b^2 - 12$?

    a. $12b^2 - 144$
    b. $12(b - 1)$
    c. $12(b - 1)(b + 1)$
    d. $12(b - 1)^2$
    e. $(4b - 3)(3b + 4)$

STOP

The answers to these questions are presented in Section QA7 (page 246)

Quantitative 8:   25 Minutes   18 Questions

<u>Directions</u>: This section contains two types of questions. You have 25 minutes to complete both types. For questions 1 – 8, choose the best answer from the choices given. For Student-Produced Response questions 9 – 18, use the grids at the bottom of the answer sheet.

- The use of a calculator is permitted.
- All numbers used are real numbers.
- Figures that accompany problems in this test are intended to provide valuable information useful in solving the problems. They are drawn as accurately as possible EXCEPT when it is stated in a specific problem that the figure is not drawn to scale. All figures lie in a plane unless otherwise indicated.
- Unless otherwise specified, the domain of any function f is assumed to be the set of all real numbers x for which f (x) is a real number.

<u>Reference Information</u>:

- Circles. Area $= \pi r^2$, Circumference $= 2 \pi r$
- Rectangles: Area = Length X Width
- Right Triangles: Area = ½ (Base) (Height)
- Cubes: Volume = Length x Width x Height
- Cylinders: Volume $= \pi r^2 h$
- Pythagorean Theorem: for right triangles $c^2 = a^2 + b^2$

1. Sue is twice as old as Grace. Lee is 5 years older than Grace. If their combined ages is 58, how old is Grace?

    a.   12
    b.   14
    c.   16
    d.   24
    e.   28

2. A Brinks truck is making a special delivery of 24 gold bars to the U.S. Treasury. Each bar is 3 feet long, 6 inches wide and 12 inches deep. If the gold is certified to weigh 3 ounces per cubic inch, how many pounds does each bar weigh?

    a.   54
    b.   486
    c.   864
    d.   1,296
    e.   20,736

3. At which of the following points do the following lines intersect? $y = 5x + 4$ $y = 5x - 4$

    a.   (0, -4)
    b.   (0, -4) (4, 0)
    c.   (0, -5) (5, 0)
    d.   (-4, 0)
    e.   The two lines do not intersect

4. What is the diameter of a circle with area 81π?

    a.   3
    b.   9
    c.   18
    d.   36
    e.   54

5. For the repeating decimal 0.04321043210432104321....., what is the 49th digit to the right of the decimal point?

     a. 0
     b. 1
     c. 2
     d. 3
     e. 4

6. If 110 of the 220 students in Algebra class are from Hawaii and 22 of the students are from Canada, what percentage of the students is from neither Hawaii nor Canada?

     a. 30%
     b. 35%
     c. 40%
     d. 45%
     e. 60%

7. If $8^{24} = 512^{16x}$, what is the value of x?

     a. 2
     b. 3
     c. 4
     d. 8
     e. 12

8. If y is 5 less than 4 times x, what is the value of x?

     a. (y - 5) / 4
     b. (y + 5) / 4
     c. 4y + 20
     d. 4y - 20
     e. 4/5 y

9. A general admission ticket to the symphony costs $32, while a student ticket costs $10.00. If a total of 800 people attended a Saturday concert and the total ticket sales were $12,400, how many student tickets were sold that day?

10. Jenny's monthly budget includes $600 for rent, $300 for her car payment, $100 for insurance, $300 for utilities, and $300 for groceries. Assuming that Jenny's monthly take-home pay is $2000, what fraction of it is left for discretionary spending?

11. The angles of a triangle are in the ratio of 3:4:5. What is the measurement (in degrees) of the largest angle?

12. What is the absolute value of twice the difference of the roots of the equation $x^2 - 2x - 15 = 0$?

13. If $(5r + 27)/3 = 15 - r + 3^2 - (r/3)$, what does r equal?

14. If the following series continues in the same pattern, what will the next term be?

      45, 47, 37, 39, 29, 31, 21....

15. What is the sum of the prime numbers between 20 and 30?

16. At a church raffle, the pastor selects one ticket randomly for a prize. If there are 40 tickets in the raffle bowl, what is the probability (in percent) that any one ticket will be selected?

17. If 714/7 = 21y/14, what does y equal?

18. Acme Grocery sells organic sesame seeds for 52.5 cents per ounce. If a wholesale customer purchases 50 pounds of the organic sesame seeds at a 20% discount, what is the total price they will pay (in dollars)?

STOP

The answers to these questions are presented in Section QA8 (page 247)

Quantitative 9:   20 Minutes   16 Questions

Directions: You have 20 minutes to answer the following 16 questions. Choose the best answer from the choices given.

- The use of a calculator is permitted.
- All numbers used are real numbers.
- Figures that accompany problems in this test are intended to provide valuable information useful in solving the problems. They are drawn as accurately as possible EXCEPT when it is stated in a specific problem that the figure is not drawn to scale. All figures lie in a plane unless otherwise indicated.
- Unless otherwise specified, the domain of any function f is assumed to be the set of all real numbers x for which f (x) is a real number.

Reference Information:

- Circles. Area $= \pi r^2$, Circumference $= 2\pi r$
- Rectangles: Area = Length X Width
- Right Triangles: Area = ½ (Base) (Height)
- Cubes: Volume = Length x Width x Height
- Cylinders: Volume $= \pi r^2 h$
- Pythagorean Theorem: for right triangles $c^2 = a^2 + b^2$

1. Three sisters, Hannah, Juliet and Patricia, have weights that are consecutive even numbers. Eighteen less than Juliet's weight equals 50 less than the sum of Hannah and Patricia's weights. What is Juliet's weight?

     a.   26
     b.   28
     c.   30
     d.   32
     e.   34

2. Ryan and Jake can paint a house in 4 days if they work together. Alone, it takes Ryan 6 days to paint the house. How many days would it take Jake to paint the house if he worked alone?

     a.   5
     b.   6
     c.   8
     d.   10
     e.   12

3. The sides of a hexagonal shaped lot are 24.5 ft, 12.0 ft, 9.75 ft, 11.9 ft, 34.0 ft and 21.6 ft. If the cost of chain link fencing is $36.00 per linear yard, how much will it cost the owner of the lot to buy a fence to secure the entire lot?

     a. $1,222
     b. $1,365
     c. $1,643
     d. $4,086
     e. $4,104

4. After announcing the availability of the Forever stamp, the US Post Office recorded $2,313,716.10 in sales for the stamps at the Glendale office in a single day. Assuming that the stamps cost 41 cents each, how many Forever stamps did the Glendale office sell that day?

     a.   564,321
     b.   948,624
     c.   746,360
     d.   5,643,210
     e.   9,486,246

5. If f (a) = 1 + 1/3 a, what is f(30)?

    a. 11/3
    b. 10
    c. 11
    d. 31/3
    e. 31

6. A line with the equation y = 14x – 28 crosses the x-axis at the point with the coordinates m, n. What is the value of n?

    a. -28
    b. -2
    c. 0
    d. 2
    e. 7

7. Find the number of sides of a polygon if the sum of the interior angles is 2,700 degrees?

    a. 14
    b. 16
    c. 17
    d. 18
    e. 19

8. A rectangle that measures 9 inches by 16 inches is completely inscribed in a circle. If all four corners of the rectangle touch the circumference of the circle, what is the area of the circle?

    a. 12 π
    b. 36 π
    c. 84 π
    d. 144π
    e. 720 π

9. If the average of seven consecutive odd numbers is 21, which of the following is the largest of the seven numbers?

    a. 19
    b. 21
    c. 23
    d. 25
    e. 27

10. During the New York City auditions for American Idol, the judges allowed an equal number of men and women to take the stage. At the end of a grueling day, the ratio of female to male singers who advanced to the next round was 3 to 2. At the very end of the day, the judges had a change of heart and agreed to add one additional female singer and one additional male singer to the group that advanced. What is the new ratio of female to male singers?

    a. 3:2
    b. 4:3
    c. 5:4
    d. 6:5
    e. It cannot be determined from the information given.

11. A computer science curriculum includes 8 courses on hardware and 4 courses on software. The remaining ¼ of the courses are on web design. What fraction of the courses is on software?

    a. 1/4
    b. 1/3
    c. 2/5
    d. 1/2
    e. 5/8

12. Jane and Harry wanted to create a memorable combination for their home safe. For the first three digits, Jane used the sum of the first 40 even integers. For the second three numbers, Harry used the sum of the first 20 odd integers. For the final three numbers, they used the difference between the first two quantities. What was the nine-digit combination for the safe?

    a. 800200600
    b. 800210590
    c. 840200600
    d. 840210590
    e. 840210630

13. For residential packing, Ace Movers uses a shipping carton that is 3 feet long, 6 feet wide and 9 feet high. What is the total surface area of the shipping carton (in cubic feet)?

    a. 156
    b. 162
    c. 164
    d. 198
    e. 200

14. What number, when squared, is equal to the cubic root of 15625?

    a. 1
    b. 5
    c. 15
    d. 25
    e. 125

15. Which of the following is the correct factorization of $k^2 - 6k + 9$?

    a. $(k - 3)(k + 3)$
    b. $(k - 3)^2$
    c. $(k + 3)^2$
    d. $3(1/k^2 + 1)$
    e. $1/9(k - 1)(k + 1)$

16. Which of the following are the solutions to the following equation? $2x^3 - 3x^2 - 5x = 0$

    a. −1, -5/2, 2
    b. 0, 1, 2
    c. 1, 5/2, 6
    d. 0, 1, -5/2
    e. 0, -1, 5/2

STOP

The answers to these questions are presented in Section QA9 (page 248)

Quantitative 10:   **25 Minutes**   **20 Questions**

Directions: You have 25 minutes to answer the following 20 questions. Choose the best answer from the options given.

- The use of a calculator is permitted.
- All numbers used are real numbers.
- Figures that accompany problems in this test are intended to provide valuable information useful in solving the problems. They are drawn as accurately as possible EXCEPT when it is stated in a specific problem that the figure is not drawn to scale. All figures lie in a plane unless otherwise indicated.
- Unless otherwise specified, the domain of any function f is assumed to be the set of all real numbers x for which f (x) is a real number.

Reference Information:

- Circles. Area $= \pi r^2$, Circumference $= 2 \pi r$
- Rectangles: Area = Length X Width
- Right Triangles: Area = ½ (Base) (Height)
- Cubes: Volume = Length x Width x Height
- Cylinders: Volume $= \pi r^2 h$
- Pythagorean Theorem: for right triangles $c^2 = a^2 + b^2$

1. On Valentine's Day, a busy florist drove his delivery truck from Palm Beach to Miami at an average rate of 45 miles per hour. On his return trip to Palm Beach, he encountered rush hour traffic, which slowed him to an average speed of 25 miles per hour. What was the driver's average speed for the trip, in miles per hour?

    a.   30
    b.   32
    c.   35
    d.   38
    e.   40

2. Nathan is seven years older than his sister Claire, who is three years younger than Jayne, who is 28 years old. How old is Nathan?

    a.   22
    b.   25
    c.   28
    d.   29
    e.   32

3. Joe's monthly budget includes $1,200 for rent, $400 for his car payment, $150 for insurance, $250 for utilities, and $200 for groceries. Assuming that Joe' monthly take-home pay is $3,300, what fraction of it is left for discretionary spending?

    a.   1/5
    b.   1/4
    c.   1/3
    d.   2/5
    e.   3/5

4. The amount of sugar in a cake batter varies directly as the weight of the batter. If there are 42 pounds of sugar in a one-ton quantity of batter, how many pounds of sugar would there be in 325 pounds of batter?

    a.   3.412
    b.   6.825
    c.   13.650
    d.   27.30
    e.   54.60

5. The vertex angle of an isosceles triangle is G degrees. How many degrees are there in one of the base angles?

    a. $90 - 2G$
    b. $180 - G$
    c. $1/2(90 - G)$
    d. $1/2(180 - G)$
    e. $180 - G$

6. If a square of side 9 and a circle of radius r have equal areas, what is the value of the r (use $\pi = 3.1416$)?

    a.   5
    b.   6
    c.   9
    d.   12
    e.   18

7. The perimeter of a rectangle is 25x. If one side has a length of x/4, what is the area of the rectangle?

    a. $125x^2/16$
    b. $5x^2/2$
    c. $100x$
    d. $100x^2$
    e. $49x^2/8$

8. A gardener will fill a plot that is 4 inches deep, 30 feet long and 10 feet wide with colorful cypress mulch. If the mulch costs $1.50 per cubic foot, how much will it cost to fill the plot?

    a. $75
    b. $150
    c. $300
    d. $1200
    e. $1800

9. A line segment has endpoints of (6, 14) and (8, 21), What are the coordinates of its midpoint?

    a.   (7, 17)
    b.   (7, 17.5)
    c.   (6, 17)
    d.   (6, 17.5)
    e.   (17, 7)

10. What is the next term in the following series? 1, 7, 13, 19,

    a.   13
    b.   21
    c.   25
    d.   27
    e.   29

11. Jim's ticket won a lottery prize worth $433,890 after taxes. Jim decides to keep one-third of the amount and to divide the remainder equally among his two parents and three sisters. How much money will his two parents receive from Jim?

     a.   14,463
     b.   28,926
     c.   57,852
     d.   115,704
     e.   289,260

12. What is the largest integer that will divide evenly into 63 and 117?

     a.   1
     b.   7
     c.   9
     d.   11
     e.   13

13. What is the product of (3/8)(4/5)(9/3)?

     a.   106/120
     b.   54/64
     c.   108/122
     d.   9/10
     e.   54/56

14. Two individual price reductions of 10% and 15% are equal to a single price reduction of:

     a.   12.5%
     b.   20%
     c.   24.5%
     d.   25%
     e.   27.5%

15. The results of a beauty pageant are determined by a personal interview, a swimsuit competition, an evening gown competition, a talent show and a quiz about current events. If the personal interview counts twice as much as each of the other selection criteria, what fraction of each contestant's final score is determined by the personal interview?

     a.   1/8
     b.   1/6
     c.   ¼
     d.   1/3
     e.   2/5

16. What is the probability of getting a red jelly bean from a dispenser that contains 80 red jelly beans, 48 green ones, 36 purple ones, 26 pink ones and 210 white ones?

     a.   1/8
     b.   1/6
     c.   1/5
     d.   1/4
     e.   1/3

17. Which of the following is equal to 0.0000321?

    a. 32.1×10^{7}
    b. $32.1 \text{ c } 10^{-7}$
    c. 321×10^{-8}
    d. 3.21×10^{-6}
    e. 3.21×10^{-5}

18. If the value of x quarters is equal to the value of x + 32 nickels, x =

    a. 8
    b. 14
    c. 18
    d. 20
    e. 25

19. Which of the following expressions is equivalent to $(a + b - 1)(a - b - 1)$?

    a. $a^2 + 2a - 2b - b^2 + 1$
    b. $a^2 - 2a + 2b + b^2 + 1$
    c. $a^2 - 2a + 2b - b^2 + 1$
    d. $a^2 - 2a - b^2 + 1$
    e. $a^2 + 2a - b^2 + 1$

20. How much greater than $11 - 9y$ is $7y + 4$?

    a. $16y - 7$
    b. $-2y - 7$
    c. $2y + 15$
    d. $6y - 15$
    e. $-16y + 1$

STOP

The answers to these questions are presented in Section QA10 (page 249)

105

Quantitative 11:   25 Minutes   18 Questions

Directions: This section contains two types of questions. You have 25 minutes to complete both types. For questions 1 – 8, solve each problem and select the best answer choice. Fill in the corresponding circle on the answer sheet. You may use any available space for scratch work. For Student-Produced Response questions 9 – 18, use the grids at the bottom of the answer sheet to record your answers.

- The use of a calculator is permitted.
- All numbers used are real numbers.
- Figures that accompany problems in this test are intended to provide valuable information useful in solving the problems. They are drawn as accurately as possible EXCEPT when it is stated in a specific problem that the figure is not drawn to scale. All figures lie in a plane unless otherwise indicated.
- Unless otherwise specified, the domain of any function f is assumed to be the set of all real numbers x for which f (x) is a real number.

Reference Information:

- Circles. Area $= \pi r^2$, Circumference $= 2 \pi r$
- Rectangles: Area = Length X Width
- Right Triangles: Area = ½ (Base) (Height)
- Cubes: Volume = Length x Width x Height
- Cylinders: Volume $= \pi r^2 h$
- Pythagorean Theorem: for right triangles $c^2 = a^2 + b^2$

1. A bridal shop sells six veils and seven headpieces for $580. The cost for eight veils and five headpieces is $548. How much would it cost to buy one veil?

    a. $30
    b. $35
    c. $36
    d. $42
    e. $45

2. Frank puts $5,000 into a college savings account that pays 4.25% simple annual interest. If he leaves the money in the account for 3.5 years, what is the total amount that Frank will have?

    a. $5014.88
    b. $5063.75
    c. $5743.75
    d. $7437.50
    e. $7543.75

3. A right triangle has side lengths of 4 and 8. What is the length of the hypotenuse?

    a. 3.46
    b. 4.89
    c. 6
    d. 8.94
    e. 12

4. Find the number of sides in a polygon if the sum of the measures of the interior angles is three times as great as the sum of the measures of the exterior angles.

    a. 6
    b. 7
    c. 8
    d. 9
    e. 10

5. $1/36 (44 + 22)^2 =$

        a. 0.02776
        b. 0.1666
        c. 1.8333
        d. 120
        e. 121

6. Three sisters took their mother for a nice dinner on Mother's Day. The total for four meals was $185.30. If the girls plan to leave a 20% tip and split the bill three ways, what dollar amount will each sister owe (assume there is no sales tax for the meal)?

        a. 46.32
        b. 55.59
        c. 61.76
        d. 68.32
        e. 74.12

7. If x + 7 is an even integer, the sum of the next three even integers is:

        a. 3x + 4
        b. 3(x +7)
        c. 3x + 28
        d. 3x + 33
        e. $(x + 7)^3$

8. If 4x + 9y = 55 and 2x + 7y = 11, what is the value of (x+y)/2?

        a. 4
        b. 7
        c. 9
        d. 11
        e. 22

9. Two delivery trucks are 640 miles apart. At midnight, they start to travel toward each other at rates of 50 and 30 miles per hour. In how many hours will they pass each other?

10. The product of two consecutive odd integers is 14 less than seven times the larger integer. Find the smaller integer.

11. What is the area of a right triangle whose legs are both equal to eight?

12. How many positive integers less than 100 are evenly divisible by 4, 8 and 12?

13. For the equation $r^2 - 5r = 14$, what is a possible value for r?

14. If $357 = m^2 + 4m$, what does m equal?

15. Which of the following fractions is the smallest? 21/27, 32/37, 67/79, 43/51, 11/14

16. Six hundred guests will eat a gourmet meal at a wedding reception. The guests will eat either shrimp or roast beef. If the ratio of shrimp eaters to roast beef eaters is 6:4, how many guests at the wedding will eat roast beef?

17. What is the probability that a coin (with one side heads and the other side tails) will come up heads on four consecutive tosses?

18. In triangle ABC, angle A is twice angle B and angle C is 30 degrees more than angle B. How many degrees are in angle A?

STOP

The answers to these questions are presented in Section QA11 (page 251)

Quantitative 12:   20 Minutes   16 Questions

Directions: You have 20 minutes to answer the following 16 questions. Choose the best answer from the options given.

- The use of a calculator is permitted.
- All numbers used are real numbers.
- Figures that accompany problems in this test are intended to provide valuable information useful in solving the problems. They are drawn as accurately as possible EXCEPT when it is stated in a specific problem that the figure is not drawn to scale. All figures lie in a plane unless otherwise indicated.
- Unless otherwise specified, the domain of any function f is assumed to be the set of all real numbers x for which f (x) is a real number.

Reference Information:

- Circles. Area $= \pi r^2$, Circumference $= 2 \pi r$
- Rectangles: Area = Length X Width
- Right Triangles: Area = ½ (Base) (Height)
- Cubes: Volume = Length x Width x Height
- Cylinders: Volume $= \pi r^2 h$
- Pythagorean Theorem: for right triangles $c^2 = a^2 + b^2$

1. Beth's Bridal Shop sells two designer gowns online: Victorian Lady and Summer Delight. Selling just these two products, the company makes $45,000 in profits each year on the sale of 450 gowns. If the profit per gown is $75 and $140 for Victorian Lady and Summer Delight, respectively, how many Victorian Lace gowns does the shop sell per year?

   a. 173
   b. 177
   c. 273
   d. 277
   e. 303

2. If the population of Smithfield, which is currently 22,000, grows by 180 people each year, in how many years will the population double?

   a. 116
   b. 122
   c. 187
   d. 1870
   e. 1222

3. Office Depot has launched a new promotion to entice customers to buy ink cartridges. For the month of April, every customer who buys a printer gets a free ink cartridge, along with a coupon for future savings. At the end of the month, the store manager had recorded the following number of printers sold each day: 11, 23, 41, 23, 43, 12 , 15, 13 45 32, 34, 12, 18 , 34, 23, 23, 45, 13, 9, 25, 23, 43, 45, 12, 34, 12, 34, 54, 34, 30. The main office asks the manager to calculate the mode of this data set. What is it?

   a. 12
   b. 23
   c. 34
   d. 43
   e. 45

4. Pam plans to invest $35,000 in an account that pays 7.5% annually. How many additional dollars much she invest for the same amount of time at 4% annual interest so that her total income for the first year is 5% of her total investment?

        a. $4375
        b. $8,750
        c. $43,750
        d. $65,000
        e. $87,500

5. Equilateral triangle XYZ has an area of 36. If U is the midpoint of XY and V is the midpoint of XZ, what is the area of triangle XUV?

        a.   3
        b.   6
        c.   9
        d.   12
        e.   18

6. In quadrilateral ABCD, the sum of angles B, C and D = 5A. What is the value of angle A?

        a.   15
        b.   20
        c.   36
        d.   45
        e.   60

7. $(5y^2)^3(2y^3)^2 =$

        a. $10y^6$
        b. $250y^6$
        c. $500y^6$
        d. $250y^{12}$
        e. $500y^{12}$

8. If $x \wedge y = xy - y + y^2$, then $2 \wedge 4 =$

        a.   4
        b.   16
        c.   20
        d.   24
        e.   68

9. Sara had to mail a package on the day that the Post Office increased its rates. The cost is 55 cents for the first ounce and 34 cents for each additional ounce. How much did Sara pay to mail a package that weighed three quarters of a pound?

        a. $3.27
        b. $3.63
        c. $4.08
        d. $4.29
        e. $4.63

Use the following table to answer questions 10 – 16.

Percentage of Diabetics (By Age)

	China	Italy	France	Germany
Under 10	5	5	2	0
10 – 18	20	30	15	13
19 – 30	35	30	28	29
31 – 50	30	30	40	48
Over 51	10	5	15	10

10. If there are 15 million diabetics in China, how many of them are less than 31 years old?

    a.   750,000
    b.   3 million
    c.   5.25 million
    d.   9 million
    e.   10 million

11. If there are 8 million diabetics in France, and they each purchase two insulin pumps per year, how many pumps are needed by the diabetics who are 51 or older?

    a.   1.0 million
    b.   1.2 million
    c.   2.4 million
    d.   4 million
    e.   4.8 million

12. Which country has the smallest percentage of diabetics under age 19?

    a.   China
    b.   Italy
    c.   France
    d.   Germany
    e.   Cannot be determined from the information provided

13. Which country has the largest number of diabetics between 31 and 50?

    a.   China
    b.   Italy
    c.   France
    d.   Germany
    e.   Cannot be determined from the information given

14. A leading economic journal recently estimated the number of diabetics in China and Germany at 8 million and 14 million, respectively. If these numbers are accurate, what is the total number of people in both nations between 19 and 30 who are diabetics?

    a.   2.8 million
    b.   4.06 million
    c.   6.08 million
    d.   6.86 million
    e.   Cannot be determined from the information given

15. If there are currently 18 million diabetics in Italy, and the Italian government offers free insulin to those who are under 10 and over 51, then how many remaining diabetics will still have to buy insulin?

    a.   900,000
    b.   1.8 million
    c.   3.6 million
    d.   12.6 million
    e.   16.2 million

16. Physicians in China recently announced that all diabetics who are younger than 19 will be required to use automatic insulin pumps, rather than traditional injections. If the total number of diabetics in China is 56 million, how many of them will be required to use the automatic insulin pumps?

    a.   2.8 million
    b.   5.6 million
    c.   11.2 million
    d.   14 million
    e.   28 million

STOP

The answers to these questions are presented in Section QA12 (page 252)

Quantitative 13:   25 Minutes   20 Questions

Directions: You have 25 minutes to answer the following 20 questions. Choose the best answer from the options given.

- The use of a calculator is permitted.
- All numbers used are real numbers.
- Figures that accompany problems in this test are intended to provide valuable information useful in solving the problems. They are drawn as accurately as possible EXCEPT when it is stated in a specific problem that the figure is not drawn to scale. All figures lie in a plane unless otherwise indicated.
- Unless otherwise specified, the domain of any function f is assumed to be the set of all real numbers x for which f (x) is a real number.

Reference Information:

- Circles. Area $= \pi r^2$, Circumference $= 2 \pi r$
- Rectangles: Area = Length X Width
- Right Triangles: Area = ½ (Base) (Height)
- Cubes: Volume = Length x Width x Height
- Cylinders: Volume $= \pi r^2 h$
- Pythagorean Theorem: for right triangles $c^2 = a^2 + b^2$

1. Karen has decided to decorate her room with a wallpaper that costs $18.45 per square foot. If her room measures 20 feet by 16 feet, how much will it cost Karen to buy the wallpaper?

    a. $59.04
    b. $354.24
    c. $590.40
    d. $1,180.80
    e. $5,904

2. When Sara and Claire got dressed for the prom, they checked out each other's makeup collections.   If Sara has six more than three times number of tubes of lipstick than Claire has, and Claire has eighteen tubes of lipstick, how many tubes does Sara have?

    a.   21
    b.   24
    c.   54
    d.   60
    e.   66

3. Five consecutive even integers have a sum of 370. What is the largest of the five integers?

    a.   70
    b.   76
    c.   78
    d.   80
    e.   82

4. One hundred vacationers on a cruise ship have signed up for the ship's activities. Sixty sign up for ballroom dancing lessons. Thirty-five sign up for aerobics class. Twenty sign up for neither ballroom dancing nor aerobics class. How many have signed up for BOTH ballroom dancing and aerobics class?

    a.   5
    b.   10
    c.   12
    d.   15
    e.   18

5. If $f(p) = p/7 + 10 - (7^3)/p$, what is f (14)?

    a. −12.5
    b. -12
    c. 0
    d. 7
    e. 343

6. What is the next term in the following series?   85, 84, 82, 79, 75…….

    a. 71
    b. 70
    c. 69
    d. 68
    e. 64

7. If x = 5, y = 2 and z = 3, what is the value of $3x^3 + 5y^4 - 2z^2$?

    a. 357
    b. 375
    c. 393
    d. 437
    e. 455

8. What are the y-intercepts of the graph for the following equation: $(x + 6)^2 + (x + 3)^2 = 1$

    a. (6, 0) (3, 0)
    b. (-6, 0) (-3, 0)
    c. (0 –6) (0, -3)
    d. (0, 6) (0, 3)
    e. There are no y-intercepts

9. Find the area of a square with a diagonal of 8.

    a. 32
    b. 36
    c. 49
    d. 64
    e. 96

10. The typical tire for a passenger car has a radius of 48 inches. How many feet will the tire cover in 300 revolutions?

    a. $2,400\pi$
    b. $4,800\pi$
    c. $9,600\pi$
    d. $14,440\pi$
    e. $28,880\pi$

11.   For the following data sat, what is the median minus the mode?   3, 5, 6, 6, 7, 7, 7, 8, 9, 12, 15

    a. 0
    b. 0.7
    c. 1
    d. 1.7
    e. 2

12. The asking prices of two cars are in the ratio of 8:9. If the two cars together cost $85,000, what does the cheaper car cost?

    a. $35,000
    b. $40,000
    c. $42,000
    d. $42,500
    e. $45,000

13. A year ago, the local police issued 1432 speeding tickets at a particular intersection. This year, after decreasing their patrol in this area, they only issued 91 tickets at the same intersection. What percent decrease does this represent?

    a. 6.35%
    b. 9.36%
    c. 63.5%
    d. 93.65%
    e. 936.5%

14. New York City and Providence are 150 miles apart. A car travels from Providence to New York City at 75 miles per hour and returns from New York City to Providence along the same route at 40 miles per hour. What is the average speed for the trip (in miles per hour)?

    a. 47
    b. 50
    c. 52
    d. 57
    e. 60

15. Every time Carla travels west on highway B, she must pay a $3.00 toll. Every time she travels east on the same road, she receives a $2.00 credit. If Carla travels west on highway B seventeen times during April and she travels east on highway B twelve times during the same period, what is Carla's net gain from traveling on highway B?

    a. $5 loss
    b. $24 loss
    c. $26 loss
    d. $24 gain
    e. $26 gain

16. Two concentric circles exist in a plane. If the larger circle has a diameter of 36 and the small circle has a diameter of 12, what is the probability that any point chosen at random from the large circle will also be in the small circle?

    a. 6.25%
    b. 11.11%
    c. 12.50%
    d. 20.00%
    e. 33.33%

17. If $x = 3$, calculate $5^x - (x^3)^{x-1}$

    a. -604
    b. 44
    c. 98
    d. 104
    e. 604

18. Simply the following expression: $(3x + y)(x + 3y) - 10xy =$

   a. 0
   b. $3x^2 - 11xy + y^2$
   c. $-21xy$
   d. $3x^2 + 3y^2$
   e. $3x^2 - 3y^2$

19. The inequality $5x - 78 > 6x + 80$ is true for what values of x?

   a. $x < 2$
   b. $x > 158$
   c. $x > -158$
   d. $x < -158$
   e. $x < 158$

20. An engineer working with farm equipment discovers that the amount of fertilizer (F) and the rate of feeding (G) for a particular grain satisfy the following two equations. What are the values of F and G?

$$F - 20G = 0, F + 20G = 200$$

   a. $F = 10, G = 5$
   b. $F = 10, G = 10$
   c. $F = 50, G = 10$
   d. $F = 100, G = 5$
   e. $F = 200, G = 5$

STOP

The answers to these questions are presented in Section QA13 (page 253)

Quantitative 14:   25 Minutes   18 Questions

Directions: This section contains two types of questions. You have 25 minutes to complete both types. For questions 1 – 8, solve each problem and select the best answer choice. Fill in the corresponding circle on the answer sheet. You may use any available space for scratch work. For Student-Produced Response questions 9 – 18, use the grids at the bottom of the answer sheet to record your answers.

- The use of a calculator is permitted.
- All numbers used are real numbers.
- Figures that accompany problems in this test are intended to provide valuable information useful in solving the problems. They are drawn as accurately as possible EXCEPT when it is stated in a specific problem that the figure is not drawn to scale. All figures lie in a plane unless otherwise indicated.
- Unless otherwise specified, the domain of any function f is assumed to be the set of all real numbers x for which f (x) is a real number.

Reference Information:

- Circles. Area = πr^2, Circumference = $2 \pi r$
- Rectangles: Area = Length X Width
- Right Triangles: Area = ½ (Base) (Height)
- Cubes: Volume = Length x Width x Height
- Cylinders: Volume = $\pi r^2 h$
- Pythagorean Theorem: for right triangles $c^2 = a^2 + b^2$

1. The Zippy Cheese Company has established a quality control program to minimize the number of underweight bars of cheese that leave their plant. During the first six weeks of the program, the number of bars that failed, by week, was 324, 119, 267, 219, 553, and 189. If management's goal is to have an overall average of 300 failing bars or less during the first seven weeks of the program, what is the highest number of bars that can fail during week seven?

    a.   297
    b.   307
    c.   359
    d.   429
    e.   548

2. Two separate pipes are used to fill a 2000-gallon swimming pool. If Pipe A fills the pool at a rate of 15 gallons of water per minute and Pipe B fills the pool at a rate of 45 gallons per minute, how many minutes will it take to fill the pool to the top, if it already has 500-gallons of water in it?

    a.   17.5
    b.   21
    c.   25
    d.   30
    e.   33.3

3. What is the area of a square with a side of length 5?

    a.   5
    b.   25
    c.   50
    d.   100
    e.   125

4. What is the radius of the circle that passes through the point (10, 8) and has its center at (2, 2)?

    a.   1
    b.   2
    c.   5
    d.   8
    e.   10

5. Which of the following numbers is closest in value to 3/8?

    a.   3/10
    b.   4/13
    c.   5/16.
    d.   7/19
    e.   0.395

6. In reading a thermometer, a nurse mistakenly recorded a temperature of 97 degrees instead of 102 degrees. What was the percentage error (to the nearest hundredths of a percent)?

    a.   0.49%
    b.   0.51%
    c.   4.90%
    d.   5.00%
    e.   5.15%

7. If $3x + 4y = 12$ and $x + 8y = 46$, what is the value of $2x + 6y$?

    a.   15
    b.   24
    c.   29
    d.   68
    e.   112

8. If $11 - 4x = 3$, what is the value of $6 - 4x$?

    a.   -8
    b.   -2
    c.   0
    d.   2
    e.   8

9. If Melanie's age three years from now plus her age two years ago plus five times her age three years ago is equal to 84 years. How old is Melanie now?

10. Stenographer 1 can type four times as fast as Stenographer 2. If they both spend an equal amount of time typing 1000 pages of data, how many pages will Stenographer 2 type?

11. In triangle FHG, one angle is equal to 60 degrees, the second angle is equal to x, and the third angle is equal to 3x. What is the value of x?

12. If $x = 2$ and $y = 3$, what is the value of the expression $2x^2 + 4xy - y^2$?

13. In geometry class, 35% of the students are athletes and 15% of the athletes run track. What percentage of students in the geometry class are athletes who run track?

14. $14 - (3)^2 + (3/6)(5/10) =$

118

15. The sum of two numbers is 238. Their difference is 46. What is the smaller number?

16. For a rectangular box with a width of ½ foot, a length of 18 inches and a height of 2 feet, what is the total volume (in cubic inches)?

17. If $a^2 - b^2 = 81$ and $a - b = 3$, what is the value of a + b?

18. If g (u) = 10u/6, what is g (24)?

STOP

The answers to these questions are presented in Section QA14 (page 254)

Directions: You have 20 minutes to answer the following 16 questions. Choose the best answer from the options given.

- The use of a calculator is permitted.
- All numbers used are real numbers.
- Figures that accompany problems in this test are intended to provide valuable information useful in solving the problems. They are drawn as accurately as possible EXCEPT when it is stated in a specific problem that the figure is not drawn to scale. All figures lie in a plane unless otherwise indicated.
- Unless otherwise specified, the domain of any function f is assumed to be the set of all real numbers x for which f (x) is a real number.

Reference Information:

- Circles. Area $= \pi r^2$, Circumference $= 2 \pi r$
- Rectangles: Area = Length X Width
- Right Triangles: Area = ½ (Base) (Height)
- Cubes: Volume = Length x Width x Height
- Cylinders: Volume $= \pi r^2 h$
- Pythagorean Theorem: for right triangles $c^2 = a^2 + b^2$

1. Valerie weighs three times as much as Tiffany. Brittany weighs six pounds more than Valerie. If their combined weights are 356, how much does Brittany weigh?

     a.   134
     b.   140
     c.   146
     d.   150
     e.   156

2. There are B tenants in an apartment building, who agree to split the cost of utilities, U, in an equal manner. If the cost of utilities increases by $142 per month, how much must each tenant pay?

     a.   142/B
     b.   142B/U
     c.   (B + 142)/U
     d.   (U + 142)/B
     e.   B(U – 142)/B

3. An adult ticket to the Brooklyn Zoo costs $12.00, while a child's ticket costs $5.50. If a total of 550 people visited the zoo on Sunday and the total ticket sales were $4800, how many children's tickets were sold that day?

     a.   273
     b.   277
     c.   280
     d.   289
     e.   300

4. According to veterinary guidelines, each dog in a boarding kennel must have 4,500 cubic feet of individual space. If the kennel room measures 32 feet by 72 feet by 96 feet, how many dogs can legally be housed there?

     a.   36
     b.   39
     c.   45
     d.   49
     e.   54

Refer to the chart below for questions 5 & 6.

Number of Cardiac Patients per Thousand Residents

Atlanta	56
Boston	94
Chicago	87
Detroit	79
Los Angeles	99
Miami	48
Sacramento	61

5. Based on the chart, which city has the third highest number of cardiac patients per thousand residents?

    a. Los Angeles
    b. Miami
    c. Chicago
    d. Detroit
    e. Atlanta

6. A physician wishes to visit the two cities on the chart that have the closest number of cardiac patients as the number in Omaha, which has 68 patients per thousand residents. According to this chart, which two cities should the physician visit?

    a. Sacramento and Atlanta
    b. Sacramento and Detroit
    c. Atlanta and Detroit
    d. Atlanta and Miami
    e. Detroit and Chicago

7. A triangle has its vertices at the following points: X (0,0), Y(6,0), Z(0,9). What is its area?

    a. 20
    b. 24
    c. 27
    d. 36
    e. 54

8. A cube and a rectangular solid are equal in volume. If the lengths of the edges of the rectangular solid are 3, 9, and 27, what is the length of an edge of the cube?

    a. 3
    b. 6
    c. 9
    d. 18
    e. 27

9. Eighty-six roses were shipped to a flower shop for use in a window display. If Jane takes three for her own use, and seventeen are discarded because they are wilted, but Barb adds back an additional five roses to the group, how many roses were available for the window display?

    a. 61
    b. 64
    c. 66
    d. 71
    e. 74

10. For all non-zero values of k, which of the following *must* be true?

I. $k^2 > k$
II. $4k > 2k$
III. $k + 6 > k$

    a.   I only
    b.   II only
    c.   III only
    d.   I and II only
    e.   I, II and III

11. A year ago, Julie had 62 recipes for her country cookbook. This year, she has 329 recipes. What percentage increase does this number represent?

    a.   4.306%
    b.   43.06%
    c.   430.6%
    d.   4306%
    e.   none of the above

12. In a kennel with 27 dogs, the average (mean) weight of the neutered dogs was 83 pounds. If the average weight of the 15 intact dogs in the kennel was 92 pounds, what was the average weight of the entire kennel?

    a.   86.5
    b.   87.0
    c.   87.5
    d.   88.0
    e.   88.5

13. There are five possible electives for Julie to take at her local community college this summer: English, Math, Statistics, History and Social Studies. Her counselor has advised Julie to choose two of them. How many possible combinations of the two courses are there?

    a.   30
    b.   25
    c.   15
    d.   12
    e.   10

14. Which of the following is/are equal to 2^6?

I. $10^2 - 24$
II. 8^3
III. $2^2 \times 4^2$

    a.   I only
    b.   II only
    c.   III only
    d.   I and III only
    e.   I, II and III

15. What is the value of x if $xy + xz = 15$ and $y + z = 3$?

    a.   1/2
    b.   1
    c.   3
    d.   5
    e.   15

16. Which of the following are the solutions to the following equation? $x^2 - 7x + 10 = 0$

    a.   5, 2
    b.   2, -5
    c.   −2, -5
    d.   −2, 5
    e.   5, ½

STOP

The answers to these questions are presented in Section QA15 (page 255)

Quantitative 16:   25 Minutes   20 Questions

Directions: You have 25 minutes to answer the following 20 questions. Choose the best answer from the options given.

- The use of a calculator is permitted.
- All numbers used are real numbers.
- Figures that accompany problems in this test are intended to provide valuable information useful in solving the problems. They are drawn as accurately as possible EXCEPT when it is stated in a specific problem that the figure is not drawn to scale. All figures lie in a plane unless otherwise indicated.
- Unless otherwise specified, the domain of any function f is assumed to be the set of all real numbers x for which f (x) is a real number.

Reference Information:

- Circles. Area $= \pi r^2$, Circumference $= 2 \pi r$
- Rectangles: Area = Length X Width
- Right Triangles: Area = ½ (Base) (Height)
- Cubes: Volume = Length x Width x Height
- Cylinders: Volume $= \pi r^2 h$
- Pythagorean Theorem: for right triangles $c^2 = a^2 + b^2$

1. If Jake leaves the prom at 11:30 pm and his house is 96 miles away, how fast does he have to drive to get home by 2 am (in miles per hour)?

     a.   36
     b.   38.4
     c.   48
     d.   76.8
     e.   96

2. An IRS auditor has requested salary information for all board members of the SAG Corporation. A review of the files revealed that three members each earned $120,000 per year, another four members each earned $90,000 per year, while an additional nine members each earned $50,000 per year. What is the mean salary of the board members?

     a. $71,000
     b. $73,125
     c. $86,625
     d. $93,125
     e. $106,000

3. Patrice earns twice as much per hour as Jenny. Jenny earns $3 more per hour than Courtney. Together, they earn $57 per hour. How much is Patrice's hourly wage?

     a.   12
     b.   15
     c.   18
     d.   21
     e.   30

4. Maria put $4390 into a Platinum CD at her local bank, which she left untouched for six years and nine months, when she withdrew the entire amount, plus all of the simple annual interest she had earned. If the total balance in Maria's account was $6175, what simple rate of annual interest did she earn?

     a.   3.82%
     b.   4.62%
     c.   5.52%
     d.   6.02%
     e.   7.12%

5. In triangle ABC, AB = 3 and BC = 5. Which of the following could possibly be the length of side AC?

    a. 6
    b. 9
    c. 10
    d. either a, b or c
    e. none of the above

6. Which of the following polygons has all sides of equal length and all angles of identical measure?

    a. hexagon
    b. octagon
    c. nonagon
    d. pentagon
    e. None of the above

7. The line represented by $3x - 9y = 12$ is parallel to which of the following lines?

    a. $y = 3x + 5$
    b. $y = 12x + 1$
    c. $y = 1/3x - 8$
    d. $y = 4/3 x - 3$
    e. $y = 3x + 4/3$

8. A delivery truck traveled west for 30 miles, then south for 50 miles, then returned directly to his starting point on a diagonal. If the truck gets 8 per gallon of gas, how many gallons of gas will the truck use on the trip?

    a. 10
    b. 12
    c. 15
    d. 18
    e. 20

9. How many inches are there in X yards, Y feet and Z inches?

    a. 36X + 12Y + Z
    b. 3X + 12Y +12 Z
    c. 3X + 36Y +12 Z
    d. (X + Y + Z)/12
    e. (X +Y)/12 + Z

10. What is the next term in the following series?   100, 90, 105, 95, 110, 100, 115......

    a. 90
    b. 95
    c. 100
    d. 105
    e. 110

11. A cattery has 85 Persian cats, 411 Siamese cats and 103 Calico cats. For a treat, the owner of the cattery purchases 88 lbs of catnip, to be distributed evenly among all of the cats. Assuming there are no other types of cats in the cattery, how much catnip (in ounces) would each cat receive?

      a.   2.35
      b.   14.08
      c.   23.50
      d.   28.38
      e.   469.33

12. Which of the following is not a factor of 420?

      a.   10
      b.   15
      c.   40
      d.   42
      e.   60

13. After making preserves with her grandmother, Gayle had enough to fill 28.5 jars. If each full jar contained 23.1 oz, how many total pounds of preserves did Gayle have?

      a.   32
      b.   41
      c.   46
      d.   56
      e.   65

14. What is 5/4 divided by 7/6?

      a.   15/30
      b.   24/28
      c.   24/35
      d.   14/15
      e.   15/14

15. The final exam for English Literature class is worth 1/3 of the overall grade. The average of 4 monthly exams counts for another third, while an oral presentation on sonnets is worth the final third. So far, Becky's exam scores are 68, 73, 80 and 95. She only scored a 70 on her oral presentation. What will Becky have to earn on the final exam to raise her average to 80?

      a.   85
      b.   86
      c.   88
      d.   91
      e.   93

16. You are arranging four brightly colored decorative tiles on the bathroom wall: they are red, green, pink and purple. How many possible ways are there to arrange them on the wall (assume no tile is repeated)?

      a.   4
      b.   8
      c.   16
      d.   24
      e.   64

Use the following table to answer questions 17 – 20.

Percentage of Contact Lens Wearers (By Age)

	U.S.	U.K.	France	India
Under 10	2	5	1	0
10 – 18	21	30	15	3
19 – 30	38	35	29	19
31 – 50	29	25	40	66
Over 51	10	5	15	12

17. If there are 18 million contact lens wearers in the U.S., how many of them are less than 18 years old?

    a.   3.24 million
    b.   3.78 million
    c.   4.14 million
    d.   21 million
    e.   23 million

18. If the number of contact lens wearers in France 5 million, and they each own exactly three pairs of lenses, how many of the pairs belong to wearers who are 51 or older?

    a.   450,000
    b.   750,000
    c.   1,500,000
    d.   2,250,000
    e.   4,500,000

19. Which of the following best explains the small percentage of teenage contact lens wearers in India, compared to those in the U.S., the U.K, and France?

    a.   They are unsafe for use
    b.   They are unavailable
    c.   They are prohibitively expensive
    d.   They are legally prohibited for minors
    e.   They are not advertised on Indian television

20. Which country has the largest number of contact lens wearers between 31 and 50?

    a.   U.S.
    b.   U.K.
    c.   France
    d.   India
    e.   Cannot be determined from the information given

STOP

The answers to these questions are presented in Section QA16 (page 256)

Quantitative 17:   **25 Minutes**   **18 Questions**

Directions: This section contains two types of questions. You have 25 minutes to complete both types. For questions 1 – 8, solve each problem and select the best answer choice. Fill in the corresponding circle on the answer sheet. You may use any available space for scratch work. For Student-Produced Response questions 9 – 18, use the grids at the bottom of the answer sheet to record your answers.

- The use of a calculator is permitted.
- All numbers used are real numbers.
- Figures that accompany problems in this test are intended to provide valuable information useful in solving the problems. They are drawn as accurately as possible EXCEPT when it is stated in a specific problem that the figure is not drawn to scale. All figures lie in a plane unless otherwise indicated.
- Unless otherwise specified, the domain of any function f is assumed to be the set of all real numbers x for which f (x) is a real number.

Reference Information:

- Circles. Area = πr^2, Circumference = $2 \pi r$
- Rectangles: Area = Length X Width
- Right Triangles: Area = ½ (Base) (Height)
- Cubes: Volume = Length x Width x Height
- Cylinders: Volume = $\pi r^2 h$
- Pythagorean Theorem: for right triangles $c^2 = a^2 + b^2$

1. A researcher pumps 100% nitrogen gas into an experimental chamber at a rate of 30 cubic inches per second. If the chamber's dimensions are 15 inches by 24 inches by 48 inches, how many minutes will it take the researcher to fill the chamber with nitrogen?

    a. 9.6
    b. 57.6
    c. 96
    d. 576
    e. 5,760

2. Dina drove 240 miles round trip to visit her family for Thanksgiving. If her car averages 30 miles per gallon of gas and Dina paid an average price of $2.85 per gallon of gas, how much did she spend for gas on her trip?

    a. $22.80
    b. $24.00
    c. $32.85
    d. $42.75
    e. $85.50

3. If the following series continues in the same pattern, what will the next term be?   2, 6, 3, 9, 6, 18, 15......

    a. 6
    b. 9
    c. 12
    d. 21
    e. 45

4. A circle with a radius of 11 has the same area as a triangle with a base of 11. What is the altitude of the triangle?

    a. 7π
    b. 11π
    c. 14π
    d. 22π
    e. 121π

5. 12.67 =

    a.   37/4
    b.   38/3
    c.   72/6
    d.   72.5
    e.   100/6

6. Which of the following expresses the ratio of 12 ounces to 6 pounds?

    a.   1/16
    b.   1/12
    c.   1/8
    d.   1/6
    e.   ¼

7. The larger of two numbers is 9 more than the smaller. Double the small number equals 11 more than the small number. What is the small number?

    a.   9
    b.   10
    c.   11
    d.   19
    e.   20

8. What is the total cost (in cents) of W watermelons, which cost X dollars each, and Y apples, which cost Z cents each?

    a.   WXYZ/100
    b.   100WX + YZ
    c.   WX + 100YZ
    d.   W + YZ/100
    e.   100WX/YZ

9. A hospital is conducting an efficiency study to determine the number of thermometers that are broken on any given day. For the first three weeks in July, the following daily values have been recorded: 5, 3, 7, 3, 6, 4, 8, 3, 7, 10, 3, 5, 9, 5, 3, 7, 2, 6, 5, 3, 7. What is the mode of this data set?

10. Gary and Bill have a law mowing business. Gary can mow a one-acre lawn in 3 hours. Bill can mow the same lawn in 4 hours. How long will it take them (to the nearest minute) to mow the lawn if they both work at the same time?

11. The perimeter of triangle ABC is 125. If AB = 45 and BC = 55, what is the length of AC?

12. What is the largest integer less than 100 that leaves a remainder of 1 when divided by 14?

13. What is the diameter of a circle with area 144π?

14. What is the value of a if ab - ac = 45 and b - c = 5?

15. What is the ratio of fifteen minutes to eight hours?

16. A restaurant received 112 cans of Coca-Cola for their busy rush hour. If waitress A served 18 cans of Coca-Cola, waitress B served 11 cans, and 5 cans were consumed by each of the three cooks, how many cans of Coca-Cola remained for the evening crowd?

17. If (2x – 4)/8 = 10 –x, then what does x equal?

18. The Glenview Airport offers two options for parking. Long-term parking costs a flat rate of $7.00 per day. Short-term parking costs $1.00 for the first two hours, and 50 cents for each additional hour. If a visitor plans to park for 6 hours at the airport, what will be the additional cost of parking in long-term parking versus short-term parking?

STOP

The answers to these questions are presented in Section QA17 (page 258)

Quantitative 18:   20 Minutes   16 Questions

Directions: You have 20 minutes to answer the following 16 questions. Choose the best answer from the options given.

- The use of a calculator is permitted.
- All numbers used are real numbers.
- Figures that accompany problems in this test are intended to provide valuable information useful in solving the problems. They are drawn as accurately as possible EXCEPT when it is stated in a specific problem that the figure is not drawn to scale. All figures lie in a plane unless otherwise indicated.
- Unless otherwise specified, the domain of any function f is assumed to be the set of all real numbers x for which f (x) is a real number.

Reference Information:

- Circles. Area $= \pi r^2$, Circumference $= 2\pi r$
- Rectangles: Area = Length X Width
- Right Triangles: Area = ½ (Base) (Height)
- Cubes: Volume = Length x Width x Height
- Cylinders: Volume $= \pi r^2 h$
- Pythagorean Theorem: for right triangles $c^2 = a^2 + b^2$

1. The Ice View Highway, which links City A and City B, provides two rest areas every twelve miles. How many rest areas would a car pass if it traveled one-half of the 4,356 miles of Ice View Highway, starting at the origin of the highway?

    a. 182
    b. 356
    c. 363
    d. 726
    e. 789

2. Seventy-five freshmen have signed up for extracurricular activities. Fifty sign up for cheerleading. Thirty sign up for the yearbook staff. Eleven sign up for both cheerleading and the yearbook staff. How many of the seventy-five freshman have signed up for NEITHER cheerleading nor the yearbook staff?

    a. 3
    b. 6
    c. 8
    d. 16
    e. 18

3. Dan brought his car to the mechanic to have his engine fixed. The mechanic quoted him the following prices for parts: $350 for a new alternator, $150 for the battery and $25 for miscellaneous parts. Assuming that the minimal charge for labor is $45 per hour (rounded to the nearest half-hour) and that the shop can complete all repairs in 3.5 hours, what is the minimum amount that Dan will have to pay to have his car fixed?

    a. $157.50
    b. $525.00
    c. $682.50
    d. $705.00
    e. $727.50

4. In a large lecture hall containing 540 female students, 27 were on birth control pills, 110 were taking antibiotics, and 220 were taking antihistamines. The remaining 183 students were not taking any medication. In simplest terms, what is the ratio of female students taking birth control pills to the total number of students in the lecture hall?

    a.   1 : 100
    b.   1 : 193
    c.   1 : 27
    d.   1 : 20
    e.   1 : 5

5. Triangles with equal angles and equal sides are called

    a. Similar triangles
    b. Congruent triangles
    c. Scalene triangles
    d. Isosceles triangles
    e. Equilateral triangles

6. If the length of a square is increased by 3 inches, but 3 inches are subtracted from its width, what is the overall effect on the area of the new rectangle?

    a.   It is 9 square inches smaller than the square
    b.   It is 33% smaller than the square
    c.   It is the same area as the square
    d.   It is 33% larger than the square
    e.   It cannot be determined from the information given.

7. In the xy-plane, a circle is centered at the origin and passes through the point (-7,0). What is the area of the circle?

    a. $49/\pi$
    b. 3.5π
    c. 7π
    d. 49π
    e. 81π

8. If $f(a) = a^2 - 4a + 3$, what is $f(-1)$?

    a.   -2
    b.   0
    c.   7
    d.   8
    e.   9

9. What is the mean of the following set of numbers? 44, 33, 58, 22, 16, 66

    a.   35.8
    b.   38.5
    c.   38.9
    d.   39.8
    e.   39.9

10. If it takes 12 people to serve 500 meals at the soup kitchen, how many people will be required to serve 14,280 meals?

    a. 29
    b. 290
    c. 343
    d. 1190
    e. 11,900

11. $23/42 - 35/84 =$

    a. $-12/84$
    b. $-11/84$
    c. $11/84$
    d. $12/84$
    e. $12/42$

12. For the repeating decimal 0.04321043210432104321....., what is the 26th digit to the right of the decimal point?

    a. 0
    b. 1
    c. 2
    d. 3
    e. 4

13. For a graduation gift, Sally's mother offered to buy her three CDs from her list of seven favorites. How many different combinations does Sally have to choose from?

    a. 21
    b. 42
    c. 840
    d. 1764
    e. 2520

14. If p =3 and q is 2, what is $(9^{p})(27^{q}) =$

    a. 3^{9}
    b. 3^{14}
    c. $(729)^{2}$
    d. 6561×2
    e. 9^{5}

15. If m (8)(10)(12)(14)= (4)(5)(6)(7), what is the value of m?

    a. 1/16
    b. 1/8
    c. ½
    d. 8
    e. 16

16. Which of the following are the solutions to the following equation? $x^2 + 3x - 18 = 0$

     a.   −2, 9
     b.   2, -9
     c.   -3, 6
     d.   3, -6
     e.   3, -9

STOP

The answers to these questions are presented in Section QA18 (page 259)

Quantitative 19:   25 Minutes   20 Questions

Directions: You have 25 minutes to answer the following 20 questions. Choose the best answer from the options given.

- The use of a calculator is permitted.
- All numbers used are real numbers.
- Figures that accompany problems in this test are intended to provide valuable information useful in solving the problems. They are drawn as accurately as possible EXCEPT when it is stated in a specific problem that the figure is not drawn to scale. All figures lie in a plane unless otherwise indicated.
- Unless otherwise specified, the domain of any function f is assumed to be the set of all real numbers x for which f (x) is a real number.

Reference Information:

- Circles. Area $= \pi r^2$, Circumference $= 2 \pi r$
- Rectangles: Area = Length X Width
- Right Triangles: Area = ½ (Base) (Height)
- Cubes: Volume = Length x Width x Height
- Cylinders: Volume $= \pi r^2 h$
- Pythagorean Theorem: for right triangles $c^2 = a^2 + b^2$

1. A vineyard wants to blend Wine A, which is 6% alcohol, with Wine B, which is 18% alcohol, to yield Wine C, which is 15% alcohol. To make a batch of Wine C that weighs 2,700 ounces, how many ounces of Wine A must be used?

    a.   0.675
    b.   6.75
    c.   67.5
    d.   135
    e.   675

2. A city park is frequently used as an exercise path. If the park is a square, with each side 2400 feet long, how many minutes would it take someone walking 600 feet per minute to walk the entire perimeter of the park?

    a.   8
    b.   12
    c.   16
    d.   20
    e.   40

3. The sum of two numbers is 13. When three times the larger number is subtracted from 6 times the smaller number, the difference is 6. What is the larger number?

    a.   3
    b.   5
    c.   6
    d.   8
    e.   11

Refer to the chart below for questions 4 and 5.

Viscosity Measurements for Sugar Syrups

Percent Solids	Relative Speed of Flow
20%	50% as fast as syrup with 10% solids
30%	50% as fast as syrup with 20% solids
40%	50% as fast as syrup with 30% solids

4. According to the table, sugar syrup with 10% solids flows how many times as fast as syrup with 40% solids?

    a. 2
    b. 3
    c. 4
    d. 8
    e. 16

5. Using the table as a guide, how fast would a sugar syrup with 50% solids flow?

    a. 50% faster than a syrup with 40% solids
    b. 50% as fast as a syrup with 40% solids
    c. 100% faster than a syrup with 40% solids
    d. 75% as fast as a syrup with 40% solids
    e. 75% faster than a syrup with 25% solids

6. In triangle ABC, one angle is equal to 80 degrees, the second angle is equal to x and the third angle is equal to 4x. What is the value of x?

    a. 10
    b. 15
    c. 16
    d. 20
    e. 24

7. If Jake walks south for 50 yards, then west for 120 yards, then walked directly back to his starting point on a diagonal, how many yards did he walk altogether?

    a. 170
    b. 255
    c. 270
    d. 290
    e. 300

8. What is the diameter of a circle with an area of 144π

    a. 7
    b. 12
    c. 15
    d. 24
    e. 48

9. Find the number of sides in a polygon if the measure of an interior angle is twice as great as the measure of an exterior angle.

    a. 4
    b. 5
    c. 6
    d. 7
    e. 8

10. If $f(j) = j^2 + 0.001j$, what is $f(0.05)$?

    a. 0.00025
    b. 0.00250
    c. 0.00255
    d. 0.00300
    e. 0.00350

11. Jason has 1,489 dimes in a large jar in his bedroom. If he adds 324 dimes on Monday, and adds another 112 dimes on Tuesday, but removes 117 dimes on Wednesday, how much money (in dollars) does Jason have left in the jar on Thursday, assuming that there are no other additions or subtractions?

    a. $180.80
    b. $181.30
    c. $192.50
    d. $193.00
    e. $196.80

12. What is the product of the prime numbers between 10 and 20?

    a.   60
    b.   3,536
    c.   4,199
    d.   46,189
    e.   508,079

13. Sara's CD collection includes 235 titles. Of these, 125 are classic rock, 25 are punk and 38 are rap. The remaining CDs are of unknown classification. What fractional part of Sara's CD collection is unknown?

    a. 1/6
    b. 1/5
    c. 1/4
    d. 2/5
    e. 3/8

14. Reduce the following fraction to its simplest form: 50,000 / 5 million

    a. 1/1000
    b. 5/1000
    c. 1/100
    d. 5/100
    e. 1/10

15. When American Idol auditions were held in New York City, the judges allowed an equal number of men and women to take the stage. At the end of a grueling day, the ratio of female to male singers who advanced to the next round was 3 to 2. At the very end of the day, the judges had a change of heart and agreed to add one additional female singer and one additional male singer to the group that advanced. If the total number of singers who advanced was 32, what was the original number of men chosen to advance?

    a. 8
    b. 10
    c. 12
    d. 18
    e. 20

137

16. Pizza Hut offers six possible toppings for their personal pan pizzas: pepperoni, sausage, onion, cheese, mushrooms and peppers. If you choose four of these toppings, how many possible combinations are there?

    a.   4
    b.   16
    c.   24
    d.   30
    e.   36

17. What number, when cubed, is equal to the square of 125?

    a.   5
    b.   15
    c.   25
    d.   35
    e.   50

18. Solve for x: $(x + 5) - (4/2)(6/3) = 12$

    a. -2
    b. 4/5
    c. 8
    d. 11
    e. 13

19. Solve the following equations for y: $2x + 4y = 18$, $4x - 6y = 8$.

    a. 2
    b. 3
    c. 4
    d. 5
    e. 6

20. What is the value of $(x + 2)(x + 5) - (x + 1)(x + 3)$?

    a. 3x + 7
    b. 3x - 7
    c. 5x - 10
    d. 5x + 10
    e. 5x - 7

STOP

The answers to these questions are presented in Section QA19 (page 260)

Directions: _This section contains two types of questions. You have 25 minutes to complete both types. For questions 1 – 8, solve each problem and select the best answer choice. Fill in the corresponding circle on the answer sheet. You may use any available space for scratch work. For Student-Produced Response questions 9 – 18, use the grids at the bottom of the answer sheet to record your answers._

- The use of a calculator is permitted.
- All numbers used are real numbers.
- Figures that accompany problems in this test are intended to provide valuable information useful in solving the problems. They are drawn as accurately as possible EXCEPT when it is stated in a specific problem that the figure is not drawn to scale. All figures lie in a plane unless otherwise indicated.
- Unless otherwise specified, the domain of any function f is assumed to be the set of all real numbers x for which f (x) is a real number.

Reference Information:

- Circles.   Area $= \pi r^2$, Circumference $= 2 \pi r$
- Rectangles: Area = Length X Width
- Right Triangles: Area = ½ (Base) (Height)
- Cubes: Volume = Length x Width x Height
- Cylinders: Volume $= \pi r^2 h$
- Pythagorean Theorem: for right triangles $c^2 = a^2 + b^2$

1. The denominator of a fraction is three times as large as the numerator. If 5 is added to both the numerator and denominator, the value of the fraction is ¾. What was the numerator of the original fraction?

     a.   1
     b.   2
     c.   3
     d.   4
     e.   5

2. If the perimeter of an isosceles triangle is 64 and its base is 16, find the length of one of the equal sides.

     a.   18
     b.   20
     c.   24
     d.   26
     e.   28

3. Rectangle CDEF has a length of 6 and a width of 2. What is its perimeter?

     a.   8
     b.   12
     c.   16
     d.   40
     e.   64

4. Find the equation of the line that is parallel to y = 14 and containing the point (9, 7).

     a.   y = 7 x + 2
     b.   y = 7
     c.   x = 14
     d.   y = -7/9 x + 14
     e.   y = 7/9 x + 14

5. 15 / (3/6) =

    a. 3
    b. 5
    c. 30
    d. 90
    e. 300

6. In a kennel with 28 dogs, of which half are neutered and half are intact, the average (mean) weight of the neutered dogs was 83 pounds. If the average weight of the 14 intact dogs in the kennel was 92 pounds, what was the average weight of the entire kennel?

    a. 86.5
    b. 87.0
    c. 87.5
    d. 88.0
    e. 88.5

7. What is the least positive integer that is divisible by both 2 and 9 and leaves a remainder of 4 when divided by 5?

    a. 18
    b. 36
    c. 45
    d. 49
    e. 54

8. A parallelogram has an interior angle of 60 degrees. What is the measure of the adjacent angle?

    a. 90
    b. 120
    c. 180
    d. 300
    e. It cannot be determined from the information given

9. Debbie put $7,500 into a CD that pays 4.95% simple annual interest. If she leaves the money in the account for 6 years, what will the CD be worth?

10. A bartender is mixing Liquor A, which is 4% alcohol, with Liquor B, which is 20% alcohol, to yield Liquor C, which is 16% alcohol. To make a 4,000 ounce batch of Liquor C, how many ounces of Liquor B must be used?

11. If the diameter of a circle increases by 100%, by what percent will the area of the circle increase?

12. If (12k – 3)/3 = 24 – k, what does k equal?

13. A chef has a wonderful recipe for meatloaf, which uses 8 oz of garlic for a loaf that serves 12 people. How much **additional** garlic (in oz) would the chef need if she quadrupled the recipe (to serve 48 people)?

14. The mean of seven numbers is 77. If 12 is subtracted from each of five of the numbers, what is the new mean?

15. If the following sequence continues indefinitely, what will the 300th term be?

        9,8,7,6,5,4,9,8,7,6,5,4,9,8,7,6,5,4,9,8,7,6,5,4,9,8,7,6,5,4, ...

16. What number, when cubed, is equal to the square root of 4096?

17. Five consecutive odd integers have a sum of 475. What is the largest of the five integers?

18. If 15 balloons cost $14.87, what do seven dozen balloons cost?

STOP

The answers to these questions are presented in Section QA20 (page 261)

Quantitative 21:   20 Minutes   16 Questions

1. Two motorcyclists are 540 miles apart. At 10:00 am they start traveling toward each other at rates of 65 and 70 miles per hour. At what time will they pass each other?

      a.   1:00 pm
      b.   1:30 pm
      c.   2:00 pm
      d.   3:30 pm
      e.   4:00 pm

2. Zoe has 30 coins, a combination of nickels and dimes, which are worth a total of $2.65. How many of Zoe's coins are dimes?

      a.   20
      b.   21
      c.   22
      d.   23
      e.   24

3. Samantha deposited a total of $25,000 in a bank CD and a money market account. The bank CD offers a 7.5% annual return, while the money market account offers a 5.25% annual return. If Samantha earns $400 more per year from the CD than the money market account, how much did she invest in the CD?

      a. $10,569
      b. $11,011
      c. $11,569
      d. $13, 431
      e. $13, 989

4. The base of a triangle is 16 more than the height. If the area of the triangle is 256 square inches, what is its height?

      a.   4
      b.   8
      c.   16
      d.   32
      e.   36

5. For a line with the equation x + 3y = 6, what is the slope?

    a.   –6
    b.   –1/3
    c.   –1/6
    d.   1/6
    e.   1

6. Find the number of sides in a polygon if the measure of an interior angle is three times as great as the measure of an exterior angle.

    a.   4
    b.   5
    c.   6
    d.   7
    e.   8

7. What is the length of the hypotenuse in an equilateral right triangle with an area of 121?

    a. $7\sqrt{2}$
    b.   7
    c. $11\sqrt{2}$
    d.   11
    e.   15

8. If the length of a rectangle increases by 25% and its width decreases by 40%, what is the overall effect on the area of the rectangle?

    a.   It increases by 5%
    b.   It remains the same
    c.   It decreases by 5%
    d.   It decreases by 15%
    e.   It decreases by 25%

9. Which of the following quantities is greater than 1/7?

    a.   0.1399
    b.   2/15
    c.   3/19
    d.   0.141
    e.   4/29

10. A buffet table contains 7 entrees, 3 soups and 2 specialty salads. The remaining ¼ of the items are desserts. What percent of the items on the buffet table are specialty salads?

    a.   3.125%
    b.   6.25%
    c.   12.5%
    d.   16.67%
    e.   20%

11. In a large lecture hall containing 550 female students, 27 were on birth control pills, 110 were taking antibiotics, and 220 were taking antihistamines. The remaining 193 students were not taking any medication. In simplest terms, what is the ratio of female students taking antihistamines to the total number of students in the lecture hall?

   a. 1 : 25
   b. 1 : 20
   c. 1 : 5
   d. 2 : 5
   e. 1 : 2

12. What is the median of the following set of numbers? 44, 33, 55, 22, 11, 66

   a. 33.0
   b. 33.5
   c. 38.0
   d. 38.5
   e. 44.0

13. A bookstore is preparing a display with five different novels by a best-selling author. How many possible arrangements are there in the display (assume no title is repeated)?

   a. 25
   b. 120
   c. 125
   d. 500
   e. 600

14. $(4x^2)^2(3x^3)^3 =$

   a. $12x^{10}$
   b. $144x^{13}$
   c. $288x^{10}$
   d. $432x^{13}$
   e. $1296x^{13}$

15. If (d)(3)(5) = (10)(e)(3), and neither d nor e are 0, what is the value of e/d?

   a. 1/3
   b. 1/2
   c. 2/3
   d. 2
   e. 3

16. For the following system of equations, what are the possible values of a? ab = 1, a = 4b

   a. ½ or −1/2
   b. 1 or -1
   c. 2 or -2
   d. 4 or -4
   e. There is no solution to the equations

STOP

The answers to these questions are presented in Section QA21 (page 262)

Quantitative 22:   25 Minutes   18 Questions

1. Jocelyn weighs 60% as much as Connie. If Jocelyn gains 8 pounds, she will weigh 75% as much as Connie. What is Jocelyn's weight (in pounds)?

    a.   32.0
    b.   35.5
    c.   40.0
    d.   43.3
    e.   53.3

2. A business executive and his client are charging their dinner tab on the executive's expense account. The company will only allow them to spend a total of $50 for the meal. Assuming that they will pay 7% in sales tax for the meal and leave a 15% tip, what is the most that their food can cost?

    a. $39.55
    b. $40.03
    c. $40.63
    d. $41.15
    e. $43.15

3. If 25 less than eight times a number is equal to 215, find the number.

    a.   20
    b.   25
    c.   30
    d.   35
    e.   40

Refer to the following table for questions 4 & 5

Joe's Budget for August 2007 (in dollars)

Rent	700
Car Payment	350
Utilities	185
Cell Phone	80
Insurance	55
Food	100
Credit Card	240
Clothes	75
Miscellaneous	321
Savings	35

4. Financial experts recommend that people Joe's age allocate at least 10% of their budget for savings. How much additional money would Joe have to save each month to reach this percentage?

    a. $35
    b. $79
    c. $150
    d. $179
    e. $214

5. To buy a house, Joe will have to assume a mortgage payment that is $300 per month higher than his current rent. Which expenses, if eliminated, will allow him to achieve this goal?

    a.   Cell phone, Food and Clothes
    b.   Credit card and Insurance
    a.   Credit card and Savings
    b.   Clothes and Credit card
    c.   Savings, Clothes, Cell phone and Food

6. Jenny colored several cartons of Easter eggs for her younger sister's kindergarten class. Her final basket included blue, green and pink eggs. If the ratio of the number of blue eggs to green eggs is 8:3, and the ratio of the number of green eggs to pink eggs is 1:2, what is the ratio of the number of blue eggs to pink eggs?

    a.   8:2
    b.   8:1
    c.   2:1
    d.   3:2
    e.   8:6

7. Carly has $38 dollars left over after spending 4/9 of her birthday money. How much money did Carly receive for her birthday?

    a. $48.40
    b. $59.10
    c. $68.40
    d. $76.00
    e. $85.50

8. What is the average of the following numbers? 23.2, 41.9, 66.2, 38.7, 90.6

    a.   47.69
    b.   49.67
    c.   51.23
    d.   52.12
    e.   52.21

9. If $x = 21$, $y = 11$ and $z = 4$, what is the value of $14x - 2y + 6(z^3 - 1)$?

10. David has 20 pennies, 12 quarters and 27 dimes. How many nickels does this amount of money equal?

11. If thirteen less than eleven times a whole number is 306, find the number.

12. A clothing shop sells six pairs of shoes and eight pairs of socks for $995. The cost for four pairs of shoes and twelve pairs of socks is $750. How much would it cost to buy one pair of shoes?

13. The bus ride from Manhattan to the Bronx is inversely proportional to the bus driver's rate of speed. During periods of low traffic, when he can drive at 70 piles per hour, the ride is 20 minutes. How long (to the closest minute) does the ride take at 30 miles per hour?

14. Find the number of sides of a polygon if the sum of the interior angles is 1,980 degrees?

15. A cube and a rectangular solid are equal in volume. If the lengths of the edges of the rectangular solid are 8, 9, and 24, what is the length of an edge of the cube?

16. For the repeating decimal 0.015689015689015689......, what is the 37th digit to the right of the decimal point?

17. Give one possible solution to the following equation: $x^2 -10x + 24 = 0$.

18. What is the sum of the following fractions: 1/2, 2/4, 2/6, 1/3, 3/12 (expressed as a fraction)?

STOP

The answers to these questions are presented in Section QA22 (page 263)

Directions: This section contains two types of questions. You have 25 minutes to complete both types. For questions 1 – 8, solve each problem and select the best answer choice. Fill in the corresponding circle on the answer sheet. You may use any available space for scratch work. For Student-Produced Response questions 9 – 18, use the grids at the bottom of the answer sheet to record your answers.

- The use of a calculator is permitted.
- All numbers used are real numbers.
- Figures that accompany problems in this test are intended to provide valuable information useful in solving the problems. They are drawn as accurately as possible EXCEPT when it is stated in a specific problem that the figure is not drawn to scale. All figures lie in a plane unless otherwise indicated.
- Unless otherwise specified, the domain of any function f is assumed to be the set of all real numbers x for which f (x) is a real number.

Reference Information:

- Circles. Area $= \pi r^2$, Circumference $= 2 \pi r$
- Rectangles: Area = Length X Width
- Right Triangles: Area = ½ (Base) (Height)
- Cubes: Volume = Length x Width x Height
- Cylinders: Volume $= \pi r^2 h$
- Pythagorean Theorem: for right triangles $c^2 = a^2 + b^2$

1. One number is equal to five times a smaller number. If three times their difference is equal to 48, what is the larger number?

     a.   -4
     b.   2
     c.   4
     d.   5
     e.   20

2. An Internet business sells discount CDs and DVDs. The cost for eight CDs and nine DVDs is $199. The cost for twelve CDs and six DVDs is $159. How much would it cost to buy one DVD?

     a. $3.05
     b. $3.95
     c. $9.30
     d. $15.00
     e. $18.60

3. Jake earns a base salary of $700 per week plus a 15% commission on sales. In a week in which Jake sold $12,4000 worth of merchandise, what was his total weekly pay (before taxes)?

     a. $824
     b. $1860
     c. $1940
     d. $2500
     e. $2560

4. Triangles with equal angles but unequal sides are called

     a. Similar triangles
     b. Congruent triangles
     c. Scalene triangles
     d. Isosceles triangles
     e. Equilateral triangles

5. What is the circumference of a circle with a diameter of $2/9\pi$?

    a. 3
    b. 2/9
    c. $4/9\pi$
    d. 18
    e. $18/\pi$

6. $6 + 1/3 - (4/9)^2 - (3/2)(5/6) =$

    a. 4.73
    b. 4.89
    c. 5.73
    d. 5.89
    e. 6.20

7. Eve's boyfriend asked her to buy five items at the grocery store, which only accepts cash. They include a frozen pizza that costs $3.25, a bottle of juice that costs $4.89, a pound of butter that costs $2.89, a six-pack of root beer that is on sale for $3.19 and two packs of gum that cost 89 cents each. If Eve also wants to buy a magazine for herself that costs $3.50, how much money does she need to have with her?

    a. $15.42
    b. $18.61
    c. $19.01
    d. $19.50
    e. $20.39

8. Eight hundred people answered a newspaper ad to audition for American Idol. Forty percent of them were assigned Whitney Houston songs. Of this 40%, one-quarter of the people sang "I Will Always Love You." How many people sang "I Will Always Love You?"

    a. 40
    b. 60
    c. 80
    d. 120
    e. 160

Refer to the following charts to answer questions 9 – 11.

Number of Financial Products Sold

	Traditional Brokerage	**Online Brokerage**
CD	200	350
Annuity	50	105
401-K	85	409

Total Value of Financial Product Sold (in millions)

	CD	**Annuity**	**401-k**
Traditional Brokerage	54	23	10
Online Brokerage	92	27	31

9. For the time period represented by these charts, what was the average value of an Annuity sold at the traditional brokerage house (in millions of dollars)?

10. For the time period represented by these charts, what was the average value of a 401-K sold at an online brokerage house (in millions of dollars)?

11. For the time period represented by these charts, what was the total value of all financial products sold by the online brokerage (in millions of dollars)?

12. American Airlines is recording the number of on-time flights into and out of the Miami airport. The daily totals for one particular week are 1135, 1059, 1432, 2310, 1587, 1986, and 2131. What is the median?

13. Sam is three times as old as Greg. Lori is 10 years older than Greg. If their combined age is 65, how old is Greg?

14. A parallelogram has an interior angle of 75 degrees. What is the measure of the adjacent angle (in degrees)?

15. Square X has a side of 19, while square Y has a side of 23. How much greater is the area of square Y than square X?

16. Give one possible solution to the following equation: $x^4 - x^2 = 0$.

17. What is the probability of getting a blue M&M from a dispenser that contains 50 red M&Ms, 75 green M&Ms, 100 blue M&Ms and 75 white M&Ms?

18. If x = 2, calculate $5^x + (x^4)^{x-1}$

STOP

The answers to these questions are presented in Section QA23 (page 264)

Quantitative 24:   25 Minutes   18 Questions

1. After careful negotiations, the Zippy Insurance Company agreed to pay 75% of Chad's accident expenses, after deducting $100 in non-covered items and a $325 administrative fee. If Chad's expenses totaled $14,625, how much did he receive from Zippy Insurance?

    a. $9,968
    b. $9,650
    c. $10,650
    d. $10,968
    e. $11,650

2. Carrie added M coins to her large collection, which gave her a total of N coins. Then, Carrie sold M – 180 of her coins to a local collector. How many coins did Carrie have left?

    a.   M - N + 180
    b.   N + M - 180
    c.   N - M + 180
    d.   N - M - 180
    e.   (M + N – 180)/2

3. David drives to work on the interstate. The time it takes him to reach his office is inversely proportional to his rate of speed. If he drives at 75 mph, it takes him 30 minutes. How long (in minutes) will it take David if he drives 45 mph?

    a.   18
    b.   45
    c.   50
    d.   75
    e.   112.50

Refer to the chart below for questions 4 – 6

Ribbons Won by the Warren High School Football Team

	2006	2007
September	21	18
October	56	29
November	34	35
December	12	26

4. According to the table, what was the % increase in the number of ribbons won by the football team in November 2006 vs. November 2007?

    a.   1.03%
    b.   2.17%
    c.   10.3%
    d.   21.7%.
    e.   217%

5. According to the table, what was the % change in the number of ribbons won by the football team in September 2006 vs. September 2007?

    a.   3% decrease
    b.   14.3% decrease
    c.   16.7% decrease
    d.   14.3% increase
    e.   16.7% increase

6. According to the table, what was the overall % change in the number of ribbons won by the football team in 2006 and 2007?

    a.   There was no change
    b.   4% decrease
    c.   12.2% decrease
    d.   16.7% decrease
    e.   87.8% decrease

7. If the prime numbers between 80 and 90 are added together, what is their sum?

    a.   81
    b.   89
    c.   164
    d.   172
    e.   176

8. At the end of a night, a waitress calculates the total amount of tip money to be $346.84. After giving the busboy 5% of the total amount, she must divide the remainder into five equal shares and place *two* of those shares into an envelope. How much will the waitress place in the envelope?

    a. $62.43
    b. $65.90
    c. $124.86
    d. $131.80
    e. $138.74

9. A line segment contains six points. S, T, U, V, W and X. How many different line segments are formed by these six points?

10. If f (z) = z^3/25, what is f (15)?

11. Marcia drove 550 miles on a business trip, using a company car that averages 25 miles per gallon. If Marcia paid an average price of $3.03 per gallon of gas, how much did she spend on gas for the trip?

12. Joe will cover his bathroom floor with ceramic tiles that measure 3 inches by 6 inches. If the room is a rectangle that measures 8 feet by 6 feet, how many tiles will Joe need to cover the floor?

13. What is the area of a square with a side of length 13?

14. Rectangle ABCD has a length of 15 and a width of 9. What is its perimeter?

15. If 17 − 5d = 2, what is the value of 9 − 2d?

16. How many 0.5 oz. chicken nuggets are in a 2 lb bag of chicken nuggets (assume the bag has zero weight?

17. When an accountant requested her client's sales records for tax season, she received a stack of invoices numbered 00236 through 00435. Upon further examination, however, the accountant realized that invoice numbers 00236 and 00237 were for transactions in the previous tax year, and should not be included in the current year's calculations. How many invoices did the bookkeeper use for this year's calculations?

18. Adam earns twice as much per hour as Josh. Josh earns $5 more per hour than Connie. Together, they earn $75 per hour. What is Adam's hourly wage?

STOP

The answers to these questions are presented in Section QA24 (page 265)

Quantitative 25:   25 Minutes   18 Questions

Directions: This section contains two types of questions. You have 25 minutes to complete both types. For questions 1 – 8, solve each problem and select the best answer choice. Fill in the corresponding circle on the answer sheet. You may use any available space for scratch work. For Student-Produced Response questions 9 – 18, use the grids at the bottom of the answer sheet to record your answers.

- *The use of a calculator is permitted.*
- *All numbers used are real numbers.*
- *Figures that accompany problems in this test are intended to provide valuable information useful in solving the problems. They are drawn as accurately as possible EXCEPT when it is stated in a specific problem that the figure is not drawn to scale. All figures lie in a plane unless otherwise indicated.*
- *Unless otherwise specified, the domain of any function f is assumed to be the set of all real numbers x for which f (x) is a real number.*

Reference Information:

- *Circles. Area $= \pi r^2$, Circumference $= 2\pi r$*
- *Rectangles: Area = Length X Width*
- *Right Triangles: Area = ½ (Base) (Height)*
- *Cubes: Volume = Length x Width x Height*
- *Cylinders: Volume $= \pi r^2 h$*
- *Pythagorean Theorem: for right triangles $c^2 = a^2 + b^2$*

1. The supermarket sells salted peanuts for fifty cents an ounce. If the local baker runs out of peanuts unexpectedly and has to buy them from this supermarket at the regular retail price, what will he pay for 42 pounds of salted peanuts?

    a. $16
    b. $24
    c. $80
    d. $186
    e. $336

2.   Cement truck 1 can pour 600 gallons of concrete mix in 2.1 hours. Cement truck 2 can pour the same amount in 2.9 hours. How many minutes longer than cement truck 1 would it take cement truck 2 to pour 130,000 quarts of concrete mix?

    a.   48
    b.   126
    c.   432
    d.   2600
    e.   6825

3. The difference between two positive consecutive integers, when each is squared, equals 23. What is the smaller number?

    a.   9
    b.   10
    c.   11
    d.   12
    e.   13

4. If x#y = 2xy + y, what is 3#7?

    a. 6
    b. 11
    c. 19
    d. 27
    e. 49

5. If the length of rectangle R is one-half the length of rectangle Z, and the width of rectangle R is one-half the width of rectangle Z, what is the ratio of the area of rectangle Z to the area of rectangle R?

    a. ¼
    b. ½
    c. 2/1
    d. 4/1
    e. It cannot be determined from the information given

6. Which of the following rectangular solids has the same volume as a sphere with a radius of 5? (Use π = 3.1416)
    a. A square with a side length of 10.
    b. A square with a diagonal of 5.
    c. A rectangular solid with a length of 5, a width of 10, and a height of 10.
    d. A rectangular solid with a length of 2, a width of 2, and a height of 131.
    e. A rectangular solid with a length of 3, a width of 3, and a height of 58.

7. How many 6 ounce rib eye steaks are in a carton of steaks that weighs 48 pounds? (Assume that all of the steaks are rib eye and that they account for the total weight of the box)

    a. 96
    b. 108
    c. 128
    d. 146
    e. 196

8. Jason inherited $8 million from his paternal grandfather. Today, he placed the entire amount in account that earns 9 1/2% simple annual interest. Assuming that Jason leaves the money in the account and does not withdraw any of the interest, how much will have (principal + interest) exactly one year from today?

    a. $8,000,760
    b. $8,007,600
    c. $8,076,000
    d. $8,760,000
    e. $8,950,000

Refer to the following charts to answer questions 9 – 11.

Number of Financial Products Sold:

	Traditional Brokerage	**Online Brokerage**
CD	200	350
Annuity	50	105
401-K	85	409

Total Value of Financial Product Sold (in millions)

	CD	**Annuity**	**401-k**
Traditional Brokerage	54	23	10
Online Brokerage	92	27	31

9. What was the total number of Annuities sold at both brokerage houses for the time period represented by these charts?

10. What was the total number of financial products sold at the online brokerage for the time period represented by these charts?

11. CDs account for what percentage of the total dollar value of financial products sold at the traditional brokerage house (for the time period represented by these charts)?

12. David scored the following number of baskets during his first six basketball games: 5, 6, 9, 12, 4, and 8. How many baskets must he score in game 7 to have an average of 10 baskets per game for the entire 7-game season?

13. A group of 700 college students was asked to name their favorite color. One hundred students said red, 225 said blue, 125 said green, and 50 students each said yellow, orange and white, respectively. The remaining students were undecided. In simplest terms, what % of students was undecided (to the nearest whole percentage)?

14. A wholesale dairy sells blocks of butter in cubic containers that have an edge of 16 inches. If the butter weighs 20 pounds per cubic foot, what is the weight of a single cube of butter (to the nearest tenth of a pound)?

15. For what value of x will the expression $8/(x-3) - 2 = 0$?

16. $(11 - 5)^3 =$

17. In quadrilateral ABCD, the sum of angles A, B and C = 7D. What is the value of angle D (in degrees)?

18. If $4y \leq 47$ and $3y \geq 33$, and y is an integer, what must y be?

STOP

The answers to these questions are presented in Section QA25 (page 266)

Quantitative 26:   **25 Minutes**   **18 Questions**

Directions: This section contains two types of questions. You have 25 minutes to complete both types. For questions 1 – 8, solve each problem and select the best answer choice. Fill in the corresponding circle on the answer sheet. You may use any available space for scratch work. For Student-Produced Response questions 9 – 18, use the grids at the bottom of the answer sheet to record your answers.

- The use of a calculator is permitted.
- All numbers used are real numbers.
- Figures that accompany problems in this test are intended to provide valuable information useful in solving the problems. They are drawn as accurately as possible EXCEPT when it is stated in a specific problem that the figure is not drawn to scale. All figures lie in a plane unless otherwise indicated.
- Unless otherwise specified, the domain of any function f is assumed to be the set of all real numbers x for which f (x) is a real number.

Reference Information:

- Circles. Area $= \pi r^2$, Circumference $= 2 \pi r$
- Rectangles: Area = Length X Width
- Right Triangles: Area = ½ (Base) (Height)
- Cubes: Volume = Length x Width x Height
- Cylinders: Volume $= \pi r^2 h$
- Pythagorean Theorem: for right triangles $c^2 = a^2 + b^2$

1. An online store sells two products: a hardcover and soft cover book of sonnets. Altogether, the company earned $65,000 in profits last year on the sale of 5000 units. If their profit on the hardcover book is $5 and their profit on the soft cover version is $15, how many soft cover books did they sell?

    a.   1500
    b.   2000
    c.   2500
    d.   3500
    e.   4000

2. Jade placed a large sum of money in a bank CD that pays 8% simple interest per year. Then, she deposited the same amount, plus an additional $5000, in a real estate investment trust (REIT) that paid 12% simple annual interest. If her total annual return from both investments is $26,000, how much money did Jade place into the bank CD?

    a.   72,000
    b.   96,000
    c.   110,000
    d.   127,000
    e.   132,000

3. Karen inherited a valuable oil painting that she wants to have framed. If the painting is a rectangle, with a width of 48 inches and a length of 64 inches, how much framing, in linear feet, does Karen need to buy (to the nearest whole foot)?

    a.   19
    b.   32
    c.   112
    d.   224
    e.   448

4. Square M is twice as large as square K. If the length of the side of square M is increased by 50% to make square S, by what percent is the area of square S greater than the sum of the areas of squares K and M?

    a.   75%
    b.   80%
    c.   110%
    d.   130%
    e.   150%

5. What is the sum of the measure of the interior angles of a polygon having 13 sides?

    a.   360
    b.   780
    c.   1,560
    d.   1,980
    e.   2,340

6. If 86,868,686 is divided by 6,868, what is the remainder?

    a.   2222
    b.   3434
    c.   4343
    d.   6832
    e.   12648

7. A plasma television that costs $1650 is reduced in price by 50%. If the price is raised back to $1650, what % increase does this represent?

    a.   50%
    b.   75%
    c.   100%
    d.   150%
    e.   200%

8. What is the next term in this series?   97, 89, 83, 79, ...

    a.   69
    b.   71
    c.   73
    d.   75
    e.   77

9. If the following sequence continues indefinitely, what will be the sum of the 500th term through the 505th term?

    4,5,6,7,8,9,4,5,6,7,8,9,4,5,6,7,8,9,4,5,6,7,8,9,4,5,6,7,8,9,.......

10. Jill's boyfriend asked her to bring four DVDs from her collection of eight to a weekend party. How many different combinations does Jill have to choose from?

11. If Greg splits his thousand dollar lottery prize evenly with his three brothers, after 30% is deducted from the winnings in taxes, how much will each of them receive (in dollars)?

12. For the line $y = -8x + 16$, what is the x-intercept?

13. Joe and Candy have a $100 gift certificate for a local restaurant, which must cover the complete cost of their meal, plus tax and tip. Assuming that they will pay 6% sales tax for the meal and leave a 20% tip, what is the most that their food can cost?

14. On a snowy Sunday night, Sam and Joe decided to compare CD collections. If Sam has 12 less than four times the number of CDs that Joe has, and Joe has 62 CDs, how many CDs does Sam have?

15. Argon gas is pumped into a tank at a rate of 60 cubic inches per second. If the chamber's dimensions are 12 inches by 24 inches by 42 inches, how many minutes will it take for the tank to be completely filled with gas (to the nearest tenth of a minute)?

16.   2.05 x 8.99 x 54.22 =

17. If x = -1 and y = -2, what is he value of $x^2 + 4xy - y^2$?

18. What is the median of the following set of numbers? 33, 78, 44, 66, 55

STOP

The answers to these questions are presented in Section QA26 (page 267)

Quantitative 27:   25 Minutes   18 Questions

Directions: _This section contains two types of questions. You have 25 minutes to complete both types. For questions 1 – 8, solve each problem and select the best answer choice. Fill in the corresponding circle on the answer sheet. You may use any available space for scratch work. For Student-Produced Response questions 9 – 18, use the grids at the bottom of the answer sheet to record your answers._

- The use of a calculator is permitted.
- All numbers used are real numbers.
- Figures that accompany problems in this test are intended to provide valuable information useful in solving the problems. They are drawn as accurately as possible EXCEPT when it is stated in a specific problem that the figure is not drawn to scale. All figures lie in a plane unless otherwise indicated.
- Unless otherwise specified, the domain of any function f is assumed to be the set of all real numbers x for which f (x) is a real number.

Reference Information:

- Circles. Area = πr^2, Circumference = $2 \pi r$
- Rectangles: Area = Length X Width
- Right Triangles: Area = ½ (Base) (Height)
- Cubes: Volume = Length x Width x Height
- Cylinders: Volume = $\pi r^2 h$
- Pythagorean Theorem: for right triangles $c^2 = a^2 + b^2$

1. A store sells both videos and DVDs. The average price of a video is $12.00, while the average price of a DVD is $15.00. If, last month, the store sold 30 more DVDs than videos, and the total receipts were $5850, how many DVDs did the store sell?

    a.   200
    b.   225
    c.   230
    d.   255
    e.   260

2. Kelly wants to have her favorite picture enlarged to the size of a wall poster. The original picture measures 2 inches by 3 inches. If the shorter side of the poster will be 4 feet long, how long (in inches) will the longer side be?

    a.   6
    b.   36
    c.   64
    d.   72
    e.   78

3. The church must replace 6 stained glass windows that were destroyed by a hurricane. The windows are squares that measure 13 feet on each side. If the stained glass costs $5.86 per square foot, how many of the windows can the church replace for $4000 (assuming there is no sales tax)?

    a.   2
    b.   3
    c.   4
    d.   5
    e.   6

4. David visited his grandmother in the hospital, where there were two places for him to park. Lot A charges $5.00 for the first hour of parking and 75 cents for each additional half hour. Lot B, on the other hand, charges a flat rate of $19.75 for an entire day of parking. Assuming that David will park his car for 7 hours that day, what will be the additional cost of parking in Lot B?

    a. $3.00
    b. $3.75
    c. $5.75
    d. $11.70
    e. $14.00

5. Which of the following is equal to 0.0000543?

    a. 54.3×10^7
    b. $54.3c\ 10^{-7}$
    c. 543×10^{-8}
    d. 5.43×10^{-6}
    e. 5.43×10^{-5}

Refer to the following table for questions 6 & 7

Joe's Budget for August 2007 (in dollars)

Rent	700
Car Payment	350
Utilities	185
Cell Phone	80
Insurance	55
Food	100
Credit Card	240
Clothes	75
Miscellaneous	321
Savings	35

6. According to the table, what percentage of Joe's budget is allocated for rent and utilities?

    a. 33%
    b. 41%
    c. 49%
    d. 55%
    e. 60%

7. According to experts, discretionary expenses include money spent for food, clothes, miscellaneous items and credit card debt. By this definition, what percentage of Joe's budget is allocated to discretionary items?

    a. 23.1%
    b. 25.2%
    c. 34.4%
    d. 39.6%
    e. 54.4%

8. If the diameter of a circle is decreased by half, what happens to its circumference?

        a.   it doubles
        b.   it remains unchanged
        c.   it also decreases by half
        d.   it decreases four-fold
        e.   it cannot be determined by the information given

9.   One can of Stardust Blue paint was just enough to cover one-quarter of Jenny's bedroom.   How many additional cans will she need to buy to finish painting her bedroom and to paint 3 additional rooms that are exactly the same size?

10. What is the sum of the measure of the interior angles of a polygon having 11 sides?

11. How much larger is the surface area (in cubic feet) of a cube with an edge of 5 feet than a cube with an edge of 3 feet?

12. If $x = 1$ and $y = 2$, what is the value of the expression $5x^2 - 3xy + 7y^2$?

13. Solve the following equations for y: $4x + 5y = 14$; $6y - 4x = 19$.

14. A year ago, *The Sopranos* won 15 Emmy awards. This year, the show won only 3 Emmy awards. What % decrease does this represent?

15. What is the average of the following numbers: 22/7, 44/6,11/7, 4/9,10/13 (to two decimal places)?

16. If the following series continues in the same pattern, what will the next term be?   1, 1, 6, 36, 41.....

17. What positive integer is 40% of 15,600?

18. If $4^x < 500$, what is the largest possible *integer value* of x?

STOP

The answers to these questions are presented in Section QA27 (page 268)

Quantitative 28:   20 Minutes   16 Questions

Directions: You have 20 minutes to answer the following 16 questions. Choose the best answer from the options given.

- _The use of a calculator is permitted._
- _All numbers used are real numbers._
- _Figures that accompany problems in this test are intended to provide valuable information useful in solving the problems. They are drawn as accurately as possible EXCEPT when it is stated in a specific problem that the figure is not drawn to scale. All figures lie in a plane unless otherwise indicated._
- _Unless otherwise specified, the domain of any function f is assumed to be the set of all real numbers x for which f (x) is a real number._

Reference Information:

- _Circles. Area $= \pi r^2$, Circumference $= 2 \pi r$_
- _Rectangles: Area = Length X Width_
- _Right Triangles: Area = ½ (Base) (Height)_
- _Cubes: Volume = Length x Width x Height_
- _Cylinders: Volume $= \pi r^2 h$_
- _Pythagorean Theorem: for right triangles $c^2 = a^2 + b^2$_

1. For her Halloween party, Janice went to a local candy store and bought X dozen candy bars at a price of Y per bar. When she left the store, Janice had Z cents left over. Assuming that she made no other purchases, how much money (in cents) did Janice have when she entered the candy store?

    a. XYZ
    b. XY + Z
    c. (12X/Y) + Z
    d. 12XY – Z
    e. 12XY + Z

2. If x + 15 is an even integer, the sum of the next three even integers is:

    a. x + 57
    b. 3x + 45
    c. 3x + 51
    d. 3x + 57
    e. $(x + 15)^3$

3. If y is 5 less than 4 times x, what is the value of x?

    a. (y - 5) / 4
    b. (y + 5) / 4
    c. 4y + 20
    d. 4y - 20
    e. 4/5 y

4. A Quick Print Copy Center owns two high-speed copiers for large jobs. Photocopier A can print 100 books in five hours, while photocopier B will take seven hours to print 50 books. How long will it take (in hours) to print 100 books if photocopiers A and B work together?

    a. 1.84
    b. 3.36
    c. 3.68
    d. 4.36
    e. 7.36

5. How much larger is the surface area (in cubic feet) of a cube with an edge of 7 feet than a cube with an edge of 9 feet?

    a. 24
    b. 343
    c. 386
    d. 449
    e. 729

6. Which of the following equations will have a horizontal line as its graph?

    a. $x = 2 - y$
    b. $x = 2 + y$
    c. $x/y = 2$
    d. $x = 2$
    e. $y = 2$

7. Which of the following relations is a function?

    a. {(s, d), (v, z), (v, e)}
    b. {(k, m), (v, x), (k, 9)}
    c. {(4, 7), (5j 6), (4, 3)}
    d. {(4, 3), (7, 6), (7, 8)}
    e. {(4, 5), (5, 6), (7, 8)}

8. What is the next term in the following series: 11, 12, 13, 24, 15, 48.......

    a. 14
    b. 17
    c. 36
    d. 96
    e. None of the above.

9. On spring break in Florida, Jennifer bought six shirts as souvenirs for her friends, which cost $14.50 each. If Jennifer works at a donut shop for $5.85 per hour, how many hours will she have to work to pay for the shirts (assuming no taxes or other deductions are withheld from her paycheck)?

    a. 5.85
    b. 6.00
    c. 8.70
    d. 14.50
    e. 14.87

10. Which of the following answer choices correctly lists the prime numbers between 60 and 80?

    a. 61, 63, 67, 71, 73
    b. 61, 67, 71, 73, 77, 79
    c. 61, 67, 69, 71, 73, 77
    d. 61, 67, 71, 73, 79
    e. 67, 71, 73, 77, 79

11. A stock decreases in value by 20 percent. By what percent must the stock price increase to reach its former value?

    a. 20%
    b. 25%
    c. 30%
    d. 40%
    e. 50%

12. If it takes a robot thirty-six minutes to travel the 18 blocks between the police station and the fire house, how long will it take the same robot (in minutes), traveling at the same rate per block, to travel from the police station to the train station that is 64 blocks away?

    a. 10
    b. 32
    c. 128
    d. 648
    e. 2304

13. If X is between 0 and −1, which of the following quantities is the largest?

    a. X^3
    b. X^5
    c. X^6
    d. X^7
    e. It cannot be determined from the information given

14. If $(7b − 4)/2 = 16 - b$, then b =

    a. 1/2
    b. 2
    c. 3
    d. 4
    e. 9

15. If H = {6, 7, 8}, J = {9, 5, 7} and K = {7, 3, 4}, what is (H∩J)∩K?

    a. {7}
    b. {7, 5, 9}
    c. {5, 6, 7, 8, 9}
    d. {3, 4, 7}
    e. {5, 6, 7, 8}

16. If $4y \le 56$ and $3y \ge 36$, which of the following could be a value of y?

    a. 8
    b. 9
    c. 10
    d. 11
    e. 12

STOP

The answers to these questions are presented in Section QA28 (page 269)

Directions: You have 25 minutes to answer the following 20 questions. Choose the best answer from the options given.

- The use of a calculator is permitted.
- All numbers used are real numbers.
- Figures that accompany problems in this test are intended to provide valuable information useful in solving the problems. They are drawn as accurately as possible EXCEPT when it is stated in a specific problem that the figure is not drawn to scale. All figures lie in a plane unless otherwise indicated.
- Unless otherwise specified, the domain of any function *f* is assumed to be the set of all real numbers *x* for which *f (x)* is a real number.

Reference Information:

1. Circles. Area $= \pi r^2$, Circumference $= 2 \pi r$
2. Rectangles: Area = Length X Width
3. Right Triangles: Area = ½ (Base) (Height)
4. Cubes: Volume = Length x Width x Height
5. Cylinders: Volume $= \pi r^2 h$
6. Pythagorean Theorem: for right triangles $c^2 = a^2 + b^2$

1. Carrie recorded the number of pushups she could do at the gym each day. For the first ten days of February, Carrie had recorded the following values: 65, 72, 36, 59, 21, 79, 44, 65, 77 and 90. What is the range of the data set?

    a. 59
    b. 60.8
    c. 65
    d. 69
    e. 70

2. What is the sum of the integers between 16 and 88, inclusive?

    a. 3,592
    b. 3,640
    c. 3,692
    d. 3,708
    e. 3,796

3. What is the area (in cubic inches) of a trapezoid with a height of 16 inches and parallel side lengths of 36 inches and 48 inches?

    a. 336
    b. 576
    c. 672
    d. 1,344
    e. 1,728

4. There are 375 more Democrats than Republicans in Wheeling County. If there are P Republicans, then, in terms of P, what percentage of Wheeling County residents are Republicans?

    a. 100P/(2P + 375)%
    b. 3P – 375%
    c. 2P(3P – 375)/100%
    d. 100/(2P + 375)%
    e. (P – 375)/(2P + 375)%

5. Which of the following relations is NOT a function?

    a. {(s, d), (v, z), (q, e)}
    b. {(k, m), (v, x), (n, k)}
    c. {(4, 7), (7 6), (4, 3)}
    d. {(3, 3), (7, 6), (8, 8)}
    e. {(4, 5), (5, 6), (7, 8)}

Use the following information to answer questions 6 – 8

$R = \{2, 5, 8, 9\}$ $S = \{4, 5, 6, 7, 11\}$ $T = \{2, 3, 10, 12\}$

6. What is $(R \cup S) \cap T$?

    a. {2}
    b. {2, 3, 10, 12}
    c. {5}
    d. {2, 5}
    e. {10, 11, 12}

7. What is $(R \cup S) \cup T$?

    a. {2}
    b. {2, 3, 4, 5, 6, 7, 8 9, 11}
    c. {2, 3, 4, 5, 6, 7, 10, 11, 12}
    d. {2, 3, 4, 5, 6, 7, 8, 9, 10, 12}
    e. None of the above

8. $(R \cup S) \cup T$ has the following number of subsets:

    a. 256
    b. 512
    c. 1024
    d. 2048
    e. 4096

9. At a prestigious summer camp with 150 students, 60 are studying French, while the rest are studying German. If 96 of the students are boys, and 2/3 of the students studying German are boys, how many of the students are girls who are studying French?

    a. 24
    b. 30
    c. 36
    d. 54
    e. 60

10. After decreasing by 23% after a tsunami, the population of Sri Lanka is now 578,845. What was the original population?

    a. 445,710
    b. 548,224
    c. 674,315
    d. 711,979
    e. 751,746

11. Dave's grandmother has $50,000 invested at 5%. How much must she invest at 8% to earn $15,000 in interest from both investments annually?

    a. $31,250
    b. $62,500
    c. $156,250
    d. $312,500
    e. $625,000

12. The cost for a pen and notebook at the campus bookstore is $10.50. If the notebook costs $10.00 more than the pen, what does the pen cost (assuming there is no sales tax)?

    a.   25 cents
    b.   50 cents
    c.   75 cents
    d. $1.00
    e. $1.50

13. Janet is packing her clothing in a shipping container that is 8 feet long, 6 feet wide and 12 feet high. What is the total surface area of the shipping container (in cubic feet)?

    a.   52
    b.   216
    c.   312
    d.   432
    e.   576

Use the following table to answer questions 14 – 16.

Percentage of Contact Lens Wearers (By Age)

	U.S.	U.K.	France	India
Under 10	2	5	1	0
10 – 18	21	30	15	3
19 – 30	38	35	29	19
31 – 50	29	25	40	66
Over 51	10	5	15	12

14. A leading economic journal recently estimated the number of contact lens wearers in France and India at 10 million and 20 million, respectively. If these numbers are accurate, what is the total number of people in both nations between 19 and 30 who wear contact lenses?

    a.   2.9 million
    b.   3.8 million
    c.   6.7 million
    d.   7.5 million
    e.   Cannot be determined from the information given

15. If there are currently 5 million people who wear contact lenses in France, and the French government bans their use in people under 10 and over 51, how many *fewer* people will be allowed to wear them?

    a.   50,000
    b.   80,000
    c.   160,000
    d.   500,000
    e.   800,000

16. Optometrists in the U.K. recently estimated that 40% of contact lens wearers who are under 10 years old choose blue lenses, which are not available to older patients. If the total number of contact lens wearers in the U.K. is1.8 million, how many of them wear blue lenses?

    a. 36,000
    b. 40,000
    c. 72,000
    d. 90,000
    e. 120,000

17. $(6^3 - 6^2)^2 / 3^4 =$

    a. 4/9
    b. 1/2
    c. 1
    d. 400
    e. 3000

18. Simplify the following expression: $abc (c/ab + a/bc + bc/abc) =$

    a. $c + a + bc$
    b. $c^2 + a^2 + bc$
    c. $c^2 + a + bc$
    d. $c^2 + a + c$
    e. $c^2 + a^2 + b$

19. If x keys cost y dollars, what do z keys cost?

    a. xy/z
    b. yz/x
    c. xyz
    d. 1/xyz
    e. xz/y

20. Which of the following expressions is equivalent to $x^3 - y^3$?

    a. $(x - y)(x^2 + xy - y^2)$
    b. $(x - y)(x^2 - xy - y^2)$
    c. $(x + y)(x^2 - xy + y^2)$
    d. $(x + y)(x^2 - xy + y^2)$
    e. $(x - y)(x^2 + xy + y^2)$

STOP

The answers to these questions are presented in Section QA29 (page 270)

Quantitative 30:   25 Minutes   20 Questions

Directions: You have 25 minutes to answer the following 20 questions. Choose the best answer from the options given.

- *The use of a calculator is permitted.*
- *All numbers used are real numbers.*
- *Figures that accompany problems in this test are intended to provide valuable information useful in solving the problems. They are drawn as accurately as possible EXCEPT when it is stated in a specific problem that the figure is not drawn to scale. All figures lie in a plane unless otherwise indicated.*
- *Unless otherwise specified, the domain of any function f is assumed to be the set of all real numbers x for which f (x) is a real number.*

Reference Information:

- *Circles. Area* $= \pi r^2$*, Circumference* $= 2 \pi r$
- *Rectangles: Area = Length X Width*
- *Right Triangles: Area = ½ (Base) (Height)*
- *Cubes: Volume = Length x Width x Height*
- *Cylinders: Volume* $= \pi r^2 h$
- *Pythagorean Theorem: for right triangles* $c^2 = a^2 + b^2$

1. The Zippy Cheese Company monitors the number of bars that each employee can wrap per hour. The nine employees on the night shift wrapped the following number of bars: 234, 433, 239, 324, 333, 245, 343, 414, and 243. What is the median of this data set?

    a. 239
    b. 243
    c. 245
    d. 324
    e. 333

2. A gourmet food company has developed a special low calorie fat that it sells in cubic blocks. If the weight of the fat is 36 pounds per cubic foot, and the edge of the cubic container is 8 inches, what is the weight of a block of the fat (in pounds)?

    a. 10.67
    b. 12
    c. 24
    d. 40.67
    e. 67.67

3. Which of the following quadratic equations has (12, 11) as its solutions?

    a. $a^2 + 11a + 156 = 0$
    b. $a^2 - 13a + 139 = 0$
    c. $a^2 + 20a + 210 = 0$
    d. $a^2 - 23a + 132 = 0$
    e. $a^2 + 32a + 196 = 0$

4. In the equation $g^2 - 7g = 18$, which of the following is a possible value for g?

    a. -9
    b. -2
    c. 0
    d. 1
    e. 2

170

5. Which of the following relations is a function?

    a. {(1, b), (1, a), (2, c)}
    b. {(k, m), (v, x), (v, k)}
    c. {(4, 7), (7 6), (4, 3)}
    d. {(3, 3), (7, 6), (8, 8)}
    e. {(7, 5), (5, 6), (7, 8)}

6. Susan purchased a new condo when she moved to Los Angeles. Two years later, after a devastating correction in the housing market, she sold it to her neighbor Nathan for 40% less than she originally paid for it. Nathan did a few quick fixes and re-sold the condo to Janice for 20% more than he paid Susan for it. The price that Janice paid for the condo was what percentage of the original price that Susan paid?

    a. 28%
    b. 40%
    c. 65%
    d. 72%
    e. 80%

7. What is the value of $c \, (c^{a+b}) / c^a$?

    a. c^{a+b}
    b. $2c^b$
    c. c^{1+b}
    d. c^{2b}
    e. c / c^b

8. For what value(s) of x will the following equation equal zero? $x^2 + 10x + 16$

    a. (0, -2)
    b. (-2, -8)
    c. (2, 8)
    d. (0, 2, -8)
    e. (0, -2, 8)

9. A scientist has a 10-ounce solution that is 15% acid. If 5 ounces of pure acid are added to the solution, what percent of the resulting mixture is acid?

    a. 6.5
    b. 37.5
    c. 43.3
    d. 65.0
    e. 75.0

10. If the surface area of a cube is 726 square feet, how many cubic feet are there in the volume of the cube?

    a. 121
    b. 1,331
    c. 1,452
    d. 2,904
    e. 7,260

11. Dave and Dina paid $365,000 for their first house. If they had waited, the sales price would have increased by 6% the first year, 8% the second year, and 4% the third year. What would Dave and Dina have paid for the house if they had waited and purchased it at the end of the third year?

     a. $386,900
     b. $416,100
     c. $417,852
     d. $430,700
     e. $434,566

12. Which of the following is the smallest integer that leaves a remainder of 4 when divided by 6?

     a.   12
     b.   26
     c.   98
     d.   112
     e.   118

13. What is the probability of getting a green jelly bean from a dispenser that contains 28 red jelly beans, 48 green ones, 36 purple ones, 26 pink ones, 30 blue ones and 28 white ones?

     a.   1/8
     b.   1/7
     c.   1/6
     d.   1/5
     e.   ¼

14. How many positive integers less than 50 are evenly divisible by 3, 6 and 9?

     a.   1
     b.   2
     c.   3
     d.   4
     e.   5

15. Arrange the following fractions in ascending order: 1/4, 2/7, 2/5, 1/3, 3/8

     a.   2/7, ¼, 1/3, 3/8, 2/5
     b.   ¼, 2/5, 1/3, 2/7, 3/8
     c.   1/4, 2/7, 1/3, 3/8, 2/5
     d.   2/7, 1/3, ¼, 2/5, 3/8
     e.   1/3, ¼, 2/7, 2/5, 3/8

16.   To get a grade of A in Spanish, Sara must achieve an average of 90 or above on six exams. Thus far, Sara's scores on the first five exams are 96, 81, 79, 87 and 100. What is the lowest possible score that Sara can get on the final exam to get an A grade in Spanish?

     a.   95
     b.   96
     c.   97
     d.   98
     e.   99

17. What is the probability that a coin with one side heads and the other side tails will turn up heads on three consecutive tosses?

    a.   1/32
    b.   1/16
    c.   1/8
    d.   ¼
    e.   ½

18. If $6^x < 1,000$, what integer is the largest possible value of x?

    a.   1
    b.   2
    c.   3
    d.   4
    e.   5

19. If x = 3 and y = 4, what is the value of the expression $3x^2 - 2xy + y^2$?

    a.   19
    b.   24
    c.   27
    d.   67
    e.   73

20. Which of the following quadratic equations has (-5, 4) as its solutions?

    a. $x^2 + 4x - 25 = 0$
    b. $x^2 + 2x + 10 = 0$
    c. $x^2 - x - 10 = 0$
    d. $x^2 - x - 20 = 0$
    e. $x^2 + x - 20 = 0$

STOP

The answers to these questions are presented in Section QA30 (page 272)

Writing 1: 25 minutes 35 questions

Directions: The following sentences test correctness and effectiveness of expression. Part of each sentence (or the entire sentence) is underlined; beneath each sentence are five ways of phrasing the underlined material. Choice A repeats the original phrasing; the other four choices are different. If you think the original phrasing produces a better sentence than any of the alternatives, select choice A; if not, select one of the other choices.

In making your selection, follow the requirements of standard written English; that is, pay attention to grammar, choice of words, sentence construction, and punctuation. Your selection should result in the most effective sentence – clear and precise, without awkwardness or ambiguity.

Example: Most teenagers struggle to be free <u>both of parental domination but also from premature responsibilities.</u>

    a. both of parental domination but also from premature responsibilities.
    b. both of parental domination and also from premature responsibilities.
    c. both of parental domination and also of premature responsibilities.
    d. of parental domination and premature responsibilities.
    e. both of parental domination and their premature responsibilities as well.

The correct answer is D.

1. Convicted felons in Florida, regardless of their subsequent good deeds, <u>never have and never will be allowed</u> to vote in local, state and national elections.

    a. never have and never will be allowed
    b. neither have nor will be allowed
    c. have never and will never be allowed
    d. never have been allowed and never will be allowed
    e. never have had anyone allow them and never will have anyone allow them

2. When they competed in the Olympics, Barb and Jane acted <u>as though they were strangers, despite the fact that they had been</u> running partners for several years.

    a. as though they were strangers, despite the fact that they had been
    b. like complete and utter strangers, although they had been
    c. kind of like strangers, despite being
    d. as though they were strangers, although they had been
    e. estranged, despite having been

3. Rachel and Amy will join <u>Cara and I</u> at the mall on Tuesday.

    a. Cara and I
    b. Cara and me
    c. I and Cara
    d. me and Cara
    e. both I and Cara

4. <u>Each of the ten pageant finalists hoped that they would win the crown, the scholarship and the brand news sports car.</u>

    a. Each of the ten pageant finalists hoped that they would win the crown, the scholarship and the brand new sports car.
    b. Each of the ten pageant finalists hoped that they would win the crown and scholarship, especially the brand new sports car.
    c. Each of the ten pageant finalists hoped that they would win the crown, and with it, the scholarship and brand new sports car.
    d. Each of the ten pageant finalists hoped that she would win the crown, the scholarship and the brand new sports car.
    e. Each of the ten pageant finalists hoped that she would win the crown, which brought with it a scholarship and brand new sports car.

5. After careful consideration, Jake and Jennifer chose a wedding menu of tossed green salad, French onion soup, roast beef au jus, <u>along with a fabulous chocolate cake.</u>

   a. along with a fabulous chocolate cake
   b. including a fabulous chocolate cake
   c. and a fabulous chocolate cake
   d. in addition to a fabulous chocolate cake
   e. with a fabulous chocolate cake

6. <u>Seeing the police car, the beer bottles were immediately tossed from the car by the worried teens</u>.

   a. Seeing the police car, the beer bottles were immediately tossed from the car by the worried teens.
   b. The beer bottles, after seeing the police car, were immediately tossed from the car by the worried teens.
   c. The worried teens, after seeing the police car, tossed from the car the beer bottles, immediately.
   d. Seeing the police car, the worried teens immediately tossed the beer bottles from the car.
   e. The beer bottles were immediately tossed from the car by the worried teens, who saw a police car.

7. Hilary Clinton, <u>the Senator from New York, and most famous of all First Ladies, who we all agree is</u> one of the most famous and notorious women of the twenty-first century.

   a. the Senator from New York, and most famous of all First Ladies, who we all agree is
   b. who is the Senator from New York and the most famous of all First Ladies, who we all agree is
   c. the Senator from New York and the most famous of all First Ladies, is also agreed to be
   d. the Senator from New York and the most famous of all First Ladies, is also, we agree,
   e. is the Senator from New York, and the most famous of all First Ladies, is

8. The Department of State worked diligently <u>to develop a consistent policy regarding emigration into the</u> United States.

   a. to develop a consistent policy regarding emigration into the
   b. to develop consistent policies regarding emigration into the
   c. to make consistent the policies regarding emigration into the
   d. to develop a consistent policy regarding immigration into the
   e. to make consistent policies about immigration from the

9. After a prolonged delay, <u>in which the airport was paralyzed by eight inches of snow, the flight to Jamaica was cleared for take-off.</u>

   a. in which the airport was paralyzed by eight inches of snow, the flight to Jamaica was cleared for take-off.
   b. in which the airport was paralyzed by eight inches of snow, the flight from Jamaica took off.
   c. in which eight inches of snow paralyzed the airport, the airline cleared the flight to Jamaica for take-off.
   d. in which the airport was paralyzed by eight inches of snow, the airport allowed the flight to Jamaica to take-off.
   e. in which eight inches of snow paralyzed the airport, the flight to Jamaica was cleared for take-off.

10. In his written decision on the landmark case, Judge Reynolds eluded to previous case law on a similar topic, which supported his own personal views.

    a. In his written decision on the landmark case, Judge Reynolds eluded to previous case law on a similar topic, which supported his own personal views.
    b. In his written decision on the landmark case, Judge Reynolds alluded to previous case law on a similar topic, which supported his own personal views.
    c. Judge Reynolds eluded to previous case law in his written decision on the landmark case, which supported his own personal views.
    d. In his written decision on the landmark case, Judge Reynolds was lucky to find previous case law that supported his own personal views, which he eluded to.
    e. When writing his decision of the landmark case, Judge Reynolds alluded to previous case law on a similar topic, which supported his own personal views.

11. Carrie considered suing the unscrupulous vendor, but she went no farther than veiled threats.

    a. Carrie considered suing the unscrupulous vendor, but she went no farther than veiled threats.
    b. Carrie considered suing the unscrupulous vendor, but she went no farther than making veiled threats.
    c. Although Carrie considered filing a lawsuit against the unscrupulous vendor, she went no farther than making veiled threats.
    d. Carrie went no further than making veiled threats against the unscrupulous vendor, but she considered suing them.
    e. Carrie considered suing the unscrupulous vendor, but she went no further than making veiled threats.

12. Because of an airline mix-up, several attendees missed the conference at which the agenda for future meetings were presented.

    a. Because of an airline mix-up, several attendees missed the conference at which the agenda for future meetings were presented.
    b. Due to an airline mix-up, several attendees missed the conference at which the agenda for future meetings were presented.
    c. Because of an airline mix-up, several attendees missed the conference for which the agenda for future meetings were presented.
    d. Due to an airline mix-up, several attendees missed the conference, which would present future meeting schedules.
    e. Because of an airline mix-up, several attendees missed the conference that presented the agenda for future meetings.

13. The reason why Americans don't worry about their weight is because they have little time to exercise, compared with most other cultures on earth.

    a. is because they have little time to exercise, compared with most other cultures
    b. is that they have little time to exercise, compared with most other cultures
    c. is because they have little time to exercise, compared to most other cultures
    d. is that they have little time to exercise, compared to most other cultures
    e. is they lack time to exercise, compared with most other cultures

14. If Zachary would have lain in that bed for one more minute, he might have developed horrible bedsores, which would have exacerbated his existing health problems.

    a. If Zachary would have lain in that bed for one more minute, he might have developed horrible bedsores, which would have exacerbated his existing health problems.
    b. If Zachary had lay in that bed for one more minute, he might have developed horrible bedsores, which would have exacerbated his existing health problems.
    c. If Zachary would have lay in that bed for one more minute, he might have developed horrible bedsores, which would exacerbate his existing health problems.
    d. If Zachary had laid in that bed for one more minute, he might have developed horrible bedsores, which would have exacerbated his existing health problems.
    e. If Zachary had lain in that bed for one more minute, he might have developed horrible bedsores, which would have exacerbated his existing health problems.

Directions: The following sentences test your ability to recognize grammar and usage errors. Each sentence contains either a single error of no error at all. No sentence contains more than one error. The error, if there is one, is underlined and lettered. If the sentence contains an error, select the one underlined part that must be changed to make the sentence correct. If the sentence is correct, select choice E. In choosing answers, follow the requirements of standard written English.

Example: The other students and Julie reluctantly accepted the offer to eat more early.
           A   B   C   D

No error
 E

The correct answer is D.

15. Inflation together with rising employee wages and spiraling health care costs are crippling
                                         A   B

America's small businesses in an unprecedented manner.
  C   D

No error
 E

16. There has been impressive advancements in antiviral treatments since Rock Hudson
     A   B   C
died of AIDS in 1986.
     D
No error
 E

17. IBM entered into a strategic alliance with Cisco Systems after its agreement to expand its list
    A   B   C   D
of approved vendors.

No error
 E

18. Bethany offered the rich dessert to whomever finished the tuna casserole.
     A   B   C   D
No error
 E

19. <u>Despite</u> <u>its low cost</u>, aloe extract <u>provides</u> a natural cure that is comparable to
     A   B   C

<u>prescription drugs</u>.
    D

<u>No error</u>
  E

20. <u>After</u> the coach's devastating accident, his highly motivated team
     A

<u>of</u> extraordinary soccer players <u>performing</u> <u>without the benefits of</u> his
B   C   D

guidance and direction.

  <u>No error</u>
    E

21. <u>Before</u> I realized he <u>wasn't coming,</u> I <u>waited on</u> him <u>for nearly</u> an hour.
    A   B   C   D

<u>No error</u>
  E

22. The widespread damage <u>from</u> Hurricane Rita, <u>which arrived</u>
                             A   B

three weeks <u>after</u> Hurricane Katrina, <u>was reported</u> by the National
          C   D

Weather Channel.

<u>No error</u>
  E

23. The annual clothing drive, <u>which was</u> originally scheduled for Friday
                                A

night, <u>is liable</u> to be postponed <u>until after</u> the holidays <u>because of</u> the
      B   C   D

devastating blizzard.

<u>No error</u>
  E

24. <u>Because</u> Jake disobeyed his mother's orders <u>by returning</u> from the
     A   B

prom three hours late, <u>she grounded him</u> <u>for an indecisive period</u> of time.
                         C   D

<u>No error</u>
  E

25. After careful consideration, the six winners of the $150 million Power Ball
       A   B
Lottery agreed to divide the winnings equally between themselves.
                     C   D
No error
    E

26. Despite the availability of low-cost contraceptives, the number of unplanned pregnancies
                              A
in Asia is higher then that in Europe, where birth control is less readily available.
         B   C   D
No error
    E

27. Although James did not agree about Bill Clinton's political agenda, he readily admitted
        A   B   C
that the former President was an articulate and dynamic public speaker.
                            D
No error
    E

28. Although Jane tries to forget, her memories the accident as if it occurred yesterday.
        A   B   C   D
No error
    E

29. Mrs. Davis told her twins frequently to take their vitamins.
                  A   B   C   D
No error
    E

Directions: The following passage is an early draft of an essay. Some parts of the passage need to be rewritten. Read the passage and select the best answers for the questions that follow. Some questions are about particular sentences or parts of sentences and ask you to improve the sentence structure or word choice. Other questions ask you to consider organization and development. In choosing answers, follow the requirements of standard written English.

Questions 30 – 35 refer to the following passage:

1 The traditional weimaraner breeding kennel, which has produced the greatest number of champion bloodlines in Germany, is comprised of both a male stud pen and several task-specific and sex-specific areas. 2 One is a male training room. 3 In the training room, male dogs and puppies which are learning to hunt work with skilled trainers and heavily scented samples of meat. 4 Sometimes competing for samples and sometimes preparing themselves for future hunts by demonstrating aggressive, "pack" type behaviors. 5 Occasionally a female weimaraner past her breeding age is admitted to the stud area. 6 Female puppies and dogs stay in the nursing kennel and learn their show routines. 7 When one of the older female dogs was accepted into the kinship of the males in the stud room, her acceptance was observed to have a calming influence on the male dogs, which were unaccustomed to such socialization. 8 At the breeder's insistence, a similar opportunity to admit the male dogs into the nursing kennel was never made available. 9 Instead, the female puppies are segregated from the male dogs until they are ready to breed.

179

30. What should be done with the first sentence of the passage?

    a.   It should remain unchanged.
    b.   It should be divided into two sentences; the first sentence should end after the word <u>Germany</u>..
    c.   It should be joined to sentence two with a comma, followed by the phrase <u>including a male training room</u>. The words <u>one is</u> should be omitted.
    d.   <u>Is comprised</u> should be changed to <u>includes</u>
    e.   <u>Has produced</u> should be changed to <u>produces</u> and <u>is comprised</u> should be changed to <u>includes</u>.

31. What changes are required in sentence 2?

    a.   It should remain unchanged.
    b.   It should be joined to sentence one with a comma, followed by the phrase <u>including a male training room.</u> The words <u>one is</u> should be omitted.
    c.   It should be omitted.
    d.   It should be followed by a comma, followed by the word <u>where.</u> The phrase <u>in the training room</u> should be omitted in sentence three.
    e.   It should be omitted. In sentence three, the words <u>In the training room</u> should be changed to <u>In the male training room</u>.

32. In sentence 4, what is the best replacement for the phrase "*Sometimes competing for samples and sometimes preparing*"?

    a.   *Despite sometimes competing and preparing*
    b.   *Although they are competing for samples and sometimes preparing*
    c.   *Sometimes they compete for samples and prepare*
    d.   *Because they compete for samples and prepare*
    e.   *By competing for samples and preparing*

33. Which of the following is the best way to revise and combine sentences 5 and 6 ?

    a.   No changes are needed.
    b.   Simply reverse the order of the sentences.
    c.   *Although female puppies and dogs usually stay in the nursing kennel and learn their show routines, occasionally a female weimaraner past her breeding age is admitted to the stud area.*
    d.   *Female puppies and dogs stay in the nursing kennel and learn their show routines, other than when an occasional female weimaraner past her breeding age is admitted to the stud area.*
    e.   Retain sentence five in its current form, but omit sentence six.

34. What changes are necessary in sentence 7?

    a.   None
    b.   *When the males in the stud room accepted one of the older female dogs into their kinship, she had a calming influence on them. Previously, the male dogs had not been unaccustomed to such socialization.*
    c.   *When one of the older female dogs was accepted into the kinship off the males in the stud room, she had a calming influence on them and provided a chance for socialization.*
    d.   End the sentence after the expression *calming influence on the male dogs.* Omit the rest of the sentence.
    e.   *When the males in the stud room accepted one of the older female dogs into their kinship, they enjoyed the calming influence of socialization for the first time.*

35. What is the best revision for sentence 9?

   a. No revisions are necessary.
   b. Replace instead with sadly
   c. Replace are segregated with are still segregated
   d. Replace are segregated with remain segregated
   e. Eliminate the sentence

STOP

The answers to these questions are presented in Section WA1 (page 273)

Writing 2:   **25 minutes**   **35 questions**

Directions: *The following sentences test correctness and effectiveness of expression. Part of each sentence (or the entire sentence) is underlined; beneath each sentence are five ways of phrasing the underlined material. Choice A repeats the original phrasing; the other four choices are different. If you think the original phrasing produces a better sentence than any of the alternatives, select choice A; if not, select one of the other choices.*

In making your selection, follow the requirements of standard written English; that is, pay attention to grammar, choice of words, sentence construction, and punctuation. Your selection should result in the most effective sentence – clear and precise, without awkwardness or ambiguity.

Example: *Most teenagers struggle to be free both of parental domination but also from premature responsibilities.*

    a. *both of parental domination but also from premature responsibilities.*
    b. *both of parental domination and also from premature responsibilities.*
    c. *both of parental domination and also of premature responsibilities.*
    d. *of parental domination and premature responsibilities.*
    e. *both of parental domination and their premature responsibilities as well.*

The correct answer is D.

1. Prison as well as restitution was the thief's dismal fate.

    a. Prison as well as restitution was the thief's dismal fate.
    b. First prison, then restitution, will be the thief's dismal fate
    c. He will be punished by prison as well as restitution.
    d. Prison and restitution was the thief's dismal fate.
    e. As his fate, he endured dismal prison as well as restitution.

2. Neither Jeremy nor Nicholas were at the party when Karen arrived.

    a. were at the party when Karen arrived
    b. were at the party when Karen arrives
    c. was at the party when Karen arrived
    d. were at the party for Karen's arrival
    e. was at the party for Karen to arrive

3. Every flight attendant except Jenny and she was delayed by bad weather.

    a. except Jenny and she
    b. except Jenny and her
    c. accept Jenny and she
    d. besides she and Jenny
    e. accept for her and Jenny

4. One cannot win the lottery if you don't buy a ticket.

    a. One cannot win the lottery if you don't buy a ticket.
    b. You cannot win the lottery if one doesn't buy a ticket.
    c. He cannot win the lottery if you don't buy a ticket.
    d. You cannot win the lottery if you don't buy a ticket.
    e. One cannot win the lottery if a ticket is not bought.

5. The editor rejected the manuscript because <u>it was pompous, offensive and lacking in style.</u>

    a. it was pompous, offensive and lacking in style.
    b. It was pompous, it offended her and lacked style.
    c. of its pomposity, offensive and lack of style.
    d. of its pomposity, offensiveness and lacking of style.
    e. it was pompous, offensive and style-lacking.

6. According to Gary, <u>a stove is needed for the senior center in good condition</u>.

    a. a stove is needed for the senior center in good condition.
    b. a stove in good condition is needed for the senior center
    c. a stove is needed by the seniors, preferably in good condition.
    d. the senior center needs a stove in good condition.
    e. the stove that is needed for the senior center is in good condition.

7. <u>A special interest group comprising members of the Republican Party, Right to Life advocates and miscellaneous religious groups hoping to influence the President's decision on reproductive freedom.</u>

    a. A special interest group comprising members of the Republican Party, Right to Life advocates and miscellaneous religious groups hoping to influence the President's decision on reproductive freedom.
    b. A special interest group included members of the Republican Party, Right to Life advocates and miscellaneous religious groups whom hoped to influence the President's decision on reproductive freedom.
    c. A special interest group, including members of the Republican Party, Right to Life advocates and miscellaneous religious groups, hoped to influence the President's decision on reproductive freedom.
    d. A special interest group comprising members of the Republican Party, Right to Life advocates and miscellaneous religious groups were hoping to influence the President's decision on reproductive freedom.
    e. A special interest group hoped to influence the President's decision on reproductive freedom, included members of the Republican Party, Right to Life advocates and miscellaneous religious groups.

8. <u>After every parent/teacher conference, David's parents chastised him about his greatest weakness: his refusal to conform with societal norms.</u>

    a. After every parent/teacher conference, David's parents chastised him about his greatest weakness: his refusal to conform with societal norms.
    b. After every parent/teach conference David's parents chastised him about his refusal to conform with societal norms, which was his greatest weakness.
    c. After every parent/teacher conference, David's parents chastised him about his refusal to conform to societal norms, which was his greatest weakness.
    d. David's greatest weakness was his refusal to conform with societal norms; after every parent/teacher conference, his parents chastised him about it.
    e. After every parent/teach conference, David's parents chastised him about his refusal to conform to societal norms, which were his greatest weakness.

9. The fledgling mail order company, <u>which was financed with borrowed money, was devastated when more then 30% of holiday buyers requested a refund</u>.

    a.   which was financed with borrowed money, was devastated when more then 30% of holiday buyers requested a refund.

    b.   which was financed with borrowed money, was devastated when more then 30% of holiday shoppers demanded refunds.

    c.   which the owners financed with borrowed money, was devastated when more then 30% of holiday buyers demanded a refund.

    d.   which the owners financed with borrowed money, was devastated when more than 30% of holiday buyers requested a refund.

    e.   which was financed with outstanding loans, was devastated when more than 30% of holiday shoppers were dissatisfied with their purchases.

10. Opponents to gun control realize that <u>they cannot hope to effect</u> the public as vehemently as they wish without alienating their representatives in Washington.

    a.   they cannot hope to effect
    b.   they cannot try to affect
    c.   they cannot hope to effecting
    d.   they cannot hope to affect
    e.   they cannot hope to have an affect on

11. <u>Once the stress of dieting and exercise are over, the players can return to their gluttonous ways.</u>

    a.   Once the stress of dieting and exercise are over, the players can return to their gluttonous ways.

    b.   After the stress of dieting and exercise are over, the players can resume their gluttonous ways.

    c.   After the stress of dieting and exercise are over, the players can return to their gluttonous ways.

    d.   Once the stress of dieting and exercise is over, the players can return to their gluttonous ways.

    e.   Once the stress of dieting and exercise is over, the players can return to gluttoning.

12. <u>Buying only clothing made in the United States is admirable, so says my mother.</u>

    a.   Buying only clothing made in the United States is admirable, so says my mother.

    b.   My mother says that we should buy clothing that is made in the United States.

    c.   According to my mother, it is an admirable goal to buy clothing that is made in the United States only.

    d.   My mother admires people who only buy clothing made in the United States.

    e.   According to my mother, an admirable goal is to only buy clothing we make here in the United States.

13. <u>The entrepreneur that built the mini-mall has requested a permit to add six hundred parking spaces.</u>

    a.   The entrepreneur that built the mini-mall has requested a permit to add six hundred parking spaces.

    b.   The entrepreneur who built the mini-mall has requested a permit to add six hundred parking spaces.

    c.   The entrepreneur that built the mini-mall has requested a permit to add a parking lot big enough to fit six hundred cars.

    d.   A permit to add six hundred parking spaces was requested by the entrepreneur who built the mini-mall.

    e.   After building the mini-mall, the entrepreneur requested a permit to add a six hundred car parking lot.

14. If Benjamin Franklin <u>were to walk the halls of a modern university, he would be delighted by</u> the novels uses of electricity, particularly computer and Internet applications.

     a.   were to walk the halls of a modern university, he would be delighted by
     b.   was to walk the halls of a modern university, he would be delighted
     c.   were to walk the halls in a modern university, he would have to be delighted by
     d.   was to walk the halls of a modern university, he would delight to see the
     e.   were to walk the halls in a modern university, he would be delighted in

Directions: *The following sentences test your ability to recognize grammar and usage errors. Each sentence contains either a single error of no error at all. No sentence contains more than one error. The error, if there is one, is underlined and lettered. If the sentence contains an error, select the one underlined part that must be changed to make the sentence correct. If the sentence is correct, select choice E. In choosing answers, follow the requirements of standard written English.*

Example: *The other* students and *Julie* reluctantly accepted the offer *to eat* *more early*.
       A   B   C   D
No error
  E

The correct answer is D.

15. <u>Despite the influx of Federal money</u> into urban schools, <u>there are many inner city students</u>
               A   B   C
<u>who do not receive</u> a good education.
     D
No error
  E

16. <u>Neither the teachers</u> <u>nor the counselors</u> <u>has finished</u> <u>their</u> student evaluations.
       A   B   C   D
No error
  E

17. <u>If one is</u> a spiritual being, <u>you honor</u> the importance <u>of daily rituals</u>, such as
     A   B   C
positive affirmations, silent prayer, <u>and loving relationships</u>.
                                  D
No error
  E

18. In rural Brazil, most designer shoes <u>are made</u> by unskilled workers, <u>few</u>
                                       A
<u>of which</u> <u>could ever hope</u> to purchase a pair <u>for their own use</u>.
  B   C   D
No error
  E

19. <u>In nursing school,</u> Diane studied the proper way <u>to dress a wound</u>, <u>the way to minimize</u>
         A   B   C
bacterial infections and <u>relieving pain through the use of pharmaceuticals</u>.
                                  D
No error
  E

20. By practicing every weekend, including nights when several parties were held, her
        A   B   C
performance improved dramatically.
                    D
No error
    E

21. Diane went to the beach with her son wearing a string bikini and a lot of lotion.
            A   B   C   D
    No error
        E

22. When they least expected, a drug was found to mitigate the spread of cancer.
        A   B   C   D
No error
    E

23. Even if they are extremely clever, most escaped criminals cannot allude the
            A   B   C
law for an extended period of time.
        D
No error
    E

24. Because of an unexpected budget cut, the grocery chain will hire
        A   B   C
less employees in 2009.
    D
No error
    E

25. Clinical psychologists investigating the disturbing increase in murder rates
                            A
among pregnant women have documented the sad reality that many expectant
        B
fathers are more than capable to killing their wives and unborn children.
            C   D
No error
    E

26. The grieving relatives of 9/11 victims graciously accepted the awards of the
                            A
American Red Cross, which alleviated their financial concerns for many years
        B   C   D
to come.

No error
    E

27. <u>After</u> several years <u>of circuit weight training</u>, Jason's stamina and muscle tone <u>are like a</u>

    A   B   C

<u>seasoned athlete.</u>

     D

<u>No error</u>

    E

Directions: The following passage is an early draft of an essay. Some parts of the passage need to be rewritten. Read the passage and select the best answers for the questions that follow. Some questions are about particular sentences or parts of sentences and ask you to improve sentence structure or word choice. Other questions ask you to consider organization and development. In choosing answers, follow the requirements of standard written English.

1 In the past ten years, home schooling has taken the place of traditional education. 2 Parents across the United States are choosing it, particularly for religious and disciplinary reasons. 3 Religious families avoid public schools because they do not want their children to adopt secular values. 4 One school of thought is that "nontraditional" kids do better in a home setting. 5 Their parents, who know them better than anyone, can best address their needs and deficiencies. 6 Kids with learning disorders learn particularly well at home.

7 Opponents to home schooling claim that it robs children of socialization. 8 They also claim the education won't be as good, because parents aren't experts in all subjects. 9 But the evidence disputes these fears. 10 Students who home school participate in clubs and athletics, where they befriend other kids. 11 They also score higher on the ACT and SAT, and do better in college than kids who went to public schools. 12 So, it stands to reason, that the families who choose home schooling are making the best choice for their own children.

28. What is the best way to revise sentence 2?

    a.   No revisions are necessary
    b.   Eliminate it
    c.   Join sentences 2 and 3 with a semi-colon
    d.   Combine sentences 2 and 3 as follows: *Many religious families in the United States do not want public schools to discipline their children or to promote secular values.*
    e.   *Many families in the United States choose it for religious and disciplinary reasons.*

29. What is the best way to handle sentence 6?

    a.   No revisions are necessary
    b.   Eliminate it
    c.   Change <u>kids</u> to <u>children</u> and <u>do</u> to <u>perform</u>
    d.   Combine it with sentence 4 as follows: *One school of thought is that "nontraditional" students, including those with learning disorders, learn particularly well at home.*
    e.   Move it ahead of sentence 5

30. What is the purpose of the first paragraph (sentences 1 – 6)?

    a.   To explain the arguments in favor of home schooling
    b.   To note the deficiencies in the public school system
    c.   To promote religious values
    d.   To document a recent educational trend
    e.   To explain the decrease in enrollment at many public schools

31. What is the purpose of sentence 7?

    a.   To start a new paragraph
    b.   To insult home schooling
    c.   To provide the first of several arguments against home schooling
    d.   To persuade the reader
    e.   To document the author's position

32. What is the best way to revise sentence 7?

    a. No revisions are necessary
    b. Add <u>On the other hand</u>, to the beginning of the sentence.
    c. Add <u>On the other hand</u>, to the beginning of the sentence and replace <u>robs children of socialization</u> with <u>offers fewer chances for children to develop social skills</u>.
    d. Replace <u>robs children of socialization</u> with <u>offers fewer chances for children to socialize.</u>
    e. Combine it with sentence 8 as follows: *Opponents to home schooling claim that it robs children of socialization and offers inferior education, because parents aren't experts in all subjects.*

33. What is the best way to revise sentence 9?

    a. No revisions are necessary
    b. Eliminate it
    c. Replace <u>But</u> with <u>Thus far,</u>
    d. Eliminate <u>But</u>.
    e. Replace <u>But the</u> with <u>The long-term</u>.

34. What is the author's tone in this passage?

    a. Objective
    b. Laconic
    c. Cynical
    d. Insightful
    e. Perfunctory

35. Which of the following best reflects the author's conclusion about home schooling?

    a. He supports public schooling enthusiastically
    b. He supports home schooling enthusiastically
    c. He believes that parents who home school do so because they believe it is in their children's best interest
    d. He believes that parents who home school do so because their children are outcasts
    e. He offers no conclusion

STOP

The answers to these questions are presented in Section WA2 (page 275)

Writing 3:   **25 minutes**   **35 questions**

Directions: *The following sentences test correctness and effectiveness of expression. Part of each sentence (or the entire sentence) is underlined; beneath each sentence are five ways of phrasing the underlined material. Choice A repeats the original phrasing; the other four choices are different. If you think the original phrasing produces a better sentence than any of the alternatives, select choice A; if not, select one of the other choices.*

In making your selection, follow the requirements of standard written English; that is, pay attention to grammar, choice of words, sentence construction, and punctuation. Your selection should result in the most effective sentence – clear and precise, without awkwardness or ambiguity.

Example: Most teenagers struggle to be free <u>both of parental domination but also from premature responsibilities.</u>

    a.   both of parental domination but also from premature responsibilities.
    b.   both of parental domination and also from premature responsibilities.
    c.   both of parental domination and also of premature responsibilities.
    d.   of parental domination and premature responsibilities.
    e.   both of parental domination and their premature responsibilities as well.

The correct answer is D.

1. <u>Either Mary or him is lying.</u>

    a.   Either Mary or him is lying.
    b.   Either Mary or he is lying.
    c.   Either him or her are lying.
    d.   Either he or Mary are lying.
    e.   Either him or Mary is lying.

2. <u>Joe and Harry ran down to the lake when they heard that a school of catfish were easy prey.</u>

    a.   Joe and Harry ran down to the lake when they heard that a school of catfish were easy prey.
    b.   Joe and Harry ran to the lake when they heard that a school of catfish were easy prey.
    c.   Joe and Harry ran down to the lake when they heard that a school of catfish was easy prey.
    d.   Joe and Harry, upon hearing that a school of catfish was easy prey, run to the lake.
    e.   Joe and Harry ran down to the lake because they hear a rumor about a catfish being easy prey.

3. <u>Bethany offered the rich dessert to whoever she wanted.</u>

    a.   Bethany offered the rich dessert to whoever she wanted.
    b.   Bethany offered the rich dessert to whomever she wanted.
    c.   Bethany offered whoever the rich dessert, as she wanted.
    d.   Bethany offered everyone the rich dessert, simply because she wanted.
    e.   Bethany offered whomever she wanted the rich dessert.

4. Mr. Davis has no objection <u>to him joining the class</u> if he is willing to complete the assignments.

    a.   to him joining the class
    b.   if he will join the class
    c.   for him to join the class
    d.   if he were to join the class.
    e.   to his joining the class.

5. After scoring poorly on the SAT, <u>David decided to walk home, and then lie down for an hour, and then call a few friends.</u>

    a.   David decided to walk home, and then lie down for an hour, and then call a few friends.
    b.   David decided to walk home, lie down for an hour, and then calling a few friends.
    c.   David decided to walk home, lay down for an hour, and then call a few friends.
    d.   David decided to walk home, and then lie down for an hour, and then calling a few friends.
    e.   David decided to walk home, lie down for an hour, and then call a few friends.

6. <u>After hiding behind the sofa for ten minutes, much to our dismay, the birthday girl already knew about the surprise party.</u>

    a.   After hiding behind the sofa for ten minutes, much to our dismay, the birthday girl already knew about the surprise party.
    b.   Much to our dismay, after hiding behind the sofa for ten minutes, the birthday girl already knew about the surprise party.
    c.   Much to our dismay, after hiding behind the sofa for ten minutes, we discovered that the birthday girl already knew about the surprise party.
    d.   After hiding behind the sofa for ten minutes, we discovered that the birthday girl already knew about the surprise party, much to our dismay.
    e.   The birthday girl already knew about our surprise party, after hiding behind the sofa for ten minutes, much to our dismay.

7. <u>After careful investigation, the teacher concluded that John's aggressive behavior was provoked from a bully in the class.</u>

    a.   After careful investigation, the teacher concluded that John's aggressive behavior was provoked from a bully in the class.
    b.   After carefully investigating John's behavior, the teacher concluded that John's was aggressive because he was provoked from a bully in the class.
    c.   After carefully investigating John's aggressive behavior, the teacher concluded that it was provoked by a bully in the class.
    d.   After careful investigation, the teacher concluded that John was acting aggressive because of provoking from a bully in the class.
    e.   After careful investigation, the teacher concluded that John's aggressive behavior was provoked by a bully in the class.

8. <u>Being that the hotel was over-booked, we stayed over</u> until the next morning, when vacancies were available.

    a.   Being that the hotel was over-booked, we stayed over
    b.   In view of the fact that the hotel was over-booked, we stayed over
    c.   Since the hotel was over-booked, we stayed over
    d.   Because the hotel was over-booked, we stood over
    e.   Being that the hotel was over-booked, we stood over

9. IRS auditors stormed the corporate offices of ABC Corporation, on account of an anonymous report of accounting irregularities.

    a. IRS auditors stormed the corporate offices of ABC Corporation, on account of an anonymous report of accounting irregularities.
    b. IRS auditors stormed the corporate offices of ABC Corporation because of an anonymous report on accounting irregularities
    c. IRS auditors stormed the corporate offices of ABC Corporation because of an anonymous report full of accounting irregularities.
    d. IRS auditors stormed the corporate offices of ABC Corporation in response to an anonymous report that accused the company of accounting irregularities.
    e. IRS auditors stormed the corporate offices of ABC Corporation in response to accounting irregularities.

10. After the award ceremony, the five scholarship recipients congratulated each other on their good fortune.

    a. the five scholarship recipients congratulated each other on their good fortune.
    b. the five scholarship recipients congratulated each other on account of their good fortune.
    c. the five scholarship winners congratulated each other on enjoying the same good fortune.
    d. the five scholarship winners congratulated one another on their good fortune.
    e. the five scholarship winners, who enjoyed the same good fortune, congratulated one another.

11. In the winter, the number of heart attacks from snow shoveling is astonishing.

    a. In the winter, the number of heart attacks from snow shoveling is astonishing.
    b. In the winter, an astonishing number of heart attacks occur because of snow shoveling.
    c. An astonishing number of people suffer heart attacks in the winter because they shovel snow.
    d. In the winter, snow shoveling causes astonishing heart attacks.
    e. Heart attacks occur because of snow shoveling in the winter at an astonishing rate.

12. Cathy has not and she will not take illegal drugs.

    a. Cathy has not ever and she will not
    b. Cathy has never yet and never will
    c. Cathy never has or will
    d. Cathy has not taken and she will not
    e. Cathy never has and she never will

13. Because Gina had laid in bed for several months, she developed atrophy in her leg muscles.

    a. Because Gina had laid in bed
    b. Because Gina lies in bed
    c. Because Gina is laying in bed
    d. Because Gina has lay in bed
    e. Because Gina had lain in bed

Directions: The following sentences test your ability to recognize grammar and usage errors. Each sentence contains either a single error of no error at all. No sentence contains more than one error. The error, if there is one, is underlined and lettered. If the sentence contains an error, select the one underlined part that must be changed to make the sentence correct. If the sentence is correct, select choice E. In choosing answers, follow the requirements of standard written English.

Example: The other students and Julie reluctantly accepted the offer to eat more early.
                A   B   C   D
      No Error
         E   *The correct answer is D.*

14. In a national interview, the actress <u>stated</u> <u>that she had had</u> a great
                                            A   B
admiration <u>for the work of</u> Katharine Hepburn, <u>who</u> she considered an icon.
                    C   D
 <u>No error</u>
    E

15. <u>If</u> the author <u>would have edited</u> her manuscript <u>better</u>, she <u>might have</u>
      A   B   C   D
<u>sold it</u> to a national women's magazine.

<u>No error</u>
   E

16.   To select the optimal profession, <u>one must be insightful enough to</u>
                                                            A
<u>assess their own talents</u> and <u>wise enough to identify</u> a way to market them
              B   C
<u>in an increasingly competitive economy</u>.
                        D
<u>No error</u>
   E

17. The shark <u>presents</u> a compelling danger to coastal areas, <u>where</u>
                    A   B
tourism and ocean sports <u>are</u> a vital part of the economy; in these densely
                            C
populated regions, <u>their eradication</u> is imperative.
                          D
<u>No error</u>
   E

18. <u>To gain support</u> for her candidate, Diane <u>attended</u> the television debate, <u>which</u> was
          A   B   C
watched by millions of people <u>in a political t-shirt</u>.
                                        D
<u>No error</u>
   E

19.   A primary cause <u>of side collisions</u> <u>is when</u> drivers pull <u>into intersections</u> <u>without</u>
                              A   B   C
<u>checking</u> for the presence of ongoing traffic.
      D
<u>No error</u>
   E

20. <u>Because of</u> an equipment malfunction, the chorus <u>could not be heard</u> by the
     A   B

occupants <u>of rows six through twelve</u> <u>in the massive auditorium</u>.
                 C   D

<u>No error</u>
  E

21. <u>To save money</u>, the trend <u>in airlines service</u> <u>is to offer</u> more electronic
       A   B   C

interactions and <u>less interactions with employees</u>.
                  D

  <u>No error</u>
    E

22. <u>Due to</u> a scheduling conflict, several participants <u>missed</u> the meeting <u>at which</u>
    A   B   C

John <u>tendered</u> his resignation.
       D

  <u>No error</u>
    E

23. <u>Perspective buyers</u> of the condominiums on Fourth Street <u>were</u>
        A

<u>justifiably concerned</u> about the impact of construction noise <u>from nearby</u>
      B   C

factories, <u>which operate</u> twenty-four hours each day.
           D

<u>No error</u>
  E

24. Diana did <u>what she was expected</u> <u>to do</u> <u>when</u> she canceled the class
                    A   B   C

<u>due to</u> insufficient enrollment.
  D
<u>No error</u>
  E

25. <u>Stephanie embarked</u> <u>on a weight loss program</u> <u>in an attempt</u> <u>at attracting</u> an eligible
         A   B   C   D
bachelor.

<u>No error</u>
  E

26. David <u>could easily have earned</u> an Olympic medal <u>for</u> gymnastics, if he
              A   B

<u>had trained</u> the same long hours <u>as</u> his competitors.
   C   D
<u>No error</u>
  E

27. The kittens <u>that</u> George and Cindy <u>purchased</u> from a backyard breeder <u>were more</u>

        A   B

<u>even-tempered and healthy</u> <u>than the local pet shop</u>.

        C   D

<u>No error</u>

   E

Directions: The following passage is an early draft of an essay. Some parts of the passage need to be rewritten. Read the passage and select the best answers for the questions that follow. Some questions are about particular sentences or parts of sentences and ask you to improve sentence structure or word choice. Other questions ask you to consider organization and development. In choosing answers, follow the requirements of standard written English.

1 For buyers with a conscience, Computer Systems is a poor choice. 2 They act like they are ethical people, but they are not. 3 Until last year, when Amnesty International caught onto them, most of their components were made in third world countries. 4 They exploited children as young as eight by paying them ten cents an hour and working them sixteen hours a day. 5 But because the components were shipped to the United States and assembled at a plant in Tennessee, Computer Systems could legitimately say that they were "Made in the U.S."

6 This is deceptive, and wrong, and the antithesis of their mission statement, which claims that they support the American economy by hiring the best workers they can find. 7 They even get huge tax breaks for the plant in Tennessee, which is an underserved area. 8 If the public knew about their sweatshops in Pakistan, I doubt they would consider Computer Systems to be an ethical company. 9 After the Amnesty International expose, they cleaned up their act. 10 They closed one of their sweatshops and moved 100 jobs back to the U.S. 11 Who knows, though, whether those jobs will stay. 12 Unless they are watched and monitored, Computer Systems may go back to their deceptive practices. 13 Consumer beware!

28. What is the best revision for sentence 1?

    a.   No revision is necessary
    b.   Eliminate it
    c.   Join sentences 1 and 2 by replacing the period with a semi-colon.
    d.   Combine sentences 1 and 2 as follows: *Buyers with a conscience should avoid unethical companies like Computer Systems.*
    e.   Combine sentences 1 and 2 as follows: *For buyers with a conscience, there are better choices than Computer Systems, which is not an ethical company.*

29. What is the best revision for sentence 4?

    a.   No revision is necessary
    b.   *Computer Systems exploited eight-year-old children by paying them ten cents an hour and making them work sixteen hours per day.*
    c.   Combine sentences 3 and 4 as follows: *Before Amnesty International intervened last year, Computer Systems made most of their components in third world countries, where children were forced to work sixteen-hour days.*
    d.   Replace <u>an</u> by <u>per</u> and <u>a</u> by <u>per</u>
    e.   Combine sentences 3 and 4 as follows: *Until Amnesty International exposed them last year, Computer Systems exploited children as young as eight years old by making them work 16 hours per day for 10 cents per hour in third world factories.*

30. Why does the author include sentence 5?

    a.   To justify his frustration with Computer Systems
    b.   To suggest a solution to the problem
    c.   To explain how Computer Systems used a "loophole" in the law to claim their products were "Made in the U.S."
    d.   To document his claim
    e.   To outrage the reader about child labor laws

31. In sentence 6, to what does the author refer by the word *this*?

   a.   Manufacturing components outside the United States
   b.   Assembling the components in Tennessee, where labor costs are higher than overseas
   c.   Hiring child workers anywhere, for any reason
   d.   Getting tax breaks for a plant overseas
   e.   Claiming products are Made in the U.S. when their components are manufactured in third world companies

32. What is the best revision for sentence 9?

   a.   No revisions are needed
   b.   Combine sentences 9 and 10 as follows: *After Amnesty International exposed their labor policies,, Computer Systems closed one of their sweatshops and moved 100 jobs back to the U.S.*
   c.   Combine sentences 9 and 10 as follows: *After the Amnesty International expose, they cleaned up their act, closed one of their sweatshops, and moved 100 jobs back to the U.S.*
   d.   *Amnesty International forced Computer Systems to clean up their act.*
   e.   *After they were exposed by Amnesty International, Computer Systems made two changes:*

33. What is the best revision for sentence 11?

   a.   No revisions are necessary
   b.   Eliminate it
   c.   Add a question mark at the end of the sentence
   d.   Eliminate sentence 11 and revise sentence 12 as follows: *Unless they are watched and monitored, however, Computer Systems may resume their deceptive practices and move the jobs back overseas.*
   e.   *But I seriously doubt those jobs will stay.*

34. What is the author's tone in the passage?

   a.   slanderous
   b.   arrogant
   c.   persuasive
   d.   angry
   e.   objective

35. Which of the following groups is the intended audience for the passage?

   a.   Wall Street investors
   b.   Potential employees of the company
   c.   Potential customers of the company's products
   d.   A law firm
   e.   College students

STOP

The answers to these questions are presented in Section WA3 (page 277)

Writing 4:   **25 minutes**   **35 questions**

Directions: The following sentences test correctness and effectiveness of expression. Part of each sentence (or the entire sentence) is underlined; beneath each sentence are five ways of phrasing the underlined material. Choice A repeats the original phrasing; the other four choices are different. If you think the original phrasing produces a better sentence than any of the alternatives, select choice A; if not, select one of the other choices.

In making your selection, follow the requirements of standard written English; that is, pay attention to grammar, choice of words, sentence construction, and punctuation. Your selection should result in the most effective sentence – clear and precise, without awkwardness or ambiguity.

Example: Most teenagers struggle to be free both of parental domination but also from premature responsibilities.

    a.   *both of parental domination but also from premature responsibilities.*
    b.   *both of parental domination and also from premature responsibilities.*
    c.   *both of parental domination and also of premature responsibilities.*
    d.   *of parental domination and premature responsibilities.*
    e.   *both of parental domination and their premature responsibilities as well.*

The correct answer is D.

1. According to Mom, a large quantity of clothing and accessories are on sale at Macy's Department Store.

    a.   According to Mom, a large quantity of clothing, shoes and accessories are on sale at Macy's Department Store.
    b.   According to Mom, a large quantity of clothing, shoes and accessories is on sale at Macy's Department Store.
    c.   Mom claims that a large quantity of clothing, shoes and accessories are on sale at Macy's Department Store.
    d.   A large quantity of clothing, shoes and accessories are on sale at Macy's Department Store, according to Mom.
    e.   According to Mom, Macy's Department Store is selling clothing, shoes and accessories on sale.

2. Even before the Friars rehearsed their dance performance, they knew that they were not prepared for such an important performance.

    a.   they knew that they were not prepared
    b.   he knew that they were not prepared
    c.   they knew that they had not been prepared
    d.   they knew that he was not prepared
    e.   they had known that they were not prepared

3. That which we cannot do without is that which binds us.

    a.   That which we cannot do without is that which binds us.
    b.   That we cannot do without binds us to it.
    c.   Which we cannot do without binds us to it.
    d.   What we cannot do without is that which binds us.
    e.   We are bound by what we cannot do without.

4. Because of the treacherous road conditions, all residents were advised to stay home, except for policemen, firemen and military personnel like us.

   a. Because of the treacherous road conditions, all residents were advised to stay home, except for policemen, firemen and military personnel like us.
   b. Due to treacherous road conditions, all residents were advised to stay home, accept for policemen, firemen and military personnel like us.
   c. Because of treacherous road conditions, all residents were advised to stay home, except for us police, firemen and military.
   d. Because of treacherous road conditions, all residents were advised to stay home, excect for policemen, firemen and we military personnel.
   e. Because of the treacherous road conditions, only policemen, firemen and military personnel like us were allowed on the road; all other residents were advised to stay home.

5. Despite the challenges of rising health care costs, the quality of care in Australia is significantly higher than most Asian nations.

   a. the quality of care in Australia is significantly higher than most Asian nations
   b. the quality of Australian health care is significantly higher than most Asian nations
   c. the quality of care in Australia is significantly higher than Asia
   d. the quality of health care in Australia is significantly higher than health care in most Asian nations
   e. the quality of care in Australia is significantly higher than the quality of care in most Asian nations

6. The movie did not realistically portray the struggles of the pioneers in the 1800's, which I saw at the metroplex last weekend.

   a. The movie did not realistically portray the struggles of the pioneers in the 1800's, which I saw at the metroplex last weekend.
   b. The movie did not realistically portray the 1800's struggles of the pioneers; I know, because it saw it last weekend at the metroplex.
   c. Last weekend's movie did not realistically portray the struggles of the pioneers in the 1800's at the metroplex.
   d. The movie, which I saw last weekend at the metroplex, did not realistically portray the struggles of the pioneers in the 1800's.
   e. I saw a movie last weekend at the metoplex that did not realistically portray the struggles of the 1800's pioneers.

7. The visiting professor, whose recent publications on women's suffrage in Guatemala, were recently published by *Redbook*.

   a. The visiting professor, whose recent publications on women's suffrage in Guatemala, were recently published by *Redbook*.
   b. The recent publications of the visiting professor, which were about women's suffrage in Guatemala, were recently published in *Redbook*.
   c. *Redbook* recently published the visiting professor's publications about women's suffrage in Guatemala.
   d. *Redbook* recently published articles about the visiting professor's suffrage in Guatemala.
   e. *Redbook* recently published articles about women's suffrage in Guatemala, which were written by the visiting professor.

8. <u>Dylan refused to invest in stocks because his father was defrauded by a con man during the 1987 stock market crash</u>.

  a. Dylan refused to invest in stocks because his father was defrauded by a con man during the 1987 stock market crash.
  b. Dylan refused to invest in stocks during the 1987 stock market crash because a con man defrauded his father.
  c. Because a con man defrauded his father, Dylan refused to invest in stocks during the 1987 stock market crash.
  d. To avoid being defrauded by a con man like his dad, Dylan refused to invest in stocks after the 1987 stock market crash.
  e. A con man defrauded Dylan's father after the 1987 stock market crash; as a result, Dylan refused to invest in stocks.

9. <u>In spite of Brittany's objections</u>, the hairdresser applied a dark henna to her hair, which made her look tired and drawn.

  a. In spite of Brittany's objections,
  b. Not listening to Brittany's objections,
  c. Ignoring Brittany's objections,
  d. Although Brittany clearly vocalized her vehement objections,
  e. Closing her mind to Brittany's objections

10. Millions of people require dental implants because <u>they have decayed teeth that have spread to their nerves</u>, and the teeth can no longer be saved.

  a. they have decayed teeth that have spread to their nerves
  b. their nerves have been infected by the decay in their teeth
  c. their tooth decay extends into their nerves
  d. they have decayed nerves
  e. their nerves have been infested by dental decay

11. Oncologists often claim that <u>it is them, not surgeons or cardiac specialists, that save most patient's lives</u>.

  a. it is them, not surgeons or cardiac specialists, that save most patient's lives.
  b. it is they, rather than surgeons or cardiac specialists, that save most patient's lives.
  c. they, rather than surgeons or cardiac specialists, save most patients' lives.
  d. they save more patients' lives than surgeons or cardiac specialists.
  e. they save most patients' lives, compared to surgeons or cardiac specialists.

12. Rebecca had to borrow a copy of *West Side Story* from the local library, <u>thinking that she didn't know where her own copy was at.</u>

  a. thinking that she didn't know where her own copy was at.
  b. because she didn't know where her own copy was at.
  c. on account of she didn't know were her own copy was.
  d. because she didn't know where to find her own copy at.
  e. because she didn't know where her own copy was.

13. Jane could easily have gotten accepted into a better law school if she <u>would have studied</u> more as a college student.

  a. would have studied
  b. studied
  c. had studied
  d. had been studying
  e. would of studied

14. Lori's angry outburst the night before her wedding <u>resulted in her guests premature retreat</u> from the rehearsal dinner.

    a. resulted in her guests premature retreat
    b. caused her guests premature retreat
    c. was the cause of her guests premature retreat
    d. caused her guests to retreat premature
    e. caused her guests' premature retreat

Directions: *The following sentences test your ability to recognize grammar and usage errors. Each sentence contains either a single error of no error at all. No sentence contains more than one error. The error, if there is one, is underlined and lettered. If the sentence contains an error, select the one underlined part that must be changed to make the sentence correct. If the sentence is correct, select choice E. In choosing answers, follow the requirements of standard written English.*

Example: <u>The other</u> students and <u>Julie</u> reluctantly accepted the offer <u>to eat</u> <u>more early</u>.
         A   B   C   D
<u>No error</u>
   E

The correct answer is D.

15. Charred remains <u>found in</u> the debris extending from Fifth Avenue <u>to</u> the Brooklyn Bridge
                    A   B
<u>suggests that</u> the fire started <u>as early as</u> 9 pm.
     C   D
<u>No error</u>
   E

16. <u>Jane</u> <u>works</u> <u>during the day</u> and <u>go to</u> school at night.
     A   B   C   D
<u>No error</u>
   E

17. <u>Since</u> no one understands the project <u>as well</u> <u>as her</u>, no one <u>except her</u> should give the
     A   B   C   D
oral presentation.

<u>No error</u>
   E

18. <u>At</u> the job fair, Mr. Davis met two candidates <u>who,</u> <u>he believed,</u> <u>could do</u> the job.
     A   B   C   D
<u>No error</u>
   E

19. <u>When</u> the election results, <u>including those for</u> the contentious Senate race in
     A   B
District 3, <u>were announced</u>, Senator Smith <u>conceded</u> defeat.
              C   D
<u>No error</u>
   E

199

20. The hiring manager <u>did not encourage</u> the applicant <u>any</u>, although her credentials
                              A   B

<u>were</u> a perfect fit <u>for the opening</u> at the firm.
C   D

<u>No error</u>
E

21. After school, Juan <u>works</u> as a maintenance manager at a car wash, <u>where</u> he
                     A   B

<u>is expected to solve</u> <u>a large amount of</u> mechanical problems.
          C   D

<u>No error</u>
E

22. <u>Although</u> she tried <u>to be brave</u>, the little girl would undoubtedly be <u>effected</u> by
       A   B   C

her <u>parents'</u> divorce.
      D

<u>No error</u>
E

23. <u>After having completed</u> his degree in History, Alex <u>sought</u> a job at a
         A   B

museum in Paris, <u>which</u> <u>would value</u> his knowledge of medieval times.
                C   D

<u>No error</u>
E

24. <u>Despite</u> the risks, Greg <u>laid</u> his expensive camera <u>on top of his car</u>, where it
      A   B   C

<u>could easily have been</u> damaged.
          D

<u>No error</u>
E

25. Clara <u>will stop</u> <u>at nothing</u> <u>in her efforts</u> <u>at eradicating</u> discrimination in the workplace.
            A   B   C   D

<u>No error</u>
E

26. If George Washington, <u>who</u> was a great proponent of firearms, <u>was</u> to come back to life, he
                          A   B

<u>would probably be appalled</u> <u>by the anti-gun movement</u>.
          C   D

<u>No error</u>
E

27. <u>Opinions on</u> Hilary Clinton are usually divided, <u>with</u> Democrats regarding her
      A   B

as a political dynamo, <u>while</u> Republicans chastising her as a <u>disingenuous carpetbagger</u>.
                     C   D

<u>No error</u>
  E

Directions: The following passage is an early draft of an essay. Some parts of the passage need to be rewritten. Read the passage and select the best answers for the questions that follow. Some questions are about particular sentences or parts of sentences and ask you to improve sentence structure or word choice. Other questions ask you to consider organization and development. In choosing answers, follow the requirements of standard written English.

1 In 2005, the Food and Drug Administration did an exhaustive study about snack food preferences in teens. 2 According to them, women like chocolate. 3 Give them candy, cakes, cookies, whatever, and they'll go to town on them. 4 Men, on the other hand, prefer salty snacks like chips and salsa. 5 They are more apt to eat salted peanuts and other fried products - not baked goods.

6 What does this mean? 7 To food companies, it means a lot. 8 They can use this information to advertise and market their products better. 9 Chocolate ads should be aimed toward women. 10 Chip ads should be tailored for men. 11 By putting money into the right type of promotional campaigns, food companies can improve their bottom lines. 12 They might also want to direct their new products accordingly, too. 13 Maybe there are new products they can sell that no one has thought of yet. 14 People spend $450 million on snack foods each year in the United States. It's a huge market. 15 Food companies can earn a larger piece of this pie by using the FDA data to their best advantage.

28. What is the best way to revise sentence 1?

    a.   No revisions are required.
    b.   Replace <u>did</u> with <u>conducted</u>
    c.   Join sentence 1 and sentence 2 with a semi-colon
    d.   Join sentence 1 and sentence 2 with a comma
    e.   Eliminate it

29. What is the best revision for sentence 3?

    a.   No revisions are required
    b.   Eliminate it
    c.   Join sentence 2 and sentence 3 with a semi-colon
    d.   Revise and connect sentences 2 and 3 as follows: *The results suggest that women like snack foods that contain chocolate, such as candy, cakes and cookies.*
    e.   Revise and connect sentences 2, 3, 4 and 5 as follows: *The results showed that women go to town on chocolate, such as candy, cakes and cookies, while men prefer salty snacks, such as chips, salsa, salted peanuts and other fried products.*

30. What is the objective of the first paragraph?

    a.   To explain the snack preferences of men and women
    b.   To present the results of the FDA study about snack preferences in teens
    c.   To promote the sale of chocolate to women
    d.   To promote the sale of salty foods to men
    e.   Both c and d.

31. What is the purpose of sentence 6?

    a. To anticipate the readers' thoughts
    b. To spike the reader's interest
    c. To explain the relevance of paragraph 1
    d. To start a new paragraph
    e. To adopt a humorous tone

32. What is the best revision for sentence 6?

    a. No revisions are needed
    b. Eliminate it
    c. Join sentences 6 and 7 with a semi-colon
    d. Join sentences 6, 7, and 8 as follows: *This information can help food companies tailor their advertising and marketing to each sex.*
    e. Join sentences 6, 7 and 8 as follows: *This information can help food companies advertise and market their products.*

33. Sentences 11, 12 and 13 can BEST be combined in what way?

    a. *To improve their bottom lines, food companies must develop unique products and put money into the right type of promotional campaigns.*
    b. *By putting their money into the right type of promotional campaigns, food companies can improve their bottom lines.*
    c. *Food companies can improve their bottom lines by developing unique products and putting money into promotional campaigns.*
    d. *If they develop new products and put money into the right type of promotional campaigns, food companies may be able to improve their bottom lines*
    e. *By targeting their product development and promotional campaigns to each sex, food companies may be able to improve their bottom lines.*

34. Sentences 14 and 15 should be combined into a single sentence that concludes the passage. Which of the following is the best option?

    a. *To earn a larger piece of the United States snack food market - $450 million each year - food companies must use the FDA data to their best advantage.*
    b. *By using the FDA data to their best advantage, food companies can earn a larger piece of the United States snack food market, which is $450 million each year.*
    c. *United States residents spend $450 million on snack foods each year; to earn a larger piece of this pie, food companies must use the FDA data to their best advantage.*
    d. *The annual snack food market in the United States is $450 million, which food companies can seize by using the FDA data to their best advantage.*
    e. *To earn the lion's share of the $450 million annual snack food market in the United States, food companies must use the FDA data to their best advantage.*

35. Which of the following new products would the author of this passage be most likely to support?

    a. Low calorie ice cream
    b. Gourmet chocolates for teenage girls
    c. Potato chips for college students
    d. Reduced fat movie popcorn
    e. Upscale yogurt with licorice topping

STOP

The answers to these questions are presented in Section WA4 (page 279)

Writing 5:   **25 minutes**   **35 questions**

1. Either Sara or you are guilty.

    a.   Either Sara or you are guilty.
    b.   Either Sara or you is guilty.
    c.   Either Sara is guilty or you are guilty.
    d.   Either you or Sara are guilty.
    e.   Either Sara is guilty or you is guilty.

2. There remain many arguments in favor of women becoming stay-at-home mothers.

    a.   There remain many arguments in favor of women becoming stay-at-home mothers.
    b.   There remains many arguments in favor of women becoming stay-at-home mothers.
    c.   There remain many arguments to favor women becoming stay-at-home mothers.
    d.   There remains many arguments that favor women becoming stay-at-home mothers.
    e.   There remain many arguments in favor of women to become stay-at-home mothers.

3. If a husband wants to send his wife a dozen roses, they can order them from a local florist.

    a.   they can order them from a local florist
    b.   they can order it from a local florist
    c.   he can order them from a local florist
    d.   they can order them at a local florist
    e.   one can order it from a local florist

4. The teacher claimed that everyone will be punished for their misdeeds.

    a.   that everyone will be punished for their misdeeds.
    b.   if everyone will be punished for their misdeeds.
    c.   about everyone being punished for their misdeeds.
    d.   that everyone will be punished for his misdeeds.
    e.   that everyone should be punished for his misdeeds.

5. The night after their breakup, Janis tried to make Steve jealous <u>by walking through a restaurant full of people in a revealing outfit.</u>

    a.   by walking through a restaurant full of people in a revealing outfit
    b.   by walking in a revealing outfit full of people in a crowded restaurant
    c.   by walking through a restaurant in a revealing outfit full of people
    d.   by wearing a revealing outfit walking through a restaurant full of people
    e.   by walking through a restaurant full of people while she was wearing a revealing outfit

6. <u>If one lives in Florida during the winter months, when temperatures are cold up north and in Chicago during the summer months, when Florida is as hot as an oven.</u>

    a.   If one lives in Florida during the winter months, when temperatures are cold up north, and in Chicago during the summer months, when Florida is as hot as an oven.
    b.   If one lives in Florida during the winter months, the temperatures are cold up north, and in Chicago during the summer months, when Florida is as hot as an oven.
    c.   A snowbird lives in Florida during the winter months, when temperatures are cold up north, and in Chicago during the summer months, when Florida is as hot as an oven.
    d.   If a snowbird lives in Florida during the winter months, when temperatures are cold up north, and in Chicago during the summer months, when Florida is as hot as an oven.
    e.   If a snowbird lives in Florida during the winter months, when temperatures are cold up north, then in Chicago during the summer months, when Florida is as hot as an oven.

7. Ryan refuses to buy footwear at Macys because <u>he was sold a pair of shoes that fell apart within two weeks.</u>

    a.   he was sold a pair of shoes that fell apart within two weeks.
    b.   he was sold by the clerk a pair of shoes that fell apart within two weeks.
    c.   he was sold a pair of shoes that two weeks later fell apart.
    d.   the clerk sold him a pair of shoes that fell apart within two weeks.
    e.   a pair of shoes that were sold to him fell apart within two weeks.

8. <u>Although he tried to hide it, Dave was completely disinterested in Joe's story about his summer vacation.</u>

    a.   Although he tried to hide it, Dave was completely disinterested in Joe's story about his summer vacation.
    b.   Although he tried to hide it, Dave was completely disinterested in hearing Joe's story about his summer vacation.
    c.   Dave was completely disinterested in Joe's story about his summer vacation, but he tried to hide it.
    d.   Dave tried to hide is complete disinterest in Joe's story about his summer vacation.
    e.   Although he tried to hide it, Dave was completely uninterested in Joe's story about his summer vacation.

9. Before he left for the mall, <u>Dave asked Carla if she wanted to accompany him.</u>

    a.   Dave asked Carla if she wanted to accompany him.
    b.   Dave asked Carla if she wanted to go.
    c.   Dave asked Carla whether she wanted to accompany him.
    d.   Dave asked Carla if she wanted to come with him.
    e.   Dave asked Carla whether she wanted to come with.

10. Although Bob and Ted worked together on the science project, Bob's conclusions were completely different than Ted's.

    a.   Although Bob and Ted worked together on the science project, Bob's conclusions were completely different than Ted's.
    b.   Despite working together on the science project, Bob's conclusions were completely different than Ted's.
    c.   Although Bob and Ted worked together on the science project, Bob's conclusions were completely different from Ted's.
    d.   Although they worked together on the science project, Bob and Ted reached conclusions that were completely different than each other's.
    e.   Bob and Ted, who worked together on the science project, reached conclusions that were completely different than each other.

11. Shortly after their guests arrived, Dina and Tom realized that they had prepared nowhere near the amount of food they needed to feed the entire group.

    a.   had prepared nowhere near the amount of food they needed
    b.   had prepared nowhere near the amount of food they would need
    c.   had prepared not enough food they would need
    d.   had not prepared the amount of food they would need
    e.   had not prepared enough food

12.   The children play quieter after lunch when I feed them a heavier snack.

    a.   The children play quieter after lunch when I feed them a heavier snack.
    b.   The children play quietly after lunch when they have ate a heavier snack.
    c.   The children play quietly after lunch when I feed them a heavier snack.
    d.   The children play most quiet after lunch when I feed them a heavier snack.
    e.   I feed the children a heavier snack to get them to play quiet after lunch.

Directions: The following sentences test your ability to recognize grammar and usage errors. Each sentence contains either a single error of no error at all. No sentence contains more than one error. The error, if there is one, is underlined and lettered. If the sentence contains an error, select the one underlined part that must be changed to make the sentence correct. If the sentence is correct, select choice E. In choosing answers, follow the requirements of standard written English.

Example: The other students and Julie reluctantly accepted the offer to eat more early.
            A   *B*   *C*   *D*

No error
  E

The correct answer is D.

13.   Although the principal praised the students' ability to handle change,
       A   B
never before has their violations of the rules been more apparent.
       C   D
No error
  E

14. Long before she went to the emergency room, Emily had suspected that
       A   B   C
her leg was broken.
       D
No error
  E

15. When she packed for the trip, Diane did not realize that the rainfall in Madrid would
              A   B   C

be just like Sydney that time of year.
   D

No error
   E

16. Whose to decide whether or not a child should receive medical care for a life threatening
     A   B   C   D

Illness: the parents, the physician, or the insurance company?

No error
   E

17. After the science fair, Mrs. Chaney praised Alison for her appearance, choice of topic and
          A   B   C

because she was organized.
        D

 No error
   E

18. Although I understand that not all hotels can offer smoke-free rooms, I do not
        A   B   C

understand why I was assigned a room by a desk clerk that reeked of cigarette smoke.
                                                    D

No error
   E

19. Rather than tell the truth, which would place her in a bad light, the
     A   B

disingenuous politician hedging her bets by remaining silent.
              C   D

No error
   E

20. Contrary to what many of Mary's neighbors suspected, the dog's aggressive
        A   B   C

behavior was not provoked from the taunts of the neighborhood children.
                    D

No error
   E

21. Using a typewriter in the computer age is in many ways like when we use
      A   B   C

a slide rule instead of a calculator.
          D

No error
   E

22. The President, as well as the Senate and House, is trying to affect positive
              A   B   C

changes in education, health care and international policy.
               D

No error
  E

23. On opening night, the cast members gave a terrific performance, although
        A   B   C

there wasn't hardly anyone in the audience.
       D

No error
  E

24. If Grace would have lain her purse on the table, it might not have been stolen in the robbery.
             A   B   C   D

No error
  E

25. If any soldier from the Civil War was to observe our computerized weapons, he
                             A   B

would be amazed by such cutting-edge technology.
   C   D

No error
  E

Directions: The following passage is an early draft of an essay. Some parts of the passage need to be rewritten. Read the passage and select the best answers for the questions that follow. Some questions are about particular sentences or parts of sentences and ask you to improve sentence structure or word choice. Other questions ask you to consider organization and development. In choosing answers, follow the requirements of standard written English.

1 One of the biggest challenges to women after menopause is the loss of bone density. 2 Menopause happens when women are between 45 and 60. 3 The changes cause calcium to leach from the bones and become brittle. 4 If this happens for too long, women's bones are no longer strong enough for them to perform their usual tasks or enjoy typical things. 5 This is called osteoporosis.

6 Experts recommend three methods of treatment for this disorder. 7 First, women should take calcium. 8 They need 1,000 mg every day. 9 It can either come from food or vitamin supplements. 10 They also need to exercise. 11 The exercise must be aerobic, like walking or running. 12 They should do it for three hours each week. 13 Preferably thirty minutes each day for six days. 14 Finally, women should consider taking estrogen after menopause. 15 By taking it, they can adjust their hormonal balance to a healthier level. 16 Supplements are not right for everyone, so patients should see their doctors before trying to order them online. 17 By doing all three things, women can avoid losing bone density and enjoy a healthy old age.

26. What should be done with the first sentence of the passage?

    a. It should remain unchanged
    b. It should be deleted
    c. It should be combined with sentence 2 as follows: *When women undergo menopause between ages 45 and 60, one of their biggest challenges is the loss of bone density.*
    d. It should be combined with sentence 3 by placing a comma between the two sentences. Sentence 2 should be omitted.
    e. It should be combined with sentences 2 and 3 as follows: *When women undergo menopause between ages 45 and 60, one of their biggest challenges is the loss of bone density, which causes calcium to leach from the bones and become brittle.*

27. Which of the following is the best revision for sentence 4?

    a. No revisions are necessary.
    b. It should be combined with sentence 5 by placing a comma between the two sentences.
    c. Replace this with bone density continues to decrease.
    d. Replace or enjoy typical things with and enjoy their typical activities.
    e. Replace this with bone density continues to decrease AND replace or enjoy typical things with and enjoy their typical activities

28. What is the best revision for sentence 5?

    a. No revisions are necessary.
    b. It should be deleted.
    c. It should be moved to the beginning of paragraph 2.
    d. This should be changed to this process.
    e. This should be changed to these changes culminate in the disease called.

29. What is the purpose of the first paragraph (sentences 1 – 5)?

    a. To define the meaning and causes of osteoporosis
    b. To explain who is at risk for osteoporosis
    c. To warn women about the dangers of menopause
    d. To sell hormonal treatments for menopause
    e. To explain why post-menopausal women break bones easily

30. What is the best revision for sentence 6?

    a. No revisions are necessary.
    b. It should be deleted.
    c. This disorder should be changed to osteoporosis.
    d. Three methods of treatment for this disorder should be changed to three methods to prevent bone loss.
    e. The phrase three methods of treatment should be changes to treatments

31. What is the best revision for sentence 7?

    a. No revisions are necessary.
    b. It should be deleted.
    c. It should be combined with sentence 8 by placing a semi-colon between the two sentences.
    d. It should be combined with sentence 8 as follows: *First, women should consume 1,000 mg of calcium every day.*
    e. It should be combined with sentences 8 and 9 as follows: *First, women should consume 1,000 mg of calcium every day, either in their food or as a vitamin supplement.*

32. What is the best revision for sentence 10?

    a. No revisions are necessary.
    b. It should be combined with sentences 11, 12 and 13 as follows: *Women also need to run or walk for three hours each week, preferably thirty minutes each day for six days.*
    c. It should be combined with sentences 11 and 12 as follows: *Women also need three hours of aerobic exercise, such as running or walking.*
    d. It should be combined with sentences 11 and 12 as follows: *Second, women need to devote three hours per week to aerobic exercise, such as running or walking.*
    e. It should be combined with sentence 11 as follows: *Second, women must embark on a regular exercise routine, such as walking or running.*

33. What is the best way to combine sentences 14 and 15?

    a.   No revisions are necessary.
    b.   Join them with a semi-colon.
    c.   Join them with a colon.
    d.   Replace the words <u>by taking it they can</u> with <u>to</u>
    e.   They should be re-written as follows: *Finally, women must take estrogen after menopause to achieve a healthier hormonal balance.*

34. What is the best way to conclude paragraph 2?

    a.   No changes are necessary.
    b.   Line 17 should be revised as follows: *By using calcium, exercise, and estrogen, women can minimize bone loss and enjoy a healthy old age.*
    c.   <u>All three things,</u> should be replaced by <u>calcium, exercise and estrogen,</u>
    d.   <u>Avoid losing bone density</u> should be replaced by <u>minimize bone loss</u>
    e.   <u>By doing all three things, women can</u> should be replaced by <u>Calcium, exercise and estrogen can help women</u>

35. The main point of the second paragraph is to:

    a.   Summarize the information in paragraph one.
    b.   Contradict the information in paragraph one.
    c.   Provide a solution to the problem described in paragraph one.
    d.   Provide supporting evidence to information in paragraph one,
    e.   Persuade the reader about the topic in paragraph one.

STOP

The answers to these questions are presented in Section WA5 (page 281)

Writing 6:   25 minutes   35 questions

Directions: *The following sentences test correctness and effectiveness of expression. Part of each sentence (or the entire sentence) is underlined; beneath each sentence are five ways of phrasing the underlined material. Choice A repeats the original phrasing; the other four choices are different. If you think the original phrasing produces a better sentence than any of the alternatives, select choice A; if not, select one of the other choices.*

In making your selection, follow the requirements of standard written English; that is, pay attention to grammar, choice of words, sentence construction, and punctuation. Your selection should result in the most effective sentence – clear and precise, without awkwardness or ambiguity.

Example: Most teenagers struggle to be free <u>both of parental domination but also from premature responsibilities.</u>

a. both of parental domination but also from premature responsibilities.
b. both of parental domination and also from premature responsibilities.
c. both of parental domination and also of premature responsibilities.
d. of parental domination and premature responsibilities.
e. both of parental domination and their premature responsibilities as well.

The correct answer is D.

1. The use of cell phones, along with other wireless devices, <u>make other methods of communication, such as pay phones and "snail mail," seem downright obsolete.</u>

    a.   make other methods of communication, such as pay phones and "snail mail," seem downright obsolete.
    b.   make pay phones and "snail mail" seem like obsolete methods of communication.
    c.   makes pay phones and "snail mail" seem like obsolete methods of communication.
    d.   makes other methods of communication appear to be adolescent, like pay phones and "snail mail."
    e.   when compared to other methods of communication, such as pay phones and "snail mail," make them seem downright obsolete.

2. People convicted for fraud <u>never have nor ever will be honest</u>.

    a.   never have nor ever will be honest.
    b.   never have been, and never will be, honest.
    c.   never have been honest and never will be honest.
    d.   never have and never will be honest.
    e.   have and will never be honest.

3. The day care center has no objection <u>to him joining the staff, as long as he is willing to assume the same duties as the female employees</u> on staff.

    a.   to him joining the staff, as long as he is willing to assume the same duties as the female employees
    b.   to him joining the staff, so long as he is willing to assume the same duties as the women
    c.   to his joining the staff, as long as he is willing to assume the same duties as the female employees
    d.   to his joining the staff, so long as he will assume the same duties as the female employees
    e.   to him joining the staff, providing that he is willing to do the same job as the female employees

4. Carolyn asked Elizabeth to mail her application immediately, because she was afraid it would arrive after the deadline.

   a. Carolyn asked Elizabeth to mail her application immediately, because she was afraid it would arrive after the deadline.
   b. Carolyn asked Elizabeth to mail her application immediately, to avoid missing the deadline.
   c. Carolyn asked Elizabeth to mail her application immediately, because she was afraid that Elizabeth would miss the deadline.
   d. Carolyn advised Elizabeth to mail her application immediately, because it would arrive after the deadline.
   e. Carolyn advised Elizabeth to mail her application immediately, to ensure that it arrived before the deadline.

5. Swimming two miles in heated pool is significantly easier than to swim the same distance in the choppy ocean.

   a. Swimming two miles in a heated pool is significantly easier than to swim the same distance in the choppy ocean.
   b. Swimming two miles in a heated pool is significantly easier than swimming the same distance in the choppy ocean.
   c. To swim two miles in a heated pool is significantly easier than for one to swim the same distance in the choppy ocean.
   d. To swim two miles in a heated pool is significantly easier than swimming the same distance in the choppy ocean.
   e. It is significantly easier to swim two miles in a heated pool than the same distance in the choppy ocean.

6. To avoid airport delays, our plans were that we would catch the red eye.

   a. To avoid airport delays, our plans were that we would catch the red eye.
   b. To avoid airport delays, our plans were for catching the red eye.
   c. To avoid airport delays, we planned to catch the red eye.
   d. Our plans were to catch the red eye so that we could avoid airport delays.
   e. We planned to catch the red eye, that's how we would avoid airport delays.

7. The five surviving U.S Presidents were formerly honored at a ceremony in Boston, where the current President praised them for their distinguished service to our nation.

   a. The five surviving U.S. Presidents were formerly honored at a ceremony in Boston, where the current President praised them for their distinguished service to our nation.
   b. At a formal ceremony in Boston, the President formally honored the five surviving U.S. Presidents, whom he praised for their distinguished service to our nation.
   c. The five surviving U.S. Presidents, who served our nation with distinction, were formally honored by our current President at a ceremony in Boston.
   d. The current President formally honored the five U.S. Presidents in Boston and praised them for their distinguished service to our nation.
   e. At a ceremony in Boston, the current President formally honored the five surviving U.S. Presidents and praised them for their distinguished service to our nation.

8. After a three-hour delay, the opening chorus of the musical was heard throughout the large auditorium.

   a. the opening chorus of the musical was heard throughout the auditorium.
   b. the opening chorus of the musical were heard throughout the auditorium.
   c. the entire auditorium heard the opening chorus of the musical.
   d. the audience heard the opening chorus of the musical throughout the auditorium.
   e. the auditorium heard the opening chorus of the musical.

9. <u>Rather than choose between three equal candidates</u>, the committee decided to award scholarships to all of them.

    a.   Rather than choose between three equal candidates,
    b.   Rather than choose among three equal candidates,
    c.   Rather than choose between three equally qualified candidates,
    d.   Rather than choose among three equally qualified candidates,
    e.   Rather than choose among the three candidates,

10. Although she was a mediocre student, Sara studied diligently to earn <u>the kind of grades that her friends in the honor society did.</u>

    a.   the kind of grades that her friends in the honor society did.
    b.   the type of grades that her friends in the honor society did.
    c.   honor society grades.
    d.   grades like her honor society friends.
    e.   grades that were similar to those of her friends in the honor society.

11. After years of backbreaking work in the fields, <u>for which she was paid little money, Clara's hands became inflicted with arthritis.</u>

    a.   for which she was paid little money, Clara's hands became inflicted with arthritis.
    b.   for which Clara was paid little money, her hands became afflicted by arthritis.
    c.   when Clara was paid little money, her hands became afflicted by arthritis.
    d.   when she was paid little money, Clara became inflicted with arthritis of the hands.
    e.   for which Clara was paid little money, her hands became afflicted with arthritis.

12. <u>According to recent polls, the top three consumer concerns are jobs, health care, and inflation, respectfully.</u>

    a.   According to recent polls, the top three consumer concerns are jobs, health care, and inflation, respectfully.
    b.   Consumers are most concerned about jobs, health care, and inflation, respectfully, according to recent polls.
    c.   According to recent polls, the top three consumer concerns, respectfully, are jobs, health care, and inflation.
    d.   According to recent polls, the top three consumer concerns are jobs, health care, and inflation, respectively.
    e.   Recent consumer polls proved that consumers are most concerned about the availability of jobs, health care, and inflation, respectively.

13. <u>Carrie, Samantha and Charlotte are all great actresses, but Samantha has the wider emotional range.</u>

    a.   Carrie, Samantha and Charlotte are all great actresses, but Samantha has the wider emotional range.
    b.   Although Carrie, Samantha and Charlotte are all great actresses, Samantha has the wider emotional range.
    c.   Carrie, Samantha and Charlotte are all great actresses, but Samantha has the widest emotional range.
    d.   Of the three actresses – Carrie, Samantha and Charlotte – Samantha has the wider emotional range.
    e.   Samantha has more emotion than Carrie and Charlotte.

14. Media reps from twelve television networks will meet on Saturday <u>to lay out their strategy for covering political news.</u>

  a. to lay out their strategy for covering political news.
  b. to lie out their strategy for covering political news.
  c. to lay out their strategy to cover political news.
  d. to lay our their strategy for political news.
  e. to lie out their strategy to cover political news.

15. <u>To snap back at one's angry husband is a less effective course than attempting to reconcile with him.</u>

  a. To snap back at one's angry husband is a less effective course than attempting to reconcile with him.
  b. To snap back at your angry husband is less effective than reconciling with him.
  c. To snap back at one's angry husband is a less effective course than to attempt to reconcile with him.
  d. Snapping back at one's angry husband is a less effective course than to attempt to reconcile with him.
  e. To snap back at one's angry husband is less effective than reconciling with him.

16. <u>If Maria would of been home when the fire started, she would have saved the old photographs that her mother dearly loved.</u>

  a. If Maria would of been home when the fire started, she would have saved the old photographs that her mother dearly loved.
  b. If Maria was home when the fire started, she would have saved the old photographs that her mother dearly loved.
  c. Had Maria been home when the fire started, she would of saved the old photographs that her mother dearly loved.
  d. If Maria had been home when the fire started, she would have saved the old photographs that her mother dearly loved.
  e. If Maria would be home when the fire started, she could have saved the old photographs that her mother dearly loved.

17. President Abraham Lincoln <u>disregarding the fervent advice of his own Cabinet regarding</u> the controversy surrounding slavery in the American colonies.

  a. disregarding the fervent advice of his own Cabinet regarding
  b. disregarding the fervent advice of the nation's Cabinet regarding
  c. disregarded the fervent advice of his own Cabinet, ending
  d. disregarding the fervent advice of his own Cabinet about
  e. disregarded the fervent advice of his own Cabinet about

18. Ross Perot is a respected American businessman and financier, <u>and is best known for running</u> for President in 1992.

  a. and is best known for running
  b. and he is best known because he was running
  c. who was best known when he was running
  d. who everyone knows ran
  e. who is best known for running.

Directions: The following sentences test your ability to recognize grammar and usage errors. Each sentence contains either a single error of no error at all. No sentence contains more than one error. The error, if there is one, is underlined and lettered. If the sentence contains an error, select the one underlined part that must be changed to make the sentence correct. If the sentence is correct, select choice E. In choosing answers, follow the requirements of standard written English.

19. Her husband <u>wanted to wash</u> the car <u>before his wife</u> <u>had come home</u> <u>from the mall</u>.
                          A   B   C   D
<u>No error</u>
E

20. The school officials <u>attributed</u> the low SAT scores to the fact that <u>not one of the more</u>
                              A   B
<u>than</u> five hundred students <u>were graduates</u> <u>of the online review class</u>.
                                      C   D
<u>No error</u>
E

21. <u>Also on</u> the agenda <u>is</u> a presentation by Jane Bowers <u>on</u> salt reduction and a
        A   B   C
discussion <u>about our upcoming</u> Christmas party in Martha's Vineyard. .
                    D
 <u>No error</u>
E

22. Dan lives in the house <u>across from Jane</u>, <u>which is adjacent</u> <u>to the green log cabin</u> owned
                                  A   B   C
<u>by</u> Desmond Harris.
D

<u>No error</u>
E

23. Rachel <u>enjoyed</u> modern dance <u>for</u> its gracefulness, <u>musicality</u> and <u>because it told a</u>
                A   B   C   D
<u>story</u>.

<u>No error</u>
E

24. We <u>took</u> a bus <u>to</u> the history museum <u>which carried</u> <u>more than</u> two thousand passengers.
          A   B   C   D
<u>No error</u>
E

25. After living in Hawaii for most of his life, where temperatures are seldom
    A   B   C
below freezing.
    D
No error
    E

26. Dr. Bancroft has designated Nurse Smith as one of the employees who are going to
              A   B   C
receive special training in handle hazardous waste.
                         D
No error
    E

27. To address the needs of Hurricane Katrina victims, a fund was established by the
        A   B   C
America Red Cross in all fifty states to buy essential medical supplies.
                                         D
No error
    E

28. Because they could not afford to stay in a hotel room for the duration of their trip,
              A   B
Frank and Jane opted to stay in a hostile at the base of the Alps.
                 C   D
No error
    E

29. By the time the doctor returned her call, Mrs. Stevens had all ready gone into labor.
      A   B   C   D
  No error
    E

30. Being that the attorneys were not prepared, they requested a three-week
    A   B   C
continuance from the Judge.
    D
No error
    E

31. Jessie could of gone to the prom with Bryan, but she didn't know he was interested.
        A   B   C   D
No error
    E

32. The football coach, <u>along with</u> several key players, <u>are scheduling</u> a conference
                              A   B
to <u>lay down</u> next <u>season's</u> recruitment regulations.
        C   D
<u>No error</u>
     E

33. <u>Irregardless of the cost</u>, Sophie <u>continued to select</u> <u>the attire she wanted</u> for her
              A   B   C
dream wedding, <u>which was scheduled</u> for New Year's Eve.
                          D

<u>No error</u>
     E

34. <u>There is</u> ongoing debate <u>about how much</u> of the decrease in teen pregnancies <u>is due</u>
        A   B   C
<u>to</u> the availability of inexpensive birth control and how much <u>is the result of</u> abstinence
                                                                              D

programs.

<u>No error</u>
     E

35. <u>The new bridal boutique on Seventh Avenue</u> <u>employs the most unique premise</u>:
                    A   B
<u>renting, rather than selling</u>, different forms <u>of designer bridal attire</u>.
                    C   D
<u>No error</u>
     E

STOP

The answers to these questions are presented in Section WA6 (page 283)

Writing 7:   25 minutes   35 questions

Directions: The following sentences test correctness and effectiveness of expression. Part of each sentence (or the entire sentence) is underlined; beneath each sentence are five ways of phrasing the underlined material. Choice A repeats the original phrasing; the other four choices are different. If you think the original phrasing produces a better sentence than any of the alternatives, select choice A; if not, select one of the other choices.

In making your selection, follow the requirements of standard written English; that is, pay attention to grammar, choice of words, sentence construction, and punctuation. Your selection should result in the most effective sentence – clear and precise, without awkwardness or ambiguity.

Example: Most teenagers struggle to be free _both of parental domination but also from premature responsibilities._

a. both of parental domination but also from premature responsibilities.
b. both of parental domination and also from premature responsibilities.
c. both of parental domination and also of premature responsibilities.
d. of parental domination and premature responsibilities.
e. both of parental domination and their premature responsibilities as well.

The correct answer is D.

1. Connie would have accepted Bill's invitation to the dance, if he waited for her reply.

    a. if he waited for her reply.
    b. if he had waited for her reply.
    c. if he would have waited for her reply.
    d. if he only would have waited for her reply.
    e. if he took the time to wait for her reply.

2. Having sunk all of their money into a losing investment, which he had promised not to do, Rick was afraid to tell his parents.

    a. Having sunk all of their money into a losing investment, which he had promised not to do, Rick was afraid to tell his parents.
    b. Having sank all of his parents' money into a losing investment, Rick was afraid to tell them because he promised not to do.
    c. After sinking their money into a losing investment, which his parents had made him promise, Rick was afraid to tell them.
    d. Having sank all of their money into a losing investment, which he had promised not to do, Rick was afraid to tell his parents.
    e. Rick was afraid to tell his parents that he sunk all of their money into a losing investment, which he had promised not to do.

3. Between the doctor, my wife and me, there is full disclosure.

    a. Between the doctor, my wife and me, there is full disclosure.
    b. Between the doctor, my wife and I, there is full disclosure.
    c. The doctor, my wife and me agreed to fully disclose all information.
    d. The doctor agreed to disclose all information to my wife and I.
    e. The doctor, my wife and I agreed to full disclosure.

4. Dr. Davis was advised to give the assignment to whoever he believed was best qualified for the job.

    a. to whoever he believed was best qualified
    b. to whomever he believed was best qualified
    c. to whoever he knew was best qualified
    d. to the person who, in his belief, was best qualified
    e. to the person, whom, in his belief, we best qualified

217

5. The candidate reacted with quickness and eloquently to her opponent's misleading statements.

    a.   The candidate reacted with quickness and eloquently to her opponent's misleading statements.
    b.   With quickness and eloquence, the candidate responded to statements from her opponent, which she believed were misleading.
    c.   The candidate reacted quickly and eloquence to the misleading statements by her opponent.
    d.   The opponent's misleading statements were met with quickness and eloquent by the candidate.
    e.   The candidate reacted quickly and eloquently to her opponent's misleading statements.

6. Despite Bill's reservations, the party went on as planned.

    a.   Despite Bill's reservations, the party went on as planned.
    b.   Despite the fact that Bill had reservations, the party went on as planned.
    c.   Although Bill had reservations, the party went on as planned.
    d.   Despite Bill's reservations, they did not prevent the party.
    e.   Despite Bill's reservations, he went to the party as planned.

7. Thin women get more modeling jobs, they look better in stylish clothes.

    a.   Thin women get more modeling jobs, they look better in stylish clothes.
    b.   Thin women get more modeling jobs because they look better in stylish clothes.
    c.   Most modeling jobs are given to thin women, who look better in stylish clothes.
    d.   Thin women get more modeling jobs: they look better in stylish clothes.
    e.   Thin women, who look better in stylish clothes, also get more modeling jobs.

8. It was reported by Channel 12 that the identity of the deceased would not be revealed until the next of kin had been notified.

    a.   It was reported by Channel 12 that the identity of the deceased would not be revealed until the next of kin had been notified.
    b.   It was reported by Channel 12 that the authorities would not reveal the identity of the deceased until their next of kin were notified.
    c.   Channel 12 reported that the authorities will not reveal the identity of the deceased until after their next of kin have been notified.
    d.   Channel 12 would not reveal the identity of the deceased until the authorities notified their next of kin.
    e.   Channel 12 reported the authority's decision not to reveal the identity of the deceased until after the next of kin had been notified first.

9. When they found $50 in the parking lot, Joe and Ted decided to divide the money equally among themselves.

    a.   equally among themselves
    b.   equally between themselves
    c.   equally
    d.   between the two of them equally
    e.   equally between them

10. Only two of the job candidates exceeded the required typing speed of 75 words per minute; not surprisingly, even the slowest of the two was an excellent typist.

    a. Only two of the job candidates exceeded the required typing speed of 75 words per minute; not surprisingly, even the slowest of the two was an excellent typist.
    b. Only two of the job candidates typed faster than the required typing speed of 75 words per minute; not surprisingly, even the slowest of the two was an excellent typist.
    c. Only two of the job candidates typed faster than the required typing speed of 75 words per minute; even the slower one was an excellent typist.
    d. Only two job candidates typed faster than 75 words per minute; not surprisingly, even the slowest candidate was an excellent typist.
    e. Only two of the job candidates typed faster than the required speed of 75 words per minute; not surprisingly, even the slower candidate was an excellent typist.

11. Kyle turned down the job offer for several reasons, beside the disappointing salary.

    a. Kyle turned down the job offer for several reasons, beside the disappointing salary.
    b. Kyle turned down the job offer for several reasons, besides the disappointing salary.
    c. Kyle turned down the job offer on account of the disappointing salary, along with several other reasons.
    d. Kyle turned downed the job offer because of the disappointing salary, and several other reasons.
    e. Kyle turned down the job offer for many reasons, not to mention the disappointing salary.

12. In his cautionary speech about the economy, the Senator eluded to problems with inflation, interest rates, and the depressed housing market.

    a. the Senator eluded to problems with inflation, interest rates, and the depressed housing market.
    b. the Senator eluded to problems relating to inflation, interest rates, and the depressed housing market.
    c. the Senator eluded to problems relating to inflation and interest rates, along with the depressed housing market.
    d. the Senator alluded to problems with inflation, interest rates, and the depressed housing market.
    e. the Senator alluded to inflation, interest rates, and the depressed housing market, which are all problematical.

13. Buying retail is more expensive and less satisfaction than to buy at a wholesale warehouse.

    a. Buying retail is more expensive and less satisfaction than to buy at a wholesale warehouse.
    b. Buying retail is more expensive and less satisfactory to me than to buy at a wholesale warehouse.
    c. Buying retail is more expensive and less satisfying that buying at a wholesale warehouse.
    d. To buy retail is more expensive and less satisfaction than to buy at a wholesale warehouse.
    e. Buying at a wholesale warehouse is less expensive but less satisfactory than buying retail.

14. By the time Alicia retires, which will probably be in 2007, her granddaughter will have been living with her for nine years.

    a. will have been living
    b. will have lived
    c. will be living
    d. would have lived
    e. would have been living

15. The phenomena. although intriguing, was a source of frustration for the eminent scientists.

   a.   The phenomena, although intriguing, was a source of frustration for the eminent scientists.
   b.   The intriguing phenomena was a source of frustration for the imminent scientists.
   c.   The phenomenon, although intriguing, were a source of frustration for the imminent scientists.
   d.   The phenomenon, although intriguing, was a source of frustration for the imminent scientists.
   e.   The phenomena, although intriguing, were a source of frustration for the eminent scientists.

16. Bill can give the prize to whomever he wants.

   a.   whomever he wants
   b.   whoever he wants
   c.   whichever person he chooses
   d.   whomever works the hardest
   e.   whoever is best

17. If my great-grandfather was to see our family farm today, he would be stunned by the high prices of utilities and real estate.

   a.   was to see
   b.   were to see
   c.   had seen
   d.   will see
   e.   would see

18. The players will eat dinner with the cheerleaders and me after the game.

   a.   cheerleaders and me
   b.   cheerleaders and I
   c.   me and the cheerleaders
   d.   I and the cheerleaders
   e.   both I and the cheerleaders

Directions: The following sentences test your ability to recognize grammar and usage errors. Each sentence contains either a single error of no error at all. No sentence contains more than one error. The error, if there is one, is underlined and lettered. If the sentence contains an error, select the one underlined part that must be changed to make the sentence correct. If the sentence is correct, select choice E. In choosing answers, follow the requirements of standard written English.

Example: The other students and Julie reluctantly accepted the offer to eat more early.
             A   B   C   D
No error
   E

The correct answer is D.

19. Going to school and keeping up with homework are important to academic success.
        A   B   C   D
No error
   E

20. What happens is going to surprise all of you.
        A   B   C   D
No error
   E

220

21. <u>My father, mother and sister</u> <u>insists that</u> Christopher Columbus died in 1532, <u>despite</u>
          A   B   C

<u>all evidence</u> <u>to the contrary</u>.
            D

<u>No error</u>
  E

22. <u>Once a teenager</u> <u>starts to smoke</u>, <u>it will most likely he</u> <u>will continue to do so</u>.
       A   B   C   D

<u>No error</u>
  E

23. <u>Along with</u> language, economics and political persuasion, <u>sociologists insist</u>
    A   B

<u>that</u> culture, including eclectic views <u>on spirituality</u>, <u>are integral</u> to personality
                                         C   D

development.

<u>No error</u>
  E

24. My grandmother <u>tried not to encourage</u> rivalry between <u>my sister and I</u>,
                       A   B

<u>because</u> she feared it <u>would ruin</u> our subsequent relationship.
  C   D

<u>No error</u>
  E

25. The licensing requirements for physicians <u>include</u> a test of the candidate's <u>didactic</u>
                                         A   B

<u>learning</u>, <u>clinical skills</u> and <u>research proficiency</u>.
             C   D

<u>No error</u>
  E

26. The <u>eminent director, whose childhood</u> in Canada <u>was the</u>
                    A   B

<u>inspiration</u> <u>for his many films</u> <u>about rural</u> challenges.
                    C   D

<u>No error</u>
  E

27. The contract <u>that the union workers</u> <u>agreed with</u> <u>was</u> an inspiration to <u>its myriad</u> members.
                        A   B   C   D

<u>No error</u>
  E

28. After careful deliberation <u>among all parties</u>, including a heated discussion <u>about</u>
                                   A

<u>the true spirit of community</u>, <u>a decision was made</u> <u>to proceed with the development</u>.
           B   C   D

<u>No error</u>
  E

29. The guests at the funeral <u>became</u> angry and confused <u>when the flag</u> failed <u>to</u>
                              A   B

<u>raise</u> <u>in honor of</u> the decorated war veteran.
  C   D

<u>No error</u>
  E

30. The Field Museum in Chicago <u>includes</u> an impressive collection
                               A

<u>of natural history exhibits and artifacts</u>, which <u>are complimented by</u>
                  B   C

native drawings <u>from each region</u>.
                D

<u>No error</u>
  E

31. <u>Although</u> several students <u>recommended</u> the hotel <u>to Jane</u>, her experience
        A   B   C

there was <u>different than what</u> she expected.
              D

<u>No error</u>
  E

32. <u>If I was her</u>, <u>I would lay my glasses</u> <u>on the table</u> <u>before I greeted</u> the dog.
        A   B   C   D

<u>No error</u>
  E

33. Janice <u>was so excited</u> <u>about being named</u> Prom Queen <u>that she couldn't hardly</u> <u>get to sleep</u>
           A   B   C   D

that night.

<u>No error</u>
  E

34. <u>In spite of Jenny wanting</u> to go <u>to the mall</u>, her mother <u>drove her straight home</u> from
                  A   B   C

school <u>to work on her</u> assignment.
          D

<u>No error</u>
  E

35. The models <u>will double</u> their workouts <u>in their efforts</u> <u>at slimming down</u> <u>before</u> the show.
              A   B   C   D

<u>No error</u>
  E

STOP

The answers to these questions are presented in Section WA7 (page 285)

The answer keys are arranged in the following order:

Critical Reading:

Answer keys RC1 – RC13 correspond to Reading Comprehension sections Read 1 – Read 13

Quantitative:

Answer keys QA1 – QA30 correspond to Quantitative sections Quant 1 – Quant 30

Writing:

Answer keys WA1 – WA7 correspond to Writing sections Writing 1 – Writing 7

RC1: Answer Key for Reading Comprehension 1

Sentence Completion

1. In this sentence, the correct word would be a synonym for magnitude, gravity or significance. Hence, answer choice D, enormity, is correct.

2. In this case, we are looking for a word that means generous or benevolent. The correct choice is answer C, munificent.

3. Here, we are seeking a positive word that relates to good performance in the workplace. The correct answer choice is B, "assiduous," which means "hard working."

4. The sentence provides plenty of key words that indicate that the first missing word is a negative one that describes the fraudulent strategies to overstate earnings at Enron. We can also conclude that the second missing word describes the type of agent who could understand (and decipher) these strategies. The correct answer, Choice C, is perfectly understandable; none of the other combinations makes a bit of sense.

5. In this question, the only key words are authority in mathematics and Nobel Prize winner. Further, there are no words that indicate a contrast, which leads us to believe that both words will go in the same direction. At first blush, the topic of the sentence seems to indicate that the words must be positive. After all, this is a Nobel Prize winner we are talking about.

Look again. There is nothing in this sentence that indicates tone, which means that **any** set of answer choices in which the words go in the same direction is fair game. Students who immediately assume that the first word HAS to be positive would eliminate answer choice E, which is the correct answer. Once they did, they would find themselves with answer choices that made little or no sense.

6. The correct answer is a synonym for rebellious, which is choice D, hedonistic

7. The correct word means strongly, which is choice D, vehemently.

8. The correct word means psychic, which is choice C, clairvoyant.

9. The correct word means selflessness, which is choice E, generosity.

10. The first word means active, while the second means many; the best choice is E, prolific – numerous.

11. The word means to satisfy, which is choice C.

12. The two words are opposites; the best choices is A, urbane – minimal.

13. The correct answer is the opposite of simple, which is choice D, elegant.

Passage-Based Reading

14. Choice B is correct. The objective of the passage is to discuss the nutritional value and health benefits of fruits and vegetables.

15. Choice D is correct. In context, neutralize mean to defuse or render harmless.

16. Choice D is correct. All of the other choices are listed in the passage as coal foods.

17. Choice A is correct. All of the other answer choices are mentioned in the passage.

18. Choice E is correct. The answer is presented on Line 20.

19. Choice C is correct. All of the other answer choices are mentioned it the passage.

20. Choice C is correct. The author is enthusiastic about the importance of fruits and vegetables in the human diet.

21. Choice B is correct. The other choices are either too broad or too specific in scope.

22. Choice C is correct. The answer is presented in the first two lines of the passage.

23. Choice D is correct. The first paragraph defines flotsam and jetsam.

24. Choice D is correct. The second paragraph explains the rights of the Crown.

25. Choice C is correct. The passage offers legal definitions of flotsam and jetsam. It was most likely intended for an academic audience.

RC2: Answer Key for Reading Comprehension 2

Sentence Completion

1. The word *although* indicates a contrast. Another clue in the sentence is the word *notorious*, which means famous in a negative way. Therefore, we can conclude that the missing word means the opposite of generous. The correct answer choice would be a synonym for cheap or tight-fisted, which is A, parsimonious.

2. The semi-colon in this sentence, along with the word *moreover*, indicates that the second clause will amplify the first. Another clue is the word *condescending*, which describes the negative attitude to which Michael's classmates are responding. Our missing word, therefore, must be a synonym for alienate, which is answer choice E.

3. In this sentence, we are looking for a word that means the opposite of ebullient (lively and excited). Acceptable words would be any terms that convey shyness or social awkwardness. The correct answer choice is A, *melancholy*.

4. The first word means worried, while the first means sudden; the closest answer choice is B, apprehensive – unexpected.

5. The word means the same as loyal, which is choice C, steadfast.

6. The word means avoided or shunned, which is choice D, ostracized.

7. The first word means secret, while the second means suspicious; the best answer is choice D, clandestine – suspicious.

8. The first word means hardworking, while the second word means lazy; the best answer is choice D, diligent – mediocre.

9. The correct word means courage, which is choice C.

Passage-Based Reading

10. Choice B is correct. The passage discusses the ownership and use of Kenilworth Castle from ancient times until modern day

11. Choice E is correct. All of the other answer choices are mentioned in Lines 4 – 5.

12. Choice D is correct. In context, *partisans* means followers.

13.Choice A is correct. All of the other answer choices are mentioned in Lines 10 – 14. Choice A is actually a trick question, though – it contains the name of the wrong Earl (Clarendon versus Leicester).   Be careful.

14.Choice C is correct. The answer is stated directly on Line 21.

15.Choice E is correct. In context, *priory* means monastery.

16. Choice B is correct. The answer is stated directly in Line 25.

17. Choice D is correct. The answer is stated in Lines 5 – 7.

18. Choice E is correct. In context, *putrefaction* means disintegration.

19. Choice B is correct. The other answer choices are presented in Lines 9 - 14.

Sentence Completion

1. The correct answer is a word that means generous, which is answer choice E, effusive.

2. The correct answer is a word that means humble or unassuming. Choice E (demure) is the best answer.

3. The correct answer is a word that means original or innovative. Hence, choice D (original) is correct.

4. The correct answer means sad, which is choice E, plaintive.

5. The two words are opposites; the correct answer is choice C, sophisticated – simple.

6. The correct answer is a negative word for excessive, which is choice E, gratuitous.

7. The correct answer means emotionally upset, which is choice C, devastated.

8. The two words support each other; the best answer is choice E, justified – astronomical.

9. The word means independent, which is choice C, self-reliant.

10. The first word is positive, while the second is negative; the correct choice is C, elation – tempered.

11. The correct answer means non-peaceful, which is choice D, turbulent.

Passage-Based Reading

12. Choice D is correct. The main point of the passage is to discuss the regulations regarding meat consumption in Europe during the sixteenth century. The other answer choices are wrong in scope.

13. Choice D is correct. The answer is presented in Lines 3 – 4.

14. Choice A is correct. In this context, axiom means a maxim, saying, or proverb.

15. Choice B is correct. The other answer choices are all presented in Lines 20 - 21.

16. Choice C is correct. Parricide means the murder of a relative.

17. Choice B is correct. The passage is an excerpt from a history book.

18. Choice D is correct. The other answer choices are limited in scope.

19. Choice E is correct. The author presents the answer in Line 4.

20. Choice C is correct. The author presents the answer in Lines 10 – 11.

21. Choice C is correct. This is common knowledge from geography and history classes.

22. Choice E is correct. The author presents the answer in Line 13.

23. Choice D is correct. The author presents the answer in Lines 17 – 19.

24. Choice A is correct. The passage discusses the origins and uses of all three temperate scales.

RC4: Answer Key for Reading Comprehension 4

Sentence Completion

1. The word because indicates both support and explanation. Hence, we know that the second part of the sentence will follow the same direction as the first part. The second clue is dollar signs, which tells us that the missing word is a synonym for lucrative or well paying (Choice C).

2. In this sentence, the missing word is a verb that means to satisfy, appease or compensate. The correct answer is D, or placate.

3. The correct answer is a synonym of cautious, which is prudent, answer choice B.

4. The correct word means quiet or alone, which is choice E, solitary.

5. The correct word means unavoidable, which is choice C, inevitable.

6. The correct word means praised, which is choice B, commended.

7. The words are opposites; the best answer is choice E, proclivity – sabotaged.

8. The first word is negative, while the second means slim; the correct choice is A, insidious – minimal.

9. The correct word means includes many styles, or choice C, eclectic.

Passage-Based Reading

10. Choice C is correct. The main point of the passage is stated in the final line. If the Italian cities had unified rather than quarreled, they might have maintained their liberty.

11. Choice A is correct. The answer is on Line 3.

12. Choice D is correct. The answers are mentioned in Lines 4 – 6.

13. Choice E is correct. The answer is presented in Lines 11 – 14.

14. Choice C is correct. In this context, regeneration means renewal.

15. Choice B is correct. All of the other answer choices are mentioned in Lines 19 – 20.

16. Choice D. The answer is presented in Line 21.

17. Choice A is correct. In this context, enfranchised means free.

18. Choice E is correct. In this context, the word yokes means oppression.

19. Choice C is correct. The author presents the information in a neutral tone.

Sentence Completion

1. The missing word indicates that the witness disputed the defendant's self-serving statements. The correct answer is B, repudiated.

2. The correct word is choice E, dolorous, which means extremely sad.

3. The correct word means uncertain or scary. The correct answer is E, suspenseful.

4.. The word banal indicates that the second word will be negative, while the word after suggests that the first word will be positive. The correct answer choice is D, captivating – disappointed.

5. The word despite indicates that the missing word will be a synonym for positive. The correct answer is D, enthusiastically.

6. The word although denotes contrast, which means we are looking for a word that means unlikely to keep a promise. The correct answer is A, skeptical.

7. In this sentence, the word won tells us that the first word is positive. Likewise, the word although indicates that the second word is negative. The correct choice is B.

8. We are looking for two words that go in the same direction. Ironically, in this case, they are not positive words. The correct answer choice is C, because a reluctant reader eschews all types of books.

9. The strongest clue is for even the largest family, which indicates that the second word is a synonym for large. The correct answer choice is C, opulent – spacious.

Passage-Based Reading

10. Choice A is correct. All of the other choices are mentioned in Lines 1 – 3.

11. Choice D is correct. In this context, deficit means deficiency.

12. Choice D is correct. The other choices are mentioned in Passage A (Lines 15 – 17 and Lines 31 – 35).

13. Choice B is correct. In this context, audit means examination.

14. Choice C is correct. The author explains his position in Lines 53 – 55.

15. Choice E is correct. The author is objective in tone.

16. Choice B is correct. The other choices are either too broad or too narrow in scope.

17. Choice A is correct. The answer is in Lines 69 – 70.

18. Choice D is correct. In this context, pretty up means to falsify (to deliver an artificial result).

19. Choice D is correct. McCormack was referring to the investor response to poor financial numbers.

20. Choice B is correct. All of the other choices are mentioned in Lines 91 – 98.

21. Choice E is correct. The answer is mentioned in Lines 94 – 95.

22. Choice D is correct. The answer is in Lines 100 – 105. Cross-cultural training is not mentioned.

23. Choice B is correct. The answer is in Line 107.

24. Choice A is correct. Passage A focused exclusively on the criminal charges that resulted from Enron. Passage B, on the other hand, presents ways to prevent similar scandals in the future.

RC6: Answer Key for Reading Comprehension 6

Sentence Completion

1. The correct word means difficult, which is choice D, onerous.

2. The correct word means careful, which is choice B, meticulous.

3. The correct word means beautiful, which is choice A, enchanting.

4. The correct word means opposite, which is choice B, antithesis.

5. The first word means natural or hidden, while the second means appeared. The correct choice is C latent-emerge.

6. The first word means honor or obey, while the second means courage. The correct choice is C, adhere-courage.

7. The correct choice means mentally unbalanced or confused, which is choice B, delusional.

8. The correct answer is a synonym for warring, which is A, contentious.

9. The words will be opposites of each other; the correct choice is D, prestigious- charlatan.

Passage-Based Reading

10. Choice C is correct. The answer is in Line 8.

11. Choice E is correct. The answer is in Line 10.

12. Choice A is correct. On Line 41, the author reports that 97% of stolen laptops are NOT recovered.

13. Choice E is correct. All of the other devices are mentioned in the passage.

14. Choice B is correct. In this context, sensitive means classified.

15. Choice A is correct. The answer is in Line 44.

16. Choice D is correct. The other choices are mentioned in Lines 56 – 59.

17. Choice C is correct.   According to Lines 65 – 66, the laptop can only be traced if the thief logs onto the Internet, when its location can be determined from its IP number. If the thief does not log onto the Internet, the unit cannot be traced.

18. Choice A is correct. The serial number corresponds with the ownership certificate, which identifies the registered user of the laptop.

19. Choice D is correct. The author states this conclusion in the final sentence of the passage.

Sentence Completion

1. The correct word means documentation, which is choice B, evidence.

2. The correct word means fickle, which is choice E, capricious.

3. The correct word means benefits, which is choice A.

4. The correct answer means many, which is choice C, plethora.

5. The correct word means excitement, which is choice D, exuberance.

6. The correct answer means the opposite of dedicated, which is choice E, cavalier.

7. The correct answer is a synonym for angry, which is choice E, irate.

8. The first word means fast or sophisticated, while the second word means the opposite; the correct combination is choice C, sophistication- mundane.

9. The correct answer is the opposite of liberal, or D, conservative.

10. Both words are positive; the correct choice is D, passionately- leniency.

11. The words will be similar to each other; the correct choice is E, support- adhered to.

12. The correct answer means strong or unpleasant, which is choice B, noxious.

Passage-Based Reading

13. Choice C is correct. The other answer choices are either too broad or too narrow in scope.

14. Choice C is correct. In Line 3, the author cites the fast speed of the test, which is the greatest advantage for law enforcement applications.

15. Choice D is correct. In this context, burgeoning means expanding.

16. Choice A is correct. The passage mentions all of the other crimes in Lines 5 – 6.

17. Choice D is correct. The FDA has not yet approved the test for over-the-counter sales.

18. Choice D is correct. The final statement in the passage confirms the author's enthusiasm about GeneTropy.

19. The main point of the passage is to explain the botanical classification of the coffee plant. Choice B is correct.

20. Lines 1 -3 mention all of the places that are listed except Slovakia. Choice B is correct.

21. Lines 5 -6 state that the aggeion is at the base of the flower. Choice C is correct.

22. According to Lines 18 – 20, the cambium produces the cells that create the annual ring, which allow us to age the tree. Choice D is correct.

23. A corolla is a petal. Choice C is correct.

24. According to Lines 35 – 37, all are Rubiaceæ except cacao. Choice A is correct.

RC8: Answer Key for Reading Comprehension 8

Sentence Completion

1. The correct answer means uncertain, which is choice B, tentative.

2. The correct answer means made worse, which is choice E, exacerbated.

3. The word considering indicates contrast; the correct answer choice is C, surprising.

4. The correct answer is the opposite of shy, which is choice B, garrulous.

5. The correct word means artificial or dishonest, which is choice A, disingenuous.

6. The word despite indicates contrast, which means that the correct answer means steadfast or resolute; the best choice is D, immutable.

7. The two words are opposites; the first means indirect, while the second means honest. The correct answer choice is, B, evasive – candor.

Passage-Based Reading

8. Choice E is correct. The remaining choices are not the correct scope to be the main idea of the passage.

9. Choice D is correct. In this context, veracious means truthful.

10. Choice A is correct. All of the other choices are mentioned in the third paragraph (Lines 8 – 13).

11. Choice B is correct. In this context, belie means contradict.

12. Choice E is correct. St. Bernard thought the jugglers were debauched or amoral (Lines 20 – 23).

13. Choice C is correct. The answer is presented in Line 27.

14. Choice D is correct. The other answer choices are too narrow in scope.

15. Choice E is correct. In this context, elegant means refined and efficient.

16. Choice C is correct. He had a stake in DC current only.

17. Choice B is correct. DC current could not transform high voltages over a long distance at a low cost.

18. Choice D is correct. The author does not discuss the safety issues related to electricity.

19. Choice A is correct. In this context, championed means advocated or supported.

RC9: Answer Key for Reading Comprehension 9

Sentence Completion

1. The correct word means the same as less expensive, which is choice A, economical.

2. The correct word means soon, which is choice E, imminent.

3. The correct answer is the opposite of simple, which is choice C, ornate.

4. The correct answer means bad or insulting, which is choice C, disparaging.

5. The correct word means quiet, which is choice A, introverted.

Passage-Based Reading

6. Choice B is correct. The other choices are either too broad or too narrow in scope.

7. Choice D is correct. The tone is light and airy.

8. Choice C is correct. The author opens with the quote, then explains why she disagrees with it.

9. Choice C is correct. All of the other choices are mentioned in the passage.

10. Choice C is correct. The term gray ghost refers to the weimaraner breed.

11. Choice E is correct. The author lists the descriptors of cat lovers in Lines 31 and 32.

12. Choice A is correct. The overall theme of the essay is the author's love for two different types of animals. Hence, the best title is one in which she states her refusal to choose. Choice C, while tempting, is not the BEST title for the passage, because only a portion of it mentions her family home.

13. Choice C is correct. Although both passages are related to childhood memories and grandparents, the topic is more specific than that. Choice E is tempting, but the legacy only relates closely to the first essay in the pair, in which the author explains that she began to keep a journal because her mother and grandmother did the same.

14. Choice E is correct. The answer is presented in the first paragraph of Passage A.

15. Choice D is correct. The other choices are presented in the first paragraph of Passage A.

16. Choice A is correct. The author is sensitive and insightful. She enjoys looking inward.

17. Choice E is correct. In this context, therapeutic means healthy.

18. Choice B is correct. The answer is presented in Line 25.

19. Choice D is correct. Passage B mentions all of the answer choices except this one.

20. Choice C is correct. The answer is presented in the first two lines of Passage B.

21. Choice C is correct. The author kept the chair because it reminded her of her wonderful times with her grandmother (Lines 34 – 35).

22. Choice A is correct. Rambling means spacious.

23. Choice B is correct. The other choices are all mentioned in Lines 32 and 34.

24. Choice A is correct. Both authors derive strength from their tangible reminders of their loved ones.

RC10: Answer Key for Reading Comprehension 10

Sentence Completion

1. The correct answer means prove, which is choice C, substantiate.

2. The correct answer means unresolved issue or, choice D, schism.

3. The correct word means exact, which is choice C, precise.

4. The correct word means seriously ill or immobile, which is choice D, debilitating.

5. The two words are both negative; the correct answer is choice D, distort – erroneous.

Passage-Based Reading

6. Choice B is correct. The other answer choices are too narrow in scope.

7. Choice C is correct. The early birds are the first ants on the scene, which secret pheromones that subsequent ants can detect.

8. Choice C is correct. Grass is a bad environment for ants, because of the risk of pesticide treatment.

9. Choice A is correct. It provides the benefits of a sidewalk in a densely populated area, where people are likely to drop food.

10. The passage explains the importance of language in society, including the need to master it in order to speak and write effectively. The best answer is Choice C – the others are incorrect in focus and scope.

11. According to Shenstone, those with the least to say tend to speak the most. Choice B is correct.

12. In context, the word "faculty" means power. Choice E is correct.

13. Taciturnity means reluctant or disinclined to talk. Choice B is correct.

14. In paragraph two, Lines 14 -16, the author reveals that Charles enjoyed Butler's work but found him dull in person. Choice C is correct.

15. According to Line 27, carelessness in grammar is inexcusable. Choice B is correct.

16. The passage directly states (in Lines 27 – 28) that language is the greatest of sciences and using words is the greatest human arts. Choice C is correct.

17. In the passage, the word "instruments" refers to the words a person uses to make is point. Choice A is correct.

18. In the passage, the word "almonder" means the source or distributor of knowledge. Choice C is correct.

19. According to the passage, "counterfeit coins" are words that are either incorrect or ill-suited to the situation. Choice C, slang, is the best answer.

Sentence Completion

1. The correct word means the opposite of attract; the best answer choice is D, repel.

2. The correct word means lacking, which is choice C, devoid.

3. The correct word is the opposite of athletic, which is choice D, sedentary.

Passage-Based Reading

4. Choice C is correct. The other choices are either too broad or narrow in scope.

5. Choice E is correct. It is clearly an article of interest for computer owners and users.

6. Choice B is correct. All of the other choices were mentioned in the second paragraph of the passage.

7. Choice E is correct. The author suspected that Lee was motivated by all three factors.

8. Choice D is correct. The author felt that Lee was living proof of Einstein's warning.

9. Choice B is correct. The author's answer is in Line 27 of the passage.

10. Choice C is correct. The article is factual in tone, citing Lee's good deeds and bad deeds.

11. Choice B is correct. In this context, the phrase is a metaphor.

12. Choice C is the best answer. Choices A and B are true, but are less specific.

13. Choice D is correct. The watch originally belonged to the author's paternal grandfather. All of the other choices are mentioned in the passage.

14. Choice B is correct. In this context, aesthetically means visually pleasing.

15. Choice D is correct. In this context, impending means imminent.

16. Choice E is correct. The author never specifically states who gave her the ring after her mother's death.

17. Choice D is correct. The answer is presented in Line 22.

18. Choice A is correct. In this context, the word infinite means unlimited.

19. Choice E is correct. Lines 4 - 5 specifically state that the watch was not visually pleasing; its value to the author was sentimental.

RC12: Answer Key for Reading Comprehension 12

Sentence Completion

1. The correct words are synonyms; Choice E is correct.

2. The correct word means fearful of small spaces, or choice C, claustrophobic.

3. The correct word means well-known, which is choice A, notorious.

4. The correct word means enhanced, which is choice C.

5. The correct word means excessive, or choice D.

6. The correct word is discretion, or choice C.

Passage-Based Reading

7. Choice A is correct. The other choices are the wrong scope for the passage.

8. Choice D is correct.

9. Choice C is correct.

10. Choice E is correct.

11. Choice D is correct. The material is technical in nature.

12. Choice E is correct. The main point of the passage is to explain the worldwide appeal of coffee.

13. Choice E. In context, corollary means source.

14. Choice D is correct. All of the other answer choices are mentioned in Lines 13 – 14.

15. Choice A is correct. In context, adjuvant means helpful or supportive.

16. Choice C is correct. The answer is stated in Lines 21 – 22.

17. Choice B is correct. Dr. Wiley feels that coffee substitutes are woefully inadequate.

18. Choice D is correct. The author is overwhelmingly enthusiastic about coffee's appeal.

19. Choice C is correct. The passage contains basic information and is light in tone; it was written for a general audience.

Sentence Completion

1. The correct answer means unbiased, which is choice B, neutrality.

2. The correct word means eager to sue, which is choice D, litigious.

3. The correct answer means inspired, which is choice D, motivated.

4. The two words are both negative; the best answer is choice B, criminal – ruined.

5. The correct word means destroyed, which is choice C, eroded.

Passage-Based Reading

6.   Choice A is correct. The answer is stated directly in Line 42.

7. Choice E is correct. In context, supplant means supersede.

8. Choice B is correct. The answer is stated in Lines 14 – 18.

9. Choice D is correct. In this context, libertine means morally depraved or dissolute.

10. Choice D is correct. All of the other answer choices are presented in Lines 20 – 28.

11. Choice D is correct. The passage is an excerpt from a psychology textbook. The tone and subject matter of the passage do not match the other four answer choices.

12. Choice E is correct. The main point of the passage is to discuss the historical evolution of the corset in women's fashion.

13. Choice C is correct. In context, cestus means girdle.

14. Choice D is correct. All of the other countries are mentioned in the passage.

15. Choice A is correct. In context, abomination means disgrace.

16. Choice B is correct. The answer is stated directly in Lines 11 – 16.

17. Choice A is correct. All of the other answer choices are mentioned in the passage.

18. Choice C is correct. All of the other answer choices are mentioned in Lines 37 – 42.

19. Choice D is correct. The author is clear that corsets are uncomfortable and unsafe.

QA1: Answer Key for Quantitative 1

1. To solve this problem, we must determine the average rate: Average Rate = Total Distance / Total Time. In this case, the test writers did not give us any specific values for distance, so we are free to pick our own. Let's assume that the total distance Pamela traveled is 100 miles, which makes each half of the trip equal to 50 miles.

For the trip from Ames Street to Alvin Circle, the Average Rate = 50 miles/ 35 miles per hour = 1.429 hours. For the return trip, the Average Rate = 50 miles / 18 miles per hour = 2.778 hours. Hence, the total time was 4.207 hours.

Going back to the original equation, for the total trip, the Average Rate = Total Distance / Total Time = 100 miles/4.207 hours = 23.77 = 24 miles per hour. The correct answer choice is C.

2. The mode is the value that occurs most frequently in the set of data. To find it, we must first arrange the values in ascending order: 28, 34, 36, 42, 43, 44, 45, 47, 54, 56, 56, 65, 67, 81, 89. Here, the mode is 56. D

3. Here, we are given current ages and asked to calculate a time when those numbers met a specified set of criteria. Liz = 42, Amelia = 24. The correct equation to express the relationship between their ages x years ago is therefore: $42 - x = 3 (24 - x)$, so $42 - x = 72 - 3x$, or $2x = 30$. $x = 15$ Choice C is correct.

4. In this case, we must solve the equation for the total time (T) that is needed to complete the job. First, figure the amount of work that each girl does as a percentage of the total amount:

Gina   Rate x Time = Work   (1/2) times T = ½ T
Hillary   Rate x Time = Work   (1/3) times T = 1/3T

Now, add them together to figure the total time for the job:

½ T + 1/3 T = 1 or 3/6T + 2/6T =1 or 3T + 2T = 5T = 6

Solving for T, we find that they can complete the job in 1.2 hours if they work together, or 72 minutes. Answer choice C is correct.

5. Many students are intimidated by this question because it uses variables instead of actual numbers. Don't let this throw you. We can solve the problem using a simple proportion. U/M =?/N   ? = NU/M. Choice B is correct.

Alternatively, we can plug numbers into the equation for the variables and see what happens. Let's let M = 10 and U = $100. The cost of a single I=Pod is therefore $100/10, or U/M. If N = 5, the cost of N I=Pods will be 5(U/M), or NU/M

6. First, we must convert our room measurements into yards: 18 feet = 6 yards, while 36 feet = 12 yards. Therefore, the area of Doug's room is (6)(12) = 72 square yards. (72)(25) = $1800. Choice C is correct.

7. This is easiest to solve using simultaneous equations. $X + Y = 48$ and $X - Y = 12$. When we add these equations together, we get $2X = 60$. $X = 30$ and $Y = 18$. Choice A is correct.

8. Area = ½ (12)(12) =72   Choice D is correct.

9. A sector is a piece of the area of a circle. If *n* is the degree measure of the sector's central angle, then the formula is: Area of a Sector = $(n/360)(\pi)(r)(r)$. Here, Area = $(24/360)(\pi)(8)(8) = 13.4$. Choice A is correct.

10. The area of a square is L x W. The difference between the areas for these two squares is (14)(14) – (12)(12) = 196 – 144 = 52. Choice B is correct.

11. $(3/6 + 4/2)^3 =$ $(5/2)(5/2)(5/2) = 125/8 = 15.625$. Choice C is correct.

12. Choice E, 1050.

13. Convert all fractions to the form with an LCD of 30. The sum is: $2/30 + 6/30 + 12/30 + 10/30 + 3/30 = 33/30 = 11/10$. Choice A is correct.

14. (0.6) 15,600= 9,360. Choice E is correct.

15. For a 2:1 ratio, the whole is 3. 2/3 of 300 = 200 singers, 1/3 of 300 = 100 dancers. Choice B is correct.

16. If $x^2 - y^2 = 16$, then $(x +y)(x - y) = 16$. If $(x - y) = 2$, then $(x + y) = 16/2 = 8$. Choice D is correct.

17. If $y = 10 + 2x$ and $y = 5x$, then $5x = 10 + 2x$, and $3x = 10$. So, $x = 10/3$. Choice C is correct.

18. The easiest way to solve this problem is to try each answer choice. We know that the product of X and Y is 30; the problem asks us to identify the *smaller* of the two numbers. Therefore, we will substitute each answer choice into the formula $(X + Y) - (X - Y) = 6$ to see which combination gives us the correct answer. When we do, we discover that $(10 + 3) - (10 - 3) = 6$. Additionally, $(10)(3) = 30$. The correct answer is 3, or choice B.

19. $(x^4y^7/x^5y^6)^4 = (y/x)^4$ $=y^4/x^4$. Choice B is correct.

20. There are four kings in a deck of 52 cards. Thus, the probability of choosing a king is 4/52, or 1/13. Choice C is correct.

QA2: Answer Key for Quantitative 2

1. The range is the positive difference between the smallest and largest values. In this case it is $98 - 12 = 86$. Choice D is correct.

2. The find the sum of the integers between 11 and 39, inclusive, we must use the formula, Sum = Average x Number of terms. The Average = $(11 + 39) / 2 = 25$. Number of terms = $39 - 11 + 1 = 29$. The Sum = 25 x 29 = 725. Choice C is correct.

3. Choice E is correct. The area of a rectangle does not give us enough information to calculate the perimeter.

4. A parabola opening upward. Choice B is correct.

5. $585 - 116 - 219 = 250$. $947 - 250 - 219 = 478$. Choice C is correct.

6. We can solve this using a proportion. 1 batch / 24 oz = x batches / 480 oz, so x = 20 times. Choice D is correct.

7. The home improvement store sold 240/300 generators, which means that (300 – 240)/300, or 60/300 did not sell. 60/300 can be reduced to **1/5**. Choice B is correct.

8. $(9-7)^3 = 8$. Choice B is correct.

9. Nancy = Cane - 3 and Cane = 35 + 8 = 43. So, Nancy = 43 – 3 = **40 years old.**

10. Use the Pythagorean theorem to find the length: $a^2 + b^2 = c^2$, or $16 + 64 = c^2$, which is the square root of 80, or **8.94**.

11. $41 + 43 + 47 = $ **131**

12. We must determine the total amount of money in the machines and subtract $50 to find the total bank deposit. 312 quarters = $78; 234 dimes = $23.40; 443 nickels = $22.15; 444 pennies = $4.44. 78 + 23.40 + 22.15 + 4.43 – 50.00 = **$77.99**.

13. 14/31 x 93/76 = (0.4516129)(1.22368) **= 0.553**.

14. $328 - 114 = 214/100 = $ **214% increase**.

15. 3/18 = 11/x, Solve for **x =66**.

16. To count the number of consecutive integers in a set, subtract the endpoints and add 1. In this case, 00435 - 00236 + 1 = **200.**

17. 8y = 24x + 16, so y = 3x + 2. The slope is **3.**

18. $(9^p)/(3^q) = (9) / (9) = $ **1**.

QA3: Answer Key for Quantitative 3

1. Choice A is correct. Average speed = Total distance / Total time. A car traveling at 75 mph will cover 150 miles in 2 hours. A car traveling at 50 mph covers the same 150 miles in 3 hours. The total travel time is therefore 5 hours. For the entire round trip, the average speed = (150 + 150) / 5 = 60 mph.

2. To solve, we just determine the difference in monthly payments. 1850/6 = $308.33 per month. 1850/15 = $123.33 per month. 308.33 – 123.33 = $185 difference. Choice C is correct.

3. Here, we must set up an equation that represents the sum of the interest from both bonds: Bond A + Bond B = Total Interest. Let's let x = Rate for A and x + 3 = Rate for B. Thus, our equation becomes: 4000x + 12000 (x +0.03) = 1600. If we solve for x, we find that x = 0.0775 = 7.75%. Bond A rate = 7.75%, Bond B = 10.75%. Choice E is correct.

4. We can solve this using a proportion. If 4 cans covered ¾ of one room, how many cans are needed to cover 3-1/4 rooms? 4 / 0.75 = x / 3.25. Solving for x = 17.3 additional cans. Choice C is correct.

5. The sum of the angles must equal 180. Thus, 4x + 5x + 6x = 180. Solving for x, we find that 15x = 180 or x=12. 4x = 48. Choice E is correct.

6.This rectangle is actually two 5-12-13 (10-24-26) triangles, in which the hypotenuse is the diagonal. The area is L x W, or 10 x 24 = 240. Choice B is correct.

7. If $f(v) = 5v^2$ - 1/8v – 3, then $f(v^3) = 5v^5$ - $1/8v^4$ – 3. Choice B is correct.

8. Slope = (10 – 3)/ (8 – 2) = 7/6. Choice C is correct.

9. 125 – 74 – 26 = 25   Choice A is correct.

10. Choice B is correct. The divisors of 60 that are prime numbers are 2,3 and 5. By definition, 1 is NOT prime.

11. Choice C is correct, 30.

12. If 0.06x = $4.32, then x = $72. Total price = $76.32. Choice D is correct.

13. The probability is 1/6, or Choice A.

14. For x = 0.1, $(1)^2$ + 100(0.01) = 2. Choice C is correct.

15. Area of Trapezoid = (Average of parallel sides) x Height. In this case, the area = {(16 + 18)/2} x (12) = (17)(12) = 204 cubic centimeters. Choice D is correct.

Alternatively, we calculate the areas of the to parts of the trapezoid (a triangle and a rectangle) and add them together. The area of the rectangle = (12)(16) = 192. The area of the triangle is ½ (2)(12) = 12. The total area is 576 + 96 = 672 cubic inches.

16. Probability = Number of Women/Number of People = 15/300 = 1/20. Choice C is correct.

QA4: Answer Key for Quantitative 4

1. In this case, we have three distinct groups, which must add up to 100%. Since the original two groups are 45% and 35%, the remaining group must be 20% of the total. Choice C is correct.

2. We can set up an equation using the information that is provided. In this case, x (x + 2) = 8(x+ 2) - 16, so x^2 + 2x = 8x + 16-16, or x^2 = 6x. So x = 6 and x+ 2 = 8. Choice A is correct.

3. The mustard would be used 1 ¾ (or 7/4) times as fast, which would deplete the supply in 4/7 the usual amount of time. 25 (4/7) = 14.3 days. Choice C is correct.

4. Volume = L x W x H, so 180,000 = (80)(120)(H), or H = 18.75 feet. 75% of 18.75 = 14.06 feet. Choice C is correct.

5. Let x be the length of the base. Perimeter = sum of all three sides = 90 = x + 2(3x - 4) = 7x – 8. Solve for x = 14. Choice B is correct.

6. If there is one adult for every five children, we must divide the capacity of the bus by 6, 124/6 = 20.6. Therefore, there can be no more than 20 children on the tour bus (4 groups, each of which contains one adult and 20 children). Choice A is correct.

7. The perimeter is simply the sum of the three side lengths, Therefore, we can solve the problem using the following equation: 35 + 40 + LN = 105. LN = 30. Choice A is correct.

8. Circumference = π x Diameter If the radius is 7, the circumference= 14π. Choice D is correct.

9. If a Ψ b = $(1 + b)^{1/2}$ then aΨ 15 = $(1 + 15)^{½}$ = 4. Choice C is correct.

10. This problem is a combination of two sub-series. In the first one, each term increases by 1 (3,4,5,6); in the second, each term increases by 2 (5,7,9,11). The next number would be 7. Choice D is correct.

11. If 113 is the mean, then it is the fifth in the series of nine consecutive odd numbers. We can simply count back to get the first in the series, which will be 105 (113 –111-109-107-105). Choice D is correct.

12. 2.05 x 8.99 x 54.22 = 999.25. Choice D is correct.

13. Choice D is correct. The three integers are 30, 60 and 90.

14. We can solve this problem using a simple proportion. First, we must determine the daily dose. 0.03125 / 3g = 1.00 / X, so X = 96 g = the daily dose of the medication. The weekly does is 96 x 7 = 672 g. Choice E is correct.

15. Choice D is correct. If 8 numbers have an average of 8, their sum is 64. Subtracting 2 from 4 of the numbers removes 2(4), or 8 from the sum. The new sum is 56 and the new mean is 56/8 =7.

16. 0.005% = 0.5/100 = 5/1000 = 1/200. Choice E is correct.

17. (2.646)(2.828)(3) = 22.45. Choice E is correct.

18. If x = 10, then x^2 + 1/x^2 = 100.+ 0.01 = 100.01. Choice B is correct.

19. Choice E is correct. First, factor the 5 out of the original equation and then divide each side by five. The trinomial y^2 – 4y + 3 factors into (y - 3)(y - 1) = 0. Setting each term to 0 yields y = 3 and y = 1. The difference is 2. Two times two equals 4.

20. x^2 – x = 12, or x^2 – x –12 = 0, or (x+3)(x-4) = 0. x =(-3, 4). Choice B is correct.

QA5: Answer Key for Quantitative 5

1. This can be solved by a simple equation: $11x - 3 = 140$, so $11x = 143$, so $x = 13$. Choice B is correct.

2. The area of the plot is 10 feet x 12 feet, or 120 square feet, or 17,280 square inches   The area of one tile is 1/2 inch x 3 inches = 1.5 square inches. The number of tiles needed = 17,280/1.5 = 11,520 tiles, which is answer choice C.

3. $V = L \times W \times H = 6 \times 14 \times 33 = 2772$ cubic inches

3.   The line has points (0,8) and (2,0). Slope = (0-8) / (2-0) = -4. Line = $y = -4x + 8$. Choice D is correct.

5. 18 x 14 = 252 minutes = 4.2 hours, or 4 hours and 12 minutes. Diane must leave home by 12:48 pm to complete the errands by 5:00 pm.   Choice C is correct.

6. $F \cup G$ = {1, 2, 4, 5, 6, 8, 9}. {1, 2, 4, 5, 6, 8, 9} $\cap$ {2, 6, 7, 10} = {2, 6}. Choice B is correct.

7. $(F \cup G) \cup H$ = {1, 2, 4, 5, 6, 7, 8, 9, 10}. Choice E is correct.

8. $(F \cup G) \cup H$ = {1, 2, 4, 5, 6, 7, 8, 9, 10}, which has 2^9 subsets, or 512. Choice B is correct.

9. We can solve this problem by using the following equation: $x + (x + 1) + (x + 2) + (x + 3) + (x + 4) = 235$, or $5x + 10 = 235$, so $x = 225/5$. The middle number is x+2, or **47.**

10. 180(8 – 2) = 1080 total degrees, so 80 + 90 + 105 + 120 + 125 + 130 + 135 + X = 1080. X = **295 degrees**.

11. **17**

12. 25P = 10(P + 45), or 15P = 450, or **P = 30**.

13. $4g^3 - 2k^2 + 9gk - 6 = (4 \times 2 \times 2 \times 2) - 2 (3)(3) + 9 (2)(3) - 6 = 32 - 18 + 54 - 6 = \textbf{62.}$

14. 3567 x 0.015 = **53.505**.

15. {(16)(101.7) + (23)(98.5)} / 39 = {1627.2 + 2265.5} / 39 = **99.8° F**

16. $84/7 (0.95 - 0.55)^2 = 12 (0.16) = \textbf{1.92}$.

17. Slope = (15 – 5)/ (6 – 4) = 10/2 = **5.**

18. To avoid counting students twice, we must divide them into four categories according to the following equation: Spanish + Math + Neither – Both = 80. Hence: 50 + 20 + Neither – 15 = 80. Neither = **25**.

QA6: Answer Key for Quantitative 6

1. A cube with a side of 30 feet has a volume of 30 x 30 x 30 = 27,000 cubic feet. Since 1 cubic foot = 7.8 gallons, 27,000 cubic feet = 210,600 gallons. If the faucet flows at a rate of 12 gallons per minute, it will take 17,550 minutes to fill the cube, or 292.5 hours. Answer choice B is correct.

2. 9x + 4x = 48000, or 13x = 48000, so x =3692.3. Edna's share = 4x = 14,769.23. Choice C is correct.

3. Choice D is correct. Let x be Cindy's age and x + 10 be Theresa's age. Five years ago, Cindy's age was x - 5 and Theresa's age was (x + 10) - 5 = x + 5. At that time, Theresa was twice as old as Cindy, which gives us the following equation: x + 5 = 2(x - 5). Solving for x, we get x = 15.

4. To determine the median, we must first, arrange the numbers in ascending order: 56, 67, 68, 72, 73, 78. Since there are an even number of values, we must take the average of the middle two numbers as our median. Here, it is 68 + 72, which have an average of 70. Choice C is correct.

5. Slope = (11-5)/(7-4) = 6/3 = 2. y-intercept = -3. Therefore, the equation for the line is y = 2x − 3. Choice E is correct.

6. The area of the original parallelogram = Base X Height. Let B = the length of the base and H = the height of the original parallelogram. If the base increases by 12%, it becomes 1.12B. If the height decreases by 18%, it becomes 0.82H. The new area is therefore: (1.12)B (0.82)H = 0.9184BH, which is 9.18% smaller than the original area. Choice A is correct.

7. The fastest way to solve this problem is to select values for the diameter of the circle and determine the effect on the area. If the diameter is 4, the radius is 2 and the area is 4 times π. Increasing the diameter by 50% to 6, makes the new radius = 3, and the new area is 9 times π. The percent increase is (9-4) / 4 = 5/4, or 125%. Choice D is correct.

8. 300/4 = 75. The final jelly bean in the vending machine will be green, or Choice D

9. The average is 0.932, which is Choice C.

10. 10 + 11 + 11 = 32 minutes en route. 11:04 – 32 minutes is 10:32 am. Choice B is correct.

11. In the first year, the price increased by 18%, which is 1000 + (18 percent of 1000) = 1180. The second year, the price increased by an additional 28%, which is 1180 + (28 percent of 1180, or 330.4) = 1510.40, or $1,511. Choice D is correct.

12. The most common mistake for this question is to simply add the two % and assume that you have the answer (50% + 20% = 70%). Wrong! Simply plugging in a few easy numbers will show us the error. Assume that the software originally cost $100. The first 50% discount reduces its price to $50. The second discount is 20% of $50, or $10, which reduces the price to $40. To calculate the *overall percentage* that the software has been reduced, we must use the original denominator of $100: $60/$100 = 60%. Choice B is correct.

13. 3^5 x 9^3 = 177,147, which is 3^{11}. Choice C is correct.

14. Just substitute each answer. X = 9. Choice D is correct.

15. If $x^3 − x = 0$, then $x(x^2 − 1) = 0$, so x(x-1)(x+1) = 0, so x =0, 1, -1. Choice C is correct.

16. (a + b −1) (a – b) = a^2 −ab + ab −b^2 −a +b = a^2 − a − b^2 + b. Choice A is correct.

QA7: Answer Key for Quantitative 7

1. To solve this problem, put the information into a grid and solve for the appropriate quantity. In this case, we are given many of the numbers - the rest we can fill-in. The problem asks us how many female students are studying marketing, which is 45, Choice C.

	Marketing	Finance	Total
Male	55	120	175
Female	45	80	125
Total	100	200	300

2. Let x = the original population. 0.62x = 1370000. Thus, x = 2,209,677. Choice C is correct.

3. Annuity A: ($750,000)(0.0845) = $63,375. Annuity B: ($750,000)(0.0865) = $64,875). $64,875 - $63375 = $1,500. Choice C is correct.

4. For this equation, we can simply use the equation for simple averages to find the missing number. 12 = (12 + 9 + 8 + 15 + 6 + 9 + 17 + 7 + x) / 9. So, 12 = (83 + x) / 9, so 108 = 83 + x, x = 25. Choice E is correct.

5. If f (d) = (d + 6)(d – 4), then f (9) = (9 + 6) (9 – 4) = (15)(5) = 75. Choice E is correct.

6. 100/7 = 14 + 2 remainder. Her birthday will fall on a Friday. (Wednesday + 2). Choice E is correct.

7. The pattern in this series is to increase by 3, then decrease by 1. Hence, the next term will be 11. Choice C is correct.

8. Let x = height of the box; length = 2x; width = 4x. $x(2x)(4x) = 8x^3 = 512$. Therefore, x = 4. Choice B is correct.

9. To solve, we use the formula to solve for the value of the missing angle: 79+ 80+ 95+147+152+ X = 720. X = 167. Choice E is correct.

10. Circumference of a circle = 2πr. In this case, $C = 2\pi(4444) = 2.79 \times 10^4$ Choice B is correct.

11. Let's assume the two numbers being averaged are x and y. From the problem, we know that (x + y)/2 = 8x – 24. If we "solve" this equation, we find that x + y = 16x – 48, or y = 15x – 48, which is Choice D. (To check, {x + (15x – 48)} / 2 = (16x – 48)/2 = 8x – 24.)

12. To answer this question, we must divide the total amount of material (55 yards) by the quantity needed to make a single dress (6-1/5 yards). When we do, we find that the seamstress has enough material to make 8 =87/100 dresses. Since she cannot sell a fraction of a dress, we must round our answer down to 8 dresses. Choice B is correct.

13. 2,000 / 2,000, 000 = 1/1000. Choice A is correct.

14. (3/4 x 800) + (1/6 x 600) = 600 + 100 = 700. Choice B is correct.

15. First, convert all of the fractions to decimal form. Then, arrange in descending order. The correct order is Choice D, 11/13, 12/15, 32/41, 21/27,48/63.

16. If 2x + 6y = 10 and 2x + 10y = 6, then we can subtract the equations to get –4y = 4, or y =-1. Choice C is correct.

17. Choice E is correct.

18. Jim's ticket was one of 16 tickets left in the bowl during the fifth drawing. His probability of winning the prize was 1/16, or 0.0625, which is 6.25%. The correct answer is E.

19. 4 x 4 x 4 = 64. Choice C is correct.

20. $12b^2 – 12 = 12(b^2 – 1) = 12(b – 1) (b + 1)$. Choice C is correct.

QA8: Answer Key for Quantitative 8

1. We will use the information to build an equation to solve for Grace's age. Let Grace's age = G. Thus, Sue's age is 2G, while Lee's age is G + 2. Since the sum of their ages is 58, G + 2G + (G + 2) = 58, or 4G + 2 = 58, so 4G = 56. Solving for G, Grace = 14, Lee = 16, Sue = 28. Choice B is correct.

2. Volume = (36)(6)(12) = 2,592 cubic inches x 3 oz/ inch = 7,776 oz./16 = 486 lbs. Choice B is correct.

3. They do not intersect. Choice E is correct.

4. Area = πr^2 = π (9)(9). Diameter = 9 + 9 = 18. Choice C is correct.

5. The repeating pattern is 04321, which includes 5 digits. The 49th digit is therefore the fourth digit in the series, which is 2, or Choice C.

6. 110/220 = ½. 22/220 = 1/10. 60% are from Hawaii & Canada. Therefore, 40% are not. Choice C is correct.

7. $8^{24} = 512^{16x}$, so $8^{24} = (8^3)^{16x}$, so 24 = 3(16x) = 48x, or x =2. Choice A is correct.

8. According to the problem, y = 4x − 5. If we solve for x, we find x = (y +5)/4. Choice B is correct.

9. Let x = the number of general tickets; therefore, the number of student tickets is 800 − x. The total ticket sales equals the sum of general and student tickets, so: 32.00x + 10.00(800 − x) = 12,400, so 32 x + 8000 − 10x = 12400, or 22x = 4400. x = 200 general tickets; 800 − 200 = **600 student tickets**.

10. Total expenses = 600 + 300 + 100 + 300 + 300 = 1600. 1600/2000 = 4/5, which leaves **1/5 for discretionary spending**.

11. 3x + 4x + 5x = 180, so 12x = 180, x = 15, 3x = 45, 4x = 60, 5x = **75**.

12. The equation factors into (x -5)(x+3) = 0. Setting each term to 0 yields x = 5 and -3. The difference between them is 8; twice this amount is **16**.

13. 5r + 27 = 45 − 3r + 27 − r, or 9r = 45, or **r = 5**.

14. The terms increase by 2, then decrease by 10. The next term will be **23**.

15. The prime numbers between 20 and 30 are 23 and 29. Their sum is **52.**

16. 1/40 = 0.025 x 100 = **2.5%.**

17. 714/7 = 21y/14, or 102 = 1.5y or **y = 68**.

18. Sesame seeds are 0.525 dollars per ounce. The cost for 50 pounds = (50)(16)(0.525) = $420 x 0.80 = **$336**.

1. We will use the information to build an equation to solve for Juliet's weight. The weights are consecutive even numbers, Hannah's weight =x, Juliet's weight = (x + 2) and Patricia's weight = (x + 4). By definition, (x+2) − 18 = {x + (x+4)} − 50, so our equation becomes x − 16 = 2x − 46. When we solve this for x, we find that x = 30, x + 2 = 32, x + 4 = 34. Since Juliet's weight (x+2) = 32, Choice D is correct.

2. Here, we must use the basic work equation to solve for Jake's time: 1/Time A + 1/Time B = 1/ Total time. 1/6 + 1/X = ¼. X = 12. Choice E is correct.

3. The perimeter of the lot is the sum of its six sides, or 24.5 + 12 + 9.75 + 11.9 + 34 + 21.6 = 113.75 feet / 3 = 37.9 yards. 37.9 x $36 = $1,365. Choice B is correct.

4. To answer, simply divide the total amount of sales by the cost per stamp: $2,313,716.10/0.41 = 5,643,210. Choice D is correct.

5. If (a) = 1 + 1/3 a, then f(30) = 1 + 1/ 3 (30) = 1 + 10 = 11. Choice C is correct.

6. To solve, find the value of x when y equals 0. The correct answer is 2, or Choice D.

7. To solve, we use the formula: 180 (X − 2) = 2,700. X = 17. Choice C is correct.

8. In this situation, the diagonal of the rectangle is equal to the diameter of the circle. Because the rectangle can also be viewed as two triangles that share the diagonal as a common side, we can use the Pythagorean theorem to calculate its length. Accordingly, the square of the diagonal is equal to (9)(9) + (16)(16) = 81 + 256 = 337. This means that the diameter of the circle is the square root of 337, or 18.36; the radius is therefore 9.18. Now, we can calculate the area of the circle, which is (9.18)(9.18)(π), = 84.3 π. Choice C is correct.

9. Let the numbers be n, n +2, n+4, n+6, n+8, n+10 and n+12. Their sum is 7n + 42, and their average, n + 6, equals 21. The largest number, n+12, is therefore 15 + 12 = 27, or Choice E.

10. The writers do not tell us anything about the original number of singers (male or female) or how many of them advanced to the next round. We simply have a ratio. Hence, the correct answer is E, we cannot determine the final ratio without additional information.

11. 12 courses (8 + 4) comprise ¾ of the curriculum, which means that there are 16 total courses. Of these, 4, or 1/4, are on software. Choice A is correct.

12. First, we must determine the first three numbers in the combination, which are equal to the sum of the first 40 even integers.

Sum = (Number of Items) (First Item + Last Item) / 2
Sum = (40)(2 + 40)/2 = (40)(42)/2 = 840 = first three digits of the combination

Next, we must determine the sum of the first 20 odd integers:

Sum = (Number of Items) (First Item + Last Item) / 2
Sum = (20)(1 + 20)/2 = (20)(21)/2 = 210 = second three digits of the combination

The final three digits in the combination are 840 − 210 = 630.
Therefore, the complete combination of the safe is 840210630. Choice E is correct.

13. The shipping carton is 3 feet long, 6 feet wide and 9 feet high. The formula for surface area is 2(L x W + L x H + W x H) = 2 { (3)(6) + (3)(9) + (6)(9) } = 2(18 + 27 + 54) = 2(99) = 198. Choice D is correct.

14. 5 x 5 = 25, which is the cubic root of 15,625. Choice B is correct.

15. $k^2 − 6k + 9 = (k − 3)^2$ Choice B is correct.

16. If $2x^3 − 3x^2 − 5x = 0$, then x $(2x^2 − 3x − 5) = 0$, so x (2x −5) (x+1) = 0. So, x = 0, -1, 5/2. Choice E is correct.

QA10: Answer Key for Quantitative 10

1. When cars travel at different speeds, they take different lengths of time to cover the same distance. Consequently, we cannot simply average the two speeds to get the correct answer. Instead, we must use the following formula to determine the average rate: Average Rate = Total Distance / Total Time

In this case, the test writers did not give us any specific numbers, so we are free to pick any value for the total distance. In this case, we will use 100 miles for the total distance, which makes each leg of the trip (the distance from Palm Beach to Miami) equal to one-half of 100, or 50 miles.

For the trip from Palm Beach to Miami, Average Rate = 50 miles/ 45 miles per hour = 1.11 hours
For the return trip from Miami to Palm Beach, Average rate = 50 miles / 25 miles per hour = 2 hours
Hence, the total time was 3.11 hours

Going back to the original equation, for the total trip, Average Rate = Total Distance / Total Time = 100 miles/3.11 hours = 32 miles per hour. The correct answer choice is B.

2. Let's take what we know to build an equation to solve for Nathan's age. In this case, N = Nathan's age, C = Claire's age and J = Jayne's age. N = C + 7, C = J –3 or 28 – 3 = 25. So, N = 25 + 7 = 32. Choice E is correct.

3. Total expenses = 1200 + 400 + 150 + 250 + 200 = 2200. 2200/3300 = 2/3, which leaves 1/3 for discretionary spending.   Choice C is correct.

4. 42 / 2000 = x / 325. x = 6.825 lb. Choice B is correct.

5. By definition, an isosceles triangle has two equal sides. Additionally, the angles opposite the equal sides, called base angles, are also equal. Since the vertex angle = G, the sum of the other two angles = 180 – G. Each base angle therefore contains 1/2(180 – G) degrees. Choice D is correct.

6. Area of square is 81, or S^2 Area of circle = πr^2 Thus, 81 = πr^2 · Radius r = the square root of (81/π)= 5.08 = 5. Choice A is correct.

7. The perimeter 25x = sum of all 4 sides. Two of the sides are x/4 + x/4, or x/2. This means that the other two sides add up to 25x – x/2, or 50x-1x = 49x. One side, therefore, is 49x/2.   Area = (x/4)(49x/2) = $49x^2$/8. Choice E is correct.

8. Area = L x W x H = (1/3)(30)(10)=100 cubic feet x $1.50 per cubic feet = $150.00. Choice B is correct.

9. (6,14), (8, 21). Midpoint = (6+8)/2, (14 +21)/2 = 14/2, 35/2 = 7, 17.5   Choice B is correct.

10. The next term is 19 + 6 = 25. Choice C is correct.

11. 433890 x 2/3 = 289,260 / 5 = 57,852 for each person. 57852 x 2 = 115,704 for both parents.   Choice D is correct.

12. The fastest way to solve this problem is to try each answer choice. Choice C is correct..

13. Choice D is correct, 9/10.

14. Two price reductions = 0.9 x 0.85 = 0.765, which is 24.5%. Choice C is correct.

15. The contest is judged on the results of 5 events. One of them, the personal interview, counts as two of the other events. Hence, it is worth 2/6 of the overall score, with each of the other 4 events being worth an additional 1/6. The correct answer is 1/3, or Choice D.

16. 80 + 48 + 36 + 26 + 210 = 400.   80/400 = 1/ 5. Choice C is correct.

17. 3.21 x 10^{-5} · Choice E is correct.

18. Choice A is correct. The value of x quarters is 25x and the value of the x + 32 nickels is 5(x + 32). These quantities are equal, so: $25x = 5(x + 32)$. Solving for x, we find $x = 8$.

19. $(a + b - 1)(a - b - 1) = a^2 - ab - a + ab - b^2 - b - a + b + 1 = a^2 - 2a - b^2 + 1$. Choice D is correct.

20. Here, we are simply being asked to find the difference between the two quantities: $7y + 4 - (11 - 9y) = 7y + 4 - 11 + 9y = 16y - 7$. Choice A is correct.

1. Let v = cost of a veil and h = cost of a headpiece. 6v + 7h = 580. 8v + 5h = 548. We want to eliminate one of the equations. To do so, we will multiply the first equation by 5 and the second equation by 7. This gives us 30v + 35h = 2900 and 56v + 35h = 3836. We can now subtract the first equation from the second to get 26v = 936= 36. The cost of one veil is $36. Choice C is correct.

2. Interest = Principal x Rate x Time. In this case, we have simple annual interest and we are asked to calculate the total amount at the end of 3.5 years:

Total = $5000 + ($5000)(0.0425)(3.5) = $5000 + $743.75 = $5743.75   Choice C is correct.

3. We can solve this problem using the Pythagorean theorem, which states that the sum of the squares of 4 and 8 (16 and 64, respectively) must equal the square of the hypotenuse. The square root of 80 is 8.94. Choice D is correct.

4. For an octagon, the sum of interior angles is 1080, which is 3 x 360. Choice C is correct.

5. $1/36 (44 + 22)^2 = 121$ Choice E is correct.

6. 185.30 x 0.2 = 37.06. Total cost = $222.36. Each share is 222.36 / 3 = $74.12. Choice E is correct.

7. (x + 9) + (x + 11) + (x + 13) = 3x + 33. Choice D is correct.

8. 4x + 9y = 55 and 2x + 7y = 11. After subtracting the two equations, we have 2x + 2y = 44, or x + y = 22, so (x + y) / 2 = 11. Choice D is correct.

9. 50x + 30x = 640. 80x = 640. Thus, x = 8. They will pass after **8 hours**

10. x(x + 2) = 7(x + 2) – 14, so $x^2 + 2x = 7x + 14 – 14$, or $x^2 = 5x$, or x = 5, x+ 2 = 7. **The smaller integer is 5.** Check (5)(7) = 35, which is 14 less than (7)(7).

11. Area = ½ (8)(8) =**32**.

12. There are **5**: they are 24, 36, 48, 72, and 96.

13. The equation $r^2 - 5r – 14 = 0$ factors into (r + 2)(r – 7) = 0. r = -2 or 7. Since the answers to grid-in questions *cannot be negative*, the only correct answer is **7**.

14. Rearrange the equation to form $m^2 + 4m – 357 = 0$. Hence (m + 21) (m - 17) = 0, so m can = either –21 or 17. Since the answers to grid-in questions *must be positive*, **m = 17**.

15. **21/27** is the smallest.

16. For a 6:4 ratio, the whole is 10. 4/10 of 600 is **240**.

17. Probability = ½ x ½ x ½ x ½ = **1/16**.

18. Knowing that the three angles must total 180 degrees, we can solve this problem using an algebraic equation. Let x = angle A, 1/2x = angle B, and 1/2x + 30 = angle C: x + 1/2x + (1/2x + 30) = 180. Solving for x, we find that: 2x + 30 = 180, or x = 75. **Angle A = 75 degrees**,

QA12: Answer Key for Quantitative 12

1. Let x = the # of Victorian Lady gowns sold and 450 – x = the # of Summer Delight gowns sold. The total profit ($45,000) is the sum of the two gowns:

75x + 140 (450 –x) = 45000, so 75x + 63,000 – 140x = 45000, or -65x = -18000, x = 277 Victorian Lady Gowns; 450 –277 = 173 Summer Delight Gowns. Choice D is correct.

2. Let x = the # of years until the population doubles: 2(22000) = 22000 + 180x, solving for x, we find 180x =22000, or x = 122.22. Choice B is correct.

3. The mode is the value that occurs most frequently in the set of data. To find it, we must first arrange the values in ascending order: 9, 11, 12, 12, 12, 12, 13, 13, 15, 18, 23, 23, 23, 23, 23, 25, 30, 32, 34, 34, 34, 34, 34, 41, 43, 45, 45, 45, 54. The value that occurs most often is 34, or C.

4. Let x = the additional dollars that Pam must invest at 4%. Her total investment is therefore 35000 + x. By definition, the sum of both interest payments will be Pam's total interest: 0.075(35000) + 0.04(x) = 0.05(35000 + x). Solving for x, 2625 + 0.04x = 1750 = 0.05x , 875 = 0.01x, so x = $87,500 Choice E is correct.

5. The area of the triangle formed by the midpoints is ¼ of the original triangle XYZ. Therefore, the area is 36/4 = 9. Choice C is correct.

6. A + B + C + D = 360. Here, A + 5A = 6A = 360. Therefore, A = 60 degrees. Choice E is correct.

7. $(5y^2)^3(2y^3)^2 = (125y^6)(4y^6) = 500y^{12}$. Choice E is correct.

8. If $x \wedge y = xy – y + y^2$, then $2 \wedge 4 = (2)(4) – 4 + 16 = 20$. Choice C is correct.

9. 55 + 11 (34) = $4.29 cost to mail a 12-ounce package. Choice D is correct.

10. (15 million)(0.05 + 0.20 + 0.35) = 9 million. Choice D is correct.

11. If France has a total of 8 million diabetics, then the number of them who are 51 or older is (8 million)(0.15) = 1.2 million. If all of these patients purchase 2 insulin pumps per year, they will require a total of 2.4 million. Choice C is correct.

12. Choice D is correct. Germany has the smallest percentage, which is 13%.

13. Choice E is correct. The chart only gives the % of diabetics in each nation; it does not reveal the actual numbers. Without them, we cannot answer this question.

14. China: 8 million diabetics x (0.35) = 2.8 million between 19 and 30
    Germany: 14 million diabetics x (0.29) = 4.06 million between 19 and 30

Therefore, the total number of people in both nations between 19 and 30 who wear contact lenses = 6.86 million. Choice D is correct.

15. 18 million (0.05) = 900,000 under age 10.
    18 million (0.05) = 900,000 over age 51.

900,000 + 900,000 = 1,800,000 people will get free insulin. The remaining 16.2 million will still need to purchase insulin. Choice E is correct.

16. 56 million (0.20 + 0.05) = 14 million diabetics under age 19. Choice D is correct.

QA13: Answer Key for Quantitative 13

1. Area = (20)(16) = 320 square feet x $18.45/square foot = $5,904. Choice E is correct.

2. We can write a simple equation to calculate the answer. Sara has 3 (18) + 6 = 60 tubes of lipstick. Choice D is correct.

3. From the data in the problem, we can write the following equation: x + (x + 2) + (x + 4) + (x + 6) + (x + 8) = 370, so 5x + 20 = 370, so 5x = 350, x = 70. x + 8 = 78. Choice C is correct.

4. The relationship of the groups is defined as follows: Group 1 + Group 2 + Neither – Both = 100. Once we establish this simple equation, we can plug in numbers to solve for the unknown, which in this case is the group defined as Both.   Group 1 + Group 2 + Neither – Both = 100. Thus, 60 + 35 + 20 – Both = 100 Both = 15, which is answer choice D.

5. If f(p) = p/7 + 10 – (7^3)/p , then f (14) = 14/7 + 10 – 343/14 = 2 + 10 – 24.5 = -12.5 Choice A is correct.

6. The first term decreases by 1, the second decreases by 2, the third decreases by 3, etc. The next term would be 75 –5 = 70. Choice B is correct.

7. If x = 5, y = 2 and z = 3, then $3x^3 + 5y^4 – 2z^2$ = (3)(5)(5)(5) + (5)(2)(2)(2)(2) – (2)(3)(3) = 375 + 80 – 18= 437. Choice D is correct.

8. None. Choice E is correct.

9. The square is the sum of two right triangles that share the diagonal as their hypotenuse. Therefore, the sum of the squares of the other two sides must equal 64. Therefore $2x^2$ = 64, where x = a side of the square. To calculate the area of the square, which is L x W, we get (5.65)(5.65) =32. Choice A is correct.

10. The tire is a circle with a radius of 48. The distance it covers in one revolution is simply the circumference of the tire. Since the circumference = $2\pi r$, we know that the tire covers $2\pi(48/12)$ = 8π feet in one revolution. Therefore, for 300 revolutions, the tire covers 2400π feet. Choice A is correct.

11.   3, 5, 6, 6, 7, 7, 7, 8, 9, 12, 15. Median = 7, Mode = 7.   7 –7 = 0. Choice A is correct.

12.   An 8/9 ratio means the total is 17. 8/17 x 85,000 = $40,000. Choice B is correct.

13. 1432 – 91 = 1341.   1341/1432 x 100 = 93.65% decrease. Choice D is correct.

14. Average speed = Total distance / Total time. The total distance is 150 (2) = 300. The time for the first half of the trip is 150/75 = 2 hours; the time for the second half of the trip is 150/40 = 3.75 hours. The average speed is 300/5.75 = **52 miles per hour**. Choice C is correct.

15. Must pay 17 (3) = $51. Get back 12 (2) = $24. Difference is $26 = loss. Choice C is correct.

16. The area of the large circle is (18)(18) π, or 324 π, while the area of the small circle is (6)(6) π, or 36 π. To determine the probability of any given point being in both circles, we simply divide the two quantities and convert to a percentage: Area of the small circle / Area of the large circle = 36 π / 324 π, or 0.111, or 11.11%. The correct answer is choice B.

17. 125 – 729 = -604. Choice A is correct.

18. (3x + y)(x + 3y) – 10xy = $3x^2$ + 9xy + xy + $3y^2$ – 10xy = $3x^2$ + $3y^2$. Choice D is correct.

19. Choice D is correct. When we simplify the expression, we get x < -158

20. If we add the equations together, we get 2F = 200, or F = 100 and G = 5. Choice D is correct.

QA14: Answer Key for Quantitative 14

1. For this problem, we can simply use the equation for simple averages to find the missing number: 300 = (324 + 119 + 267 + 219 + 553 + 189 + x) / 7, So 300 = (1671 + x) / 7, so 2100 = 1671 + x, so x = 429. Choice D is correct.

2. Here, we must use the basic work equation to solve for the total time: 1/Time A + 1/Time B = 1/ Total time. 15/1500 + 45/1500 = 1/X. Thus, X = 25 minutes. Choice C is correct.

3. Area = L x W = 5 x 5 = 25. Choice B is correct.

4. This problem gives us two pieces of information about the circle – its center coordinates (2, 2) and a point on its circumference (10, 8). We can use the distance formula to find the radius of the circle:

Radius = √{(10- 2)(10 - 2) + (8 - 2)(8 - 2)}
Radius = √{(8)(8)+(6)(6)} = √(64 + 36) = √100 = 10

Thus, the radius of the circle is 10. Choice E is correct.

5. 3/8 = 0.375. The closest answer choice is D, 7/19, which is 0.368.

6. 97/102 = 0.951. The % error = 1 – 0.951 = 4.90%, which is Choice C.

7. Add the equations together, then divide by 2: 2x + 6y = 29. Choice C is correct.

8. If 11 – 4x = 3, then x = 2. 6 – (4)(2) = -2. Choice B is correct.

9. In this problem, we will let Melanie's current age = x. Her age a year from now will be x + 3. Her age two years ago was x – 2. Her age five years ago was x – 3. By definition, our equation is:

(x +3) + (x – 2) + 5(x – 3) = 84
x + 3 + x – 2 + 5x – 15 = 84
7x = 98
x = **14** = Melanie's current age.

10. Let x = # of pages that Stenographer 2 types. 4x = # pages that Stenographer 1 types. x + 4x = 1500, so x= **200 pages**.

11. The sum of the angles must be 180, so 180 = 60 + x + 3x, or 4x = 120, so x = **30**.

12. 2(2)(2) + (4)(2)(3) – (3)(3) = 8 + 24 – 9 = **23.**

13. 0.35 x 0.15 = **5.25%.**

14. 14 - $(3)^{2}$ + (3/6)(5/10) = 14 – 9 + 0.25 = **5.25.**

15. This is easiest to solve using simultaneous equations. X + Y = 238 and X – Y = 46. When we add these equations together, we get 2X = 284, so X = 142 and Y = 96. The smaller number is **96**.

16. Volume of rectangular solid = 6 x 18 x 24 = **2592** cubic inches.

17. $a^{2} – b^{2}$ = (a +b)(a - b) = 81. If (a - b) = 3, then 3(a + b) = 81, or **a + b = 27**.

18. If g (u) = 10u/6, then g (24) = 10 (24) / 6 = 240/6 = **40**.

QA15: Answer Key for Quantitative 15

1. We will use the information we have to build an equation to solve for Brittany's weight. Let Tiffany's weight $= T$. Valerie's weight $= 3T$. Brittany's weight $= 3T + 6$. Since the sum of the three weights is 356, our equation becomes: $T + 3T + (3T + 6) = 356$, so $7T + 6 = 356$. So $T = 50$. Tiffany weights 50, Valerie weighs 150, Brittany weighs 156. Choice E is correct.

2. Since we are not given exact numbers for B and U, we can use the plug-in technique to determine the relationship. Let's randomly let $B = 10$ and $U = 100$. If the U increases by \$142, then each tenant owes $1/10 (U + 142)$, or $(U+142)/B$. Answer choice D is correct.

3. Let x the number of adult tickets; therefore, the number of child's tickets is $550 - x$. The total ticket sales equal the sum of adult and children's tickets, so: $12.00x + 5.5 (550 - x) = 4800$. Solve for $x = 273 = \#adults$. $550-273 = 277$ children. Choice B is correct.

4. Volume $= 32 \times 72 \times 96 = 221,184 / 4500 = 49$ dogs. Choice D is correct.

5. Chicago. Choice C is correct.

6. Sacramento and Detroit. Choice B is correct.

7. Area $= \frac{1}{2}$ (Base)(Height) $= \frac{1}{2} (6)(9)= 27$. Choice C is correct.

8. Choice C is correct. Volume of rectangular solid $= 3 \times 9 \times 27 = 729 =$ also the volume of the cube. So, the length of an edge of the cube is the cubic root of 729, or 9.

9. $86 - 3 - 17 + 5 = 71$. Choice D is correct.

10. For this question, we are asked to determine which of the statements are true for all k not equal to zero, which INCLUDES negative numbers and fractions. If we simply plug in positive numbers in place of k, we would conclude that all three statements were correct. However, if we substitute values such as $\frac{1}{2}$ and -6 in place of k, we quickly discover that the only statement that is true for positive numbers, negative numbers and fractions is III. Hence, C is the correct answer choice.

11. $329 - 62 = 267/62 = 4.306 \times 100 = 430.6\%$ increase. Choice C is correct.

12. Because the number of neutered and intact dogs in the kennel is not the same, we must take a *weighted average* for each of the two groups.

Total kennel average $=$(Sum of intact weights + Sum of neutered weights) / Total # of dogs
Total kennel average $= \{(15)(92) + (12)(83)\} / 27 = 88$, which is Choice D.

13. For 5 items, there are 10 possible combinations of any 2 of them. In this case, they are: English/Math, English/Statistics, English/History, English/Social Studies, Math/Statistics, Math/History, Math/Social Studies, Statistics/History, Statistics/Social Studies, and History/Social Studies. Choice E is correct.

14. Choice C is correct.

15. $xy + xz = 15$, so $x (y + z) = 15$. Since $(y + z) = 3$, $3x = 15$ and $x =5$. Choice D is correct.

16. If $x^2 -7x + 10= 0$, then $(x -2)(x - 5) = 0$. So, $x = 5$, or 2. Choice A is correct.

1. Here, we can simply plug the numbers into the rate equation: Rate x Time = Distance, or Rate x 2.5 =96 Hence, Rate = 38.4 mph   Choice B.

2. The mean equals the sum of all of the salaries divided by the number of salaries (in this case, 16).   So, 3 (120,000) + 4 (90000) + 9 (50000) /16 = 360000+ 360000 + 450000 / 16 = $73,125. Choice B.

3. Let x = Courtney's hourly wage. Jenny's wage = x + 3. Since Patrice earns twice as much as Jenny, her hourly wage is 2 (x + 3). Therefore: x + (x + 3) + 2 (x + 3) = 57. Solving for x, x = 12, which means Courtney earns $12 per hour, Jenny earns 12 + 3 = $15 per hour and Patrice earns 2(15) = $30 per hour. Choice E is correct.

4. Interest = Principal x Rate x Time. In this case, we know the beginning and ending amounts and are being asked to calculate the rate of simple annual interest that was earned over 6.75 years.

Total = $6175 = $4390 + ($4390)(X)(6.75), so 6175 = 4390 + 29632.50X, or X =1785/29632.5 = 0.0602 = 6.02% Choice D is correct.

5. The length of the third side of the triangle must be less than the sum of the other two sides. Thus, the length must be less than 5 + 3 = 8. Choice A is correct.

6. Octagon. Choice B is correct.

7. Parallel lines have the same slope. In this case, the slope of 3x –9y = 12 is 1/3, because the equation simplifies to 9y = 3x – 12, or y = 1/3x – 4/3.   Choice C also has a slope of 1/3.

8. The area the truck traveled is a right triangle with sides equal to 30, 40 and 50. Therefore, the total distance traveled is the perimeter of that triangle, or 30 + 40 + 50 = 120 miles/ 8 mpg = 15 gallons. Choice C is correct.

9. To solve, we must convert all of the terms to inches and add them together. Let's start with what we know. The term for inches is represented by Z. There are 12 inches in 1 foot. Hence, our coefficient for Y is 12. There are 3 feet in one yard and 12 inches in one foot. Hence, our coefficient for X is 3 x 12 = 36. The number of inches in a distance of X yards, Y feet and Z inches is therefore 36X + 12Y + Z. Choice A is correct.

10. The steps in these series are: subtract 10, then add 15, repeat. The next term would be 105. Choice D is correct.

11. 85 + 411 + 103 = 599 cats.   88 lb x 16 oz/lb = 1408 oz.   1408 / 599 = 2.35. Choice A is correct.

12. Choice C, 40.

13. 28.5 x 23.1 = 658.35/16 = 41.14 pounds. Choice B is correct.

14. Choice E is correct, 15/14.

15. Let's let x = the final exam grade. The average of Becky's four exams is (70 + 71 + 85 + 90)/4 = 79. Finally, her score for the oral presentation is 70. Since the final exam grade, oral presentation score and the average of her four exam grades all equal one third of Becky's final grade, we simply need to solve the following equation for x: 1/3 (79) + 1/3 (70) + 1/3 (x) = 80. Hence, x = 91. Choice D is correct.

16. For permutations, the correct formula is 4!/(4- 4)! = (4 x 3 x 2 x 1) / 1 = 24. Choice D is correct.

17. (18 million)(0.02 + 0.21) = 4.14 million. Choice C is correct.

18. If France has a total of 5 million contact lens wearers, then the number of them who are 51 or older is (5 million)(0.15) = 750,000. If all of these patients own 3 pairs each, then the number of pairs is 2,250,000. Choice D is correct.

19. Choice D is correct. Contact lenses are obviously available and affordable in India, because older patients wear them. The more logical explanation for the large discrepancy in use is that the law restricts their use to those 18 and over.

20. Choice E is correct. The chart only gives the % of contact lens wearers in each nation; it does not reveal the actual numbers.   Without them, we cannot answer this question.

QA17: Answer Key for Quantitative 17

1. Volume = (15)(24)(48) = 17,280 cubic inches /30 = 576 seconds = 9.6 minutes. Choice A is correct.

2. 240 miles/30 miles per gallon x $2.85 per gallon = $22.80. Choice A is correct.

3. The series goes according to these steps: multiply the term by 3, subtract 3, multiply the new term by 3, subtract 3, multiple the new term by 3, subtract 3, etc. The next term would be 45. Choice E is correct.

4. Area of triangle = ½ x Base x Height. In this case, the area of the triangle is the same as that of the circle, which is πr^2, or 121π. Hence, 121π = ½ x 11 x Height.   Height = 22π. Choice D is correct.

5. 12.67 = 38/3. Choice B is correct.

6. 6 pounds = 96 oz. 12/96 = 1/8. Choice C is correct.

7. Let x = the smaller number and the larger number = x + 9. We also know that 2x = (x + 9) + 11. Solve for x. x = 20. Choice E is correct.

8. The fastest way to solve this problem is to substitute numbers for the variables and see what we get. Let's assume that we have 10 watermelons that cost $3.00 each and 5 apples that cost 60 cents each. Hence, W = 10, X = 3.00, Y = 5 and Z = 0.60. The total cost of W watermelons is 100(10)(3) = 100WX The total cost of C apples is (5)(60) = YZ. Therefore, the total cost of the watermelons and apples is 100(10)(3) + (5)(6) = 100WX + YZ. Choice B is correct.

9. First, arrange the values in ascending order: 2, 3, 3, 3, 3, 3, 3, 4, 5, 5, 5, 5, 6, 6, 7, 7, 7, 7, 8, 9, 10. Then, find the value that occurs most often; in this case, it is **3,** which is the mode.

10. In this case, we must solve for the total time that is needed to complete the job. First, we figure the amount of work that each man does as a percentage of the total amount:

Gary   Rate x Time = Work   (1/3) times T = 1/3 T
Bill   Rate x Time = Work   (1/4) times T = 1/4T

Now, we can add them together to figure the total time for the job: 1/3 T + 1/4 T = 1 or   4/12T + 3/12T = 1 or   4T + 3T = 12 or 7T = 12, T = 1.71 hours = 60 minutes + 42.8 minutes = 102.8 minutes = **103 minutes**.

11. 45 + 55 + AC = 125. AC =**25.**

12. **99** (14 x 7 = 98; 98 + 1 = 99)

13. Area = π(12)(12). Diameter = 12 + 12 = **24.**

14. ab - ac = a (b - c) = 45. Since (b - c) = 5, we can substitute it back into the equation to get 5a = 45, or **a =9**.

15. Fifteen minutes = ¼ hour = **1/32** of 8 hours.

16. 112 – 18 – 11 – (3)(5) = **68.**

17. (2x – 4)/8 = 10 – x, so 2x – 4 = 80 – 8x, so 10x = 84, or **x = 8.4**.

18. Short-term parking for 6 hours costs $1.00 + 4(0.50) = $3.00. Long-term parking costs $7.00, which is **$4.00 more**.

QA18: Answer Key for Quantitative 18

1. This problem can be solved using a proportion. If there are 2 rest areas every 12 miles, there will be x number of rest areas on 4356/2, or 2178 miles of highway? 2/12 = x/2178, solving for x = 363. Choice C is correct.

2. Group 1 + Group 2 + Neither – Both = 75. In this case, 50 + 30 + Neither - 11 = 75. Neither = 6. Choice B is correct.

3. The cost of repairs = Total cost of parts + Total cost of labor. The total for the parts is $350 + $150 + $25 = $525. The total cost for labor = ($45) (3.5) = $157.50. The total cost to fix the car is $525 + $157.50 = $682.50, or Choice C.

4. 27 / 540 = 1 / 20. Choice D is correct.

5. Triangles with equal sides and equal angles are congruent. Choice B is correct.

6. We can solve this by plugging in numbers. Let's assume the original square was 10 inches x 10 inches; it's area was therefore 100 square inches. If we add 3 inches to its length and subtract 3 inches from its width, its new area is (10 + 3)(10 – 3) = (13)(7)= 91. This is 9% less, which is answer choice A.

7. A circle that is centered at the origin and passes through point (-7, 0) has a radius of 7. Therefore, its area is 49 π, which is answer Choice D.

8. f(-1) = (-1)(-1) -4(-1) + 3 = 1 + 4 + 3 = 8. Choice D is correct.

9. The mean is 39.8, or Choice D.

10. We can solve by using a proportion. 12/500 = x / 14,280. x= 342.7 = 343. Choice C is correct.

11. Choice C is correct, 11/84.

12. The repeating pattern is 04321, which includes 5 digits. The 26th digit is 0, or Choice A.

13. Use the factorial formula to solve: 7! / 3! = (7 x 6 x 5 x 4 x 3 x 2 x 1) / (3 x 2 x 1) = 840. Choice C is correct.

14. (9)(9)(9) (27)(27) = 531,441, which is (729)^2. Choice C is correct.

15. m =1/16. Choice A is correct.

16. If x^2 + 3x – 18= 0, then (x + 6)(x - 3) = 0. So, x = 3, -6. Choice D is correct.

1. Let x = the oz of Wine A needed and 2700 – x = oz of Wine B needed. Thus, our equation becomes: 0.06x + 0.18(2700 – x) = 0.15(2700). Solve for x = 675 oz of Wine A. Choice E is correct.

2. If the park is a square with a side length of 2400 feet, the perimeter is 2400 (4), or 9600 feet. Someone walking 600 feet per minute would take 9600/600, or 16 minutes to walk the perimeter of the park. Choice C is correct.

3. Let x = the smaller number and 13 – x equal the larger number. Six times the smaller number is therefore 6x. Three times the larger number is 3(13 – x). Further, we know that the difference between these two quantities is equal to 6. We must therefore solve the following equation: 6x – 3(13-x) = 6, so 6x –39 + 3x = 6, or 9x = 45, or x = 5 and 13 – 5 = 8. Choice D is correct.

4. The data indicate that each 10% increase in solids decreases the flow by 50%. Therefore, the syrup with 10% solids would flow 8 times as fast (2 x 2 x 2) as the syrup with 40% solids. Hence, the correct answer choice is D.

5. A syrup with 50% solids would flow 50% as fast as a syrup with 40% solids. Choice B is correct.

6. The sum of the angles must be 180; hence, we must solve the equation: x + 4x + 80 = 180. When we do, we find that x = 20. Choice D is correct.

7. The area that Jake walked is a right triangle with sides equal to 50, 120 and 130. Therefore, the total distance Jake walked is the perimeter of that triangle, which is 50 + 120 + 130 = 300 yards. Choice E is correct.

8. Area of circle = πr^2 In this case, the radius is the square root of 144, or 12. The diameter is 12 x 2 = 24. Choice D is correct.

9. For a hexagon, an exterior angle = 360/6 = 60; interior angle = 180-60 = 120. Choice C is correct.

10. If f(j) = j^2 + 0.001j, then f (0.05) = (0.05)(0.05) + (0.001)(0.05) = 0.0025 + 0.00005 = 0.00255. Choice C is correct.

11. 1489 + 324 + 112 – 117 = 1808 = $180.80. Choice A is correct.

12. The prime numbers between 10 and 20 are 11, 13, 17, and 19. Their product is (11)(13)(17)(19)= 46,189. Choice D is correct.

13. 235 – 125 – 25 – 38 = 47. 47 / 235 = 0.20 = 1/5. Choice B is correct.

14. 50,000 / 5, 000, 000 = 1/100. Choice C is correct.

15. The 3:2 ratio of female to male singers applies to a population of 32 – 2, or 30. Hence, the original 30 selected to advance included 18 women and 12 men (a 3:2 ratio). The correct answer for the original number of men chosen to advance is choice C, 12.

16. Use the factorial formula to solve: 6! / 4! = (6 x 5 x 4 x 3 x 2 x 1) / (4 x 3 x 2 x 1) = 30. Choice D is correct.

17. 25 x 25 x 25 = 125 x 125. Choice C is correct.

18. (x + 5) – 4 = 12, thus x = 11. Choice D is correct.

19. To solve the equations for y, we must eliminate x and add the equations together. To do so, we must multiple the first equation by two and subtract it from the second equation. When we do, we find y = 2. Choice A is correct.

20. (x + 2)(x +5) – (x + 1) (x + 3) = $(x^2 + 7x + 10)$ - $(x^2 + 4x +3)$ = 3x + 7. Choice A is correct.

QA20: Answer Key for Quantitative 20

1. The original fraction is x/3x. The new fraction is (x + 5)/(3x + 5), which equals ¾. We must solve the equation for x. When we cross-multiply, we get: 4x + 20 = 9x + 15, or x = 1. Choice A is correct.

2. Perimeter = sum of all three sides = 16 + 2x. 64 = 16 + 2x. x = 24. Choice C is correct.

3. Perimeter = 2(6) + 2(2) = 16. Choice C is correct.

4. y = 14 is horizontal, which means that a line parallel to it must also be horizontal. Hence, the answer is y = 7. Choice B is correct.

5. 15 / (3/6) = 30. Choice C is correct.

6. In this case, the number of intact dogs (14) is equal to the number of neutered dogs (also 14), which means that we can simply take the average of 83 + 92 and apply it to the entire kennel. The result is 87.5, or choice C, which is the correct answer.

7. To solve this problem, we must check our answer choices against both criteria in the problem: they must 1) be divisible by 2 and 9 AND 2) they must leave a remainder of 4 when they are divided by 5. Choices C and D are not divisible by 2, so we do not need to examine them further. Of the remaining choices, only Choice E (54) meets both criteria. .

8. The adjacent angle is 180 – 60 =120. Choice B is correct.

9. Interest = Principal x Rate x Time. In this case, we have simple annual interest and we are asked to calculate the total amount at the end of 6 years: Total = $7,500 + ($7,500)(0.0495)(6) = $7,500 + $2227.50 = **$9727.50.**

10. Let x = the oz of Liquor A needed; 4,000 – x = oz of Liquor B needed. 0.04x + 0.20(4000 – x) = 0.16(4000). Solve for x. 0.04 x + 800 – 0.2x = 640. –0.16x = -160, x = 10 ounces of Liquor A. 4000 – 10 = **3990 ounces of Liquor B**.

11. The fastest way to solve is to select values for the diameter of the circle and determine the effect on the area. If the diameter is 4, the radius is 2 and the area is 4 times π. Increasing the diameter by 100% to 8 makes the new radius = 4, and the new area is 16 times π. The percent increase is (16-4) / 4 = 12/4, or **300%.**

12. 12k – 3 = 72 – 3k, or 15k = 75, or **k = 5.**

13. 8/12 = x/48. x = 32. 32 - 8 = **24 additional ounces**.

14. For the original numbers, (7)(77) = 539 = sum. New sum= 539 – (12)(5) = 479. 479/7=**68.43**.

15. The series includes 6 digits that repeat indefinitely in the order: 9,8,7,6,5,4. 300/6 = 50 + no remainder. The 300th digit will be **4.**

16. The correct answer is **4**. 4 x 4 x 4 = 64, which is the square root of 4096.

17. x + (x + 2) + (x + 4) + (x + 6) + (x + 8) = 475, so 5x + 20 = 475, so 5x = 455, x = 91, X + 2 = 93, X = 4, 95, X + 6 = 97, x + 8 = 99. The largest number is **99**.

18. We can solve this problem by using a proportion: 15/14.87 = 84/x, so x = **$83.27**.

QA21: Answer Key for Quantitative 21

1. Here, we can use the rate equation to determine the time at which the two motorcyclists will pass each other. By definition, they are traveling the same distance, which is 540 miles. Also by definition, that distance equals the SUM of the quantities (Rate x Time) for each motorcycle. Hence, our equation becomes: $65x + 70x = 540$, or $x = 4$. They will pass after 4 hours, which will be 2:00 pm. C

2. We must set up an equation to solve this problem. If $x = $ # nickels, then $30 - x = $ # dimes. Therefore, $5x = $ value of nickels. $300 - 10x = $ value of dimes. If the total value of the coins is $2.65, then the equation becomes: $5x + 300 - 10x = 265$. Solving for x, there are $x = 7$ nickels. $30 - x = 23$ dimes. Choice D is correct.

3. Let $x = $ the amount in the bank CD and $25000 - x = $ the amount in the money market. Interest = Principal x Rate x Time. In this case, we know the interest rates on the two products and the difference between them. So, we can use this information to set up an equation to solve for the initial amount of money invested: $(0.075)(1)x = (0.0525)(25000 - x)(1) + 400$, so $0.075x = 1312.5 - 0.0525x + 400$, or $0.1275x = 1712.5$, so $x = 13431.37$ in the CD. Choice D is correct.

4. Area = ½(Base)(Height). Here, we will let $x = $ the height and $x+16 = $ the base. $256 = ½ x(x + 16)$, or $512 = x^2 + 16x$, or $0 = x^2 + 16x - 512$. $0 = (x -16) (x +32)$. The height = 16 inches. The base = 32 inches. Choice C is correct.

5. The slope is $-1/3$. Choice B is correct.

6. For an octagon, an exterior angle = $360/8 = 45$; interior angle = $180 - 45 = 135$. Choice E is correct.

7. In an equilateral right triangle, $x^2 = 121$, so the two side lengths are 11. The hypotenuse is 15.56, or $11 \sqrt{2}$. Choice C is correct.

8. The area of a rectangle is equal to its length times its width. Therefore, the new area will be equal to the new length (which is 1.25 times its old length) times its new width (which is 0.60 times its old width). Multiplying them together, we find that the new area is $(1.25)(0.60)$, or 0.75 times the original area. Thus, answer choice E is correct.

9. $3/19$ is greater than $1/7$. Choice C is correct.

10. $7 + 3 + 2 = 12$ items = ¾ of the total number of items. Hence, the overall total is 16. $2/16 = 1/8 = 12.5\%$. Choice C is correct.

11. $220 / 550 = 2 / 5$. Choice D is correct.

12. The median is the average of 33 and 44, which is 38.5, or Choice D.

13. For permutations, the correct formula is $5!/(5- 5)! = (5 \times 4 \times 3 \times 2 \times 1) / 1 = 120$. Choice B is correct.

14. $(4x^2)^2(3x^3)^3 = (16x^4)(27x^9) = 432x^{13}$. Choice D is correct.

15. The equation reduces to $d = 2e$, so $e/d. = ½$. Choice B is correct.

16. If $ab = 1$ and $a = 4b$, then $b = 1/a$ and $a = 4/a$ and $a^2 = 4$, so $a = 2$ or -2. Choice C is correct.

1. We can use the information to write an equation to solve for Jocelyn's weight. Let C = Connie's weight and J = Jocelyn's weight. From the problem, we know that J = 0.6C. We also know that J + 8 = 0.75C. Thus, 0.6C + 8 = 0.75C. Solving for C, Connie's weight = 53.3 lbs and Jocelyn's weight = 32 lb. Choice A is correct.

2. The total bill, which can be no more than $50, includes the cost of the meal, 7% sales tax and a 15% tip. If we let x = the cost of the food, then the tax = 0.07x. The tip is 15% of the total cost of the food and the 7% tip. Algebraically, we can represent the tip as 0.15 (x + 0.07x) = 0.1605x. Since the total bill can be no more than $50, our final equation for the meal is: Meal + Tax + Tip = 50, or x + 0.07x + 0.1605x = 50. Solving for x, the cost of the meal must be less than $40.63. Answer Choice C is correct.

3. This can be solved by a simple equation: 8x – 25 = 215. x = 30. Choice C is correct.

4. 10% of $2141 = $214 – 35 = $179. Choice D is correct.

5. Credit Card + Clothes = $ 240 + $75 = $315. Choice D is correct.

6. To find the ratio of blue eggs to pink eggs, we must re-state both ratios so that the number of green eggs is the same in both.   Blue eggs to green eggs = 8:3. Green eggs to pink eggs = 1:2.

In this case, the numbers corresponding to green eggs are 3 and 1, respectively. The easiest way to re-state the ratios is to use their least common multiple of 3 and 1, which is 3.

Blue eggs to green eggs = 8:3. Green eggs to pink eggs = 3:6 (which is the same as 1:2)

The ratios are now stated in a form in which the same number (3) refers to green eggs. The ratio of blue to green to pink eggs is 8:3:6. The ratio of blue eggs to pink eggs is 8:6, which is answer choice E.

7. 5/9 of the birthday money = $38.   Thus, we can set up a ratio to determine the original whole: 5/9 = 38/X. Hence, X = $68.40, which is Choice C.

8. The average is 52.12, which is Choice D.

9. 14(21) – 2(11) + 6(64-1) = 294 – 22 + 378 = **650.**

10. Determine the number of nickels for each type of coin; then, add the amounts together: 20 pennies = 4 nickels, 12 quarters = 60 nickels, 27 dimes = 54 nickels. Total nickels = 4 + 60 + 54 = **118.**

11. 11x – 13 = 306, then 11x = 319, so x = **29**

12. Let e = the cost of one pair of shoes and f = the cost of one pair of socks. Then mathematically, we can state that 6e + 8f = 995 and 4e + 12f = 750. To solve, we must eliminate one of these equations. We can do this by multiplying the first one by 3 and the second one by 2. When we do, we get 18e + 24f = 2985 and 8e + 24f = 1500. If we subtract the second equation from the first, we get 10e = 1485. One pair of shoes, e, therefore costs **$148.50.**

13. 70/30 = x/20. x = 46.7 = **47 minutes.**

14. 180 (X – 2) = 1,980, so X - 2 = 11, or X = **13 sides**.

15. V = L x W x H = 8 x 9 x 24 = 1728 cubic inches. The side length for the cube is the cubic root of this number, which is **12.**

16. For the repeating decimal 0.015689015689015689……, the repeating pattern is 015689, which is a string of 6 digits. Hence, 37th digit to the right of the decimal point will be **0.**

17. The equation can be simplified to (x -6)(x-4) = 0. Thus, the possible solutions are **4 or 6**.

18. ½ + 2/4 + 2/6 + 1/3 + 3/ 12 = 6/12 + 6 /12 + 4/12 + 4/12 + 3/12 = **23/12.**

QA23: Answer Key for Quantitative 23

1. Let's call the two numbers x and 5x. We also know that 3(x – 5x) = 48. Solve for x: -12x = 48. x = -4 5x = -20. The larger number is –4. A

2. Let c = the cost of 1 CD and d = the cost of 1 DVD. 8c + 9d = 199 12c + 6d = 159. We will now multiply the first equation by 3 and the second equation by 2, which gives us: 24c + 27d = 597 and 24c + 12d = 318. If we subtract the second equation from the first one, we get 15d = 279. d = $18.60. Choice E is correct.

3. First, let's calculate Jake's commission for the week, which is 12400(0.15) = 1860. Now, we can calculate his total weekly pay: 700 + 1860 = $2560. Choice E is correct.

4. Triangles with equal angles but unequal sides are similar. Choice A is correct.

5. Circumference is π x Diameter, or $2\pi/9\pi$ = 2/9. Choice B is correct.

6. 6 + 1/3 - $(4/9)^2$ - (3/2)(5/6) = 6 + 1/3 – 0.1975 – 1.25 = 4. 89. Choice B is correct.

7. 3.25 + 4.89 + 2.89 + 3.19 + 2(0.89) + 3. 5 = $19.50. Choice D is correct.

8. 800 x 0.4 = 320. 320 x 0.25 = 80. Choice C is correct.

9. The average value = 23/50 = **0.46** million dollars

10. The average value = 31/409 = **0.076** million dollars

11. Total value of financial products sold by online brokerage = 92 + 27 + 31 = **150** million.

12. First, arrange the numbers in ascending order: 1059, 1135, 1432, 1587, 1986, 2131, 2310. The middle number, **1587**, is the median.

13. Let Greg's age = G. Sam's age is 3G, while Lori's age is G + 10. G + 3G + (G + 10) = 65. 5G + 10 = 65, so 5G = 55, so **Greg = 11**, Sam = 33 and Lori is 21. 11 + 33 + 21 = 65.

14. The adjacent angle = 180 –75 = **105 degrees**.

15. Area of Y = 23 x 23 = 529. Area of X = 19 x 19 = 361. 529 – 361 = **168.**

16. $x^2 (x^2 – 1)$ = 0, or $x^2 (x + 1)(x – 1)$ = 0 Solutions are 0, 1, -1. Since answers to grid-in questions *cannot be negative*, the correct answers are **0 or 1.**

17. 50 + 75 + 100 + 75 = 300. 100/300 = **1/3**.

18. $5^x + (x^4)^{x-1}$ = 25 + 16 = **41.**

1. First, we must subtract the deductions from the total: 14625 – 100 – 325 = 14,200. Chad received 75% of this amount, or $10,650. Choice C is correct.

21. The fastest way to solve this problem is to substitute numbers for the variables. Then, we can convert the relationship back to letters. Let's say M = 200 and N = 500. Therefore, (M – 180) = 20. When Carrie sold the coins, she reduced her collection by the following amount: 500 – (M – 180) = 500 – M + 180. Converting this back to letters, she had N – M + 180 coins left. Choice C is correct.

3. 75 / 45 = x / 30, so x = 50 minutes. Choice C is correct.

4. 35/34 x 100 = 1.03% increase. Choice A is correct.

5. 18/21 = 85.4%, which is a 14.3% decrease from the previous year. Choice B is correct.

6. The team won 123 ribbons in 2006; 108 ribbons in 2007. 108/123 = 87.5%, which is a 12.2 % decrease. Choice C is correct.

7. Choice D is correct. 83 + 89 = 172.

8. 346.84 – 17.34 = 329.50 / 5 = 65.90 x 2 = $131.80. Choice D is correct.

9. **15** (ST, SU, SV, SW, SX, TU, TV, TW, TX, UV, UW, UX, VW, VX, WX)

10. If f (z) = z^3/25, then f (15) = { (15)(15)(15) } / 25 = 3375/25 = **135.**

11. 550 miles/25 miles per gallon x $3.03 per gallon = **$66.66**

12. The area of the room is 8 x 6 = 48 square feet. The area of one tile is (0.25) x (0.5) = 0.125 square feet. 48/0.125 = **384 tiles**.

13. Area = L x W = 13 x 13 = **169**.

14. Perimeter = 2(15) + 2(9) = **48**.

15. If 17 – 5d = 2, then 5d = 15, so d = 3. Therefore 9 – 2d = 9 – 6 = **3.**

16. If each nugget weighs 0.5 oz, then 1 lb contains 32 nuggets; therefore, 2 lb = **64 nuggets**.

17. The answer would be 00435 –00236 + 1 = 200 – 2 = **198.**

18. Let x = Connie's hourly wage. Josh's wage = x + 5. Since Adam earns twice as much as Josh, his hourly wage is 2 (x + 5). Therefore: x + (x + 5) + 2 (x + 5) = 75, so 4x + 15 = 75, or 4x = 60. X = Connie's wage = $15, Josh's wage = $20. **Adam's wage = $40**. As a check, we can verify that $15 + $20 + $40 = $75.

QA25: Answer Key for Quantitative 25

1. Peanuts are 0.50 per ounce. The cost for 42 pounds = (42)(16)(0.5) = $336   Choice E is correct.

2. Although the original information is given in hours and gallons, the answer choices are presented in terms of minutes and quarts. This means that both values must be converted:

Truck 1 2.1 hours/600 gallons = 126 min/600 gallons = 126 min / 2400 qt
Truck 2 2.9 hours/600 gallons = 174 min/600 gallons = 174 min / 2400 qt

In this case, the questions asks us to calculate the *difference in times* that the trucks would take to pour 130,000 quarts of concrete. To solve, we must determine the time required by each truck and compare the numbers.

Truck 1 126 min / 2400 qt = 6825 min / 130,000 qt; Truck 2   174 min / 2400 qt = 9425 min / 130,000 qt
9425 – 6825 = 2600, which is answer choice D.

3. In this case, the fastest way to solve this problem is to plug in the answer choices and test them. When we try answer choice C, we get the right answer. (12)(12) - (11)(11) = 144 – 121= 23.

4. If x#y = 2xy + y, then 3#7: (2)(3)(7) + 7 = 49. Choice E is correct.

5. The area of a rectangle = L x W. If we use 5 and 6 as the length and width for rectangle R, its area is 30. Rectangle Z would have an area of (10)(12) = 120, four times that of R. Choice D is correct.

6. The volume of a sphere = $4/3\pi r^3$. Hence, the volume of a sphere with a radius of 5 = 4/3(3.1416)(5)(5)(5) = 524. The correct answer choice must ALSO have a volume of 524.

The best way to solve the problem is to quickly check each answer choice. By definition, the volume of a rectangular solid = Length x Width x Height. When we check each answer choice, we find that Choice D is the correct answer: Volume = (2)(2)(131) = 524. Also note: Choice E is close (volume = 522), but it is not the *best* answer. That's what makes this problem so tricky – you need to check *all* of the answer choices for the best match.

7. (48 pounds)(16 ounces/ pound) = 768 total ounces/ 6 ounces per steak = 128. Choice C is correct.

8. $8,000,000 x 0.095 = $760,000 interest. Total = $8,760,000. Choice D is correct.

9. Total Annuities = 50 + 105 = **155**.

10. Total number of products sold = 350 + 105 + 409 = **864**.

11. 54 / (54+ 23 + 10) = 54/87= **62.1%.**

12. 10 = (5 + 6 + 9 + 12 + 4 + 8 + x)/7, So, 10 = (44 + x)/7, so 70 = 44 + x, or x = 26. David must score **26 baskets** in the final game.

13. 700 – 100 – 225 – 125 – 50 – 50 – 50 = 100. 100/700 = 14.28% = **14% were undecided**.

14. Volume = (4/3)(4/3)(4/3) = 2.37 cubic feet x 20 pounds/cubic foot = **47.4 lb.**

15. 8/(x-3) – 2 = 0, so 8/(x-3) = 2, and 8 = 2(x-3), so 8 = 2x – 6, so 14 = 2x or **x = 7**.

16. 6 x 6 x 6 = **216.**

17. A + B + C + D = 360. Here, D + 7D = 360, or 8D = 360. D = **45 degrees**.

18. For both equations to be true, y must be **11.**

1. Let x = # of soft cover books and 5000 – x = the # of hardcover books. The sum of their individual profits equals the total annual profit, or: 15x + 5(5000 – x) = 65000, so 15x + 25000 –5x = 65000, or 10x = 40000, x = 4000 soft cover books. Choice E is correct.

2. Let x = the amount in the bank CD; x + 5000 = the amount in the REIT. Interest = Principal x Rate x Time. In this case, we know the total amount that Jade earned per year, which is the sum of the two individual investments. So,

X(0.08)(1) + (x + 5000)(0.12)(1) = 26,000, or 8x + 12(x + 5000) = 2,600,000, or 20x = 2540000, x = 127,000 in bank CD. Choice D is correct.

3. The perimeter of a rectangle is 2L + 2W = 2(48) + 2 (64) = 224 inches / 12 = 18.7 = 19 linear feet. Choice A is correct.

4. Choice B is correct. If we plug in side lengths of 20, 40 and 60 for squares K, M and S, respectively, their areas are 400, 1,600 and 3,600, respectively. The area of S is greater than the sum of the area of K and M by 1,600, or (3,600 – 2,000). The percentage difference is 1,600/2,000 x 100 = 80%.

5. To solve, we use the equation 180 (13-2) = 1,980. Choice D is correct.

6. We can solve this problem by dividing the two quantities: 86868686/6868 = 12648.323529. 0.323529 x 6868 = 2222. Choice A is correct. (To check: 12648 x 6,868 = 86866464 + 2222)

7. The increase from $825 to $1650 would be 100%. Choice C is correct.

8. The series lists the prime numbers less than 100 in descending order. The next term would be 73, or Choice C.

9. The series includes 6 digits that repeat indefinitely in the order: 4,5,6,7,8,9. The sum of any six consecutive digits will therefore be the sum of 4+5+6+7+8+9 =**39**.

10. Use the factorial formula to solve: 8! / 4! = (8 x 7 x 6 x 5 x 4 x 3 x 2 x 1) / (4 x 3 x 2 x 1) = **1680**.

11. 1000 – 300 = 700 / 4 = **175**.

12. The x-intercept is the value of x when y = 0. In this case, it is **2**.

13. The total bill, which can be no more than $100, includes the cost of the meal, 6% sales tax and a 20% tip. If we let x = the cost of the food, then the tax = 0.06x. The tip is 20% of the total cost of the food and the 6% tip. Algebraically, we can represent the tip as 0.20 (x + 0.06x) = 0.212x.

Since the total bill can be no more than $100, our final equation for the meal is: Meal + Tax + Tip = 100, or x + 0.06x + 0.212x = 100, or 1.272x = 100. Solving for x, the cost of the meal must be less than **$78.62**. (Tax = $4.72, Tip = 16.67)

14. Sam has 4 (62) – 12 = **236 CDs.**

15. Volume = (12)(24)(42) = 12,096 cubic inches/60 cubic inches per second = 201.68 seconds = 3.36 = **3.4 minutes**.

16. 2.05 x 8.99 x 54.22 = **999.35.**

17. (-1)(-1) + (4)(-1)(-2) - (-2)(-2) = 1 + 8 – 4 = **5.**

18. First, arrange the numbers in ascending order: 33, 44, 55, 66, 78. The middle number, **55,** is the median.

QA27: Answer Key for Quantitative 27

1. Let x be the number of videos sold and x + 30 = the number of DVDs sold. 12x + 15(x +30) = $5850. Solve for x = 200, x + 30 = 230. Choice C is correct.

2. 2/48 = 3/x, so x = 72 inches. Choice D is correct.

3. Area of each window = (13)(13) = 169 square feet x $5.86 = $990.34 per window. The church can replace 4 windows for $3961.36. Choice C is correct.

4. To solve, simply calculate the total amount to park in Lot A vs. Lot B for 7 hours. For Lot A, the cost is $5.00 + (0.75)(12) = $14.00. Lot B, on the other hand, costs $19.75. The difference is $5.75, which is choice C.

5. **5.43 x 10^{-5}** Choice E is correct.

6. 885/2141 = 41%. Choice B is correct.

7. 100 + 240 + 75 + 321 = 736/2141= 34.4%. Choice C is correct.

8. It also decreases by half. Choice C is correct.

9. Each room requires four cans of paint. First, Jenny needs 3 extra cans to finish painting the first room. Then, she needs 4 cans per room for the 3 additional rooms, for a total of 3 + 12 = **15 additional cans.**

10. 180 (11-2) = **1620 degrees**.

11. Area 1 = 5 x 5 x 5 = 125. Area 2 = 3 x 3 x 3 = 27. 125 – 27 = **98 cubic feet**.

12. 5(1)(1) – (3)(1)(2) + (7)(2)(2) = 5 – 6- + 28 = **27**.

13. We can add the equations together to get 11y = 33, so **y = 3**.

14. 15-3 = 12. 12/15 x 100 = **80% decrease**.

15. (22/7 + 44/6 +11/7 + 4/9 +10/13) / 5 = (3.142 + 7.333 + 1.571 + 0.444 + 0.769) / 5 = (13.259) / 5 = **2.65**.

16. The terms are squared, then increased by 5. The next term will be **1681**, which is the square of 41.

17. (0.4) 15,600 = **6,240**.

18. (4)(4)(4)(4) = 256. (4)(4)(4)(4)(4) = 1024. Thus, the largest integer value of x is **4.**

1. We can solve this problem by plugging in numbers or by doing a few simple "backwards" calculations. First, let's try Option 1, the plug- in approach. Let's assume that Janice bought 10 dozen candy bars at a price of 50 cents per bar. Let's also assume that she had 20 cents left over. Hence, X = 10, Y = 50 and Z = 20.   Janice therefore spent (12)(10)(50 cents), which is 12XY. If she had 20 cents left over, then her original amount of money was 12XY + Z. Choice E is correct.

Option 2. If you don't want to plug in numbers, you can just reason the problem through.   Janice bought X dozen candy bars, which = 12X. If they cost Y cents each, then she spent 12XY. Finally, she had Z cents left over, which we must add to her total amount of money. When we do, we get the same answer as we did with the plug-in method: 12XY + Z.

2. If (x + 15) is even, then the next consecutive even integer is (x + 17). The following consecutive even integer is (x + 19) and the next consecutive even integer is (x + 21). Therefore, the sum of the next three even integers is: (x + 17) + (x + 19) + (x + 21) = 3x + 57. Choice D is correct.

3. According to the problem, y = 4x – 5. If we solve for x, we find x = (y +5)/4. Choice B is correct.

4. Here, we can use the basic equation for work problems, in which 1/Time A + 1/Time B = 1/Total Time to complete the job. In this case, machine A takes 5 hours to copy 100 books, while machine B takes 7 hours to print 50 books, or 14 hours to print 100. Hence, 1/5 + 1/14 = 1/Total Time, or 0.2714 = 1/A, A = 3.68 hours Choice C is correct.

5. Area 1 = 7 x 7 x 7 = 343. Area 2 = 9 x 9 x 9 = 729. 729 – 343 = 386 cubic feet. Choice C is correct.

6. Choice E is correct. y =2

7. To be a function, a relation must not repeat any of the first elements of its ordered pairs. Only Choice E meets this criterion.

8. If you look carefully, you will see that this example is actually a combination of TWO sub-series. The odd numbers (11, 13, 15 ….) increase by two, while the even numbers double (12, 24, 48, ….). The next number in the series will be 15 + 2, or 17. Choice B is correct.

9. 14.50 x 6 = $87.00 spent. 87/5.85 = 14.87 hours. Choice E is correct.

10. Choice D is correct.

11. Let's solve this by using $100 as the initial price of the stock: The 20% decrease reduced the stock price to $80. For the stock to reach $100 again, there must be a $20 increase. $20 is what % of $80? 20/80 x 100 = 25%. Choice B is correct.

12. We can solve this using a proportion. 36/18 = x/64.   x = 128 minutes. Choice C is correct.

13. x^6 must be the largest, because it is the only answer choice that is positive. Choice C is correct.

14. (7b – 4)/2 = 16 - b, so 7b – 4 = 32 – 2b, or 9b – 36, or b =4. Choice D is correct.

15. (H∩J)∩K is the set of elements that are in all three set. In this case, only 7 is in H,J, and K, which means that (H∩J)∩K = {7}. Choice A is correct.

16. Of the answers listed, only 12 fits both equations. Choice E is correct.

QA29: Answer Key for Quantitative 29

1. The range is the positive difference between the smallest and largest values. In this case it is 90 – 21 = 69. Choice D is correct.

2. The find the sum of the integers between 16 and 88, inclusive, we must use the formula, Sum = Average x Number of terms. The Average = 16 + 88 / 2 = 52. Number of terms = 88 – 16 + 1 = 73. The Sum = 52 x 73 = 3,796. Choice E is correct.

3. Area of Trapezoid = (Average of parallel sides) x Height. In this case, the area = {(36 + 48)/2} x (16) = (42)(16) = 672 cubic inches. Choice C is correct.

Alternatively, we can calculate the areas of the individual parts of the trapezoid (a triangle and a rectangle) and add them together. The area of the rectangle = (36)(16) = 576. The area of the triangle is ½ (12)(16) = 96. The total area is 576 + 96 = 672 cubic inches.

4. For simplicity, let's assume that there are 100 Republicans in Wheeling County, which makes P = 100.

Republicans (P)	100
Democrats (P + 375)	475
Total (2P + 375)	575

The number of residents who are Republicans is therefore 100 / 575, or P/(2P + 375). If we convert this to a percentage, we get 100P/(2P + 375). Choice A is correct.

5. To be a function, a relation must not repeat any of the first elements of its ordered pairs. Thus, we must find the answer choice that violates this rule, which is Choice C.

6. $R \cup S$ = {2, 4, 5, 6, 7, 8, 9, 11}. {2, 4, 5, 6, 7, 8, 9, 11} $\cap$ {2, 3, 10, 12} = {2}. Choice A is correct.

7. ($R \cup S$) $\cup$ T = {2, 3, 4, 5, 6, 7, 8, 9, 10, 11, 12}, which is not one of the four answer choices. Choice E is therefore correct.

8. ($R \cup S$) $\cup$ T = {2, 3, 4, 5, 6, 7, 8, 9, 10, 11, 12}, which has 2^{11} subsets, or 2048. Choice D is correct.

9. To solve this problem, put the information into a grid and solve for the appropriate quantity. In this case, we are given many of the figures – the rest we can fill-in. The problem asks us how many girls are studying French, which is 24, Choice A.

	French	German	Total
Boys	36	60	96
Girls	24	30	54
Total	60	90	150

10. Let x = the original population. 0.77x = 578,845. Thus, x = 751,746. Choice E is correct.

11. In this problem, the interest payments from both investments must equal $15,000 per year. To solve, we will let x = the amount of money that Dave's grandmother will invest at 8%. Our equation becomes:

5%($50,000) + 8%(x) = $15,000
(0.05)($50,000) + (0.08)(x) = $15,000
2500 + 0.08x = $15,000
0.08x = $12,500
X = $156,250. Choice C is correct.

12. First, let's define our variables. We will let the cost of the pen = x. Therefore, the cost of the notebook = x + $10.00. If the cost of both items is $10.50, our equation becomes:

Cost of Pen + Cost of Notebook = Total Cost
x + (x + $10.00) = $10.50
2x + $10.00 = $10.50

2x = $0.50
X = $0.25 = Choice A

13. The shipping container is 8 feet long, 6 feet wide and12 feet high. The formula for surface area is 2(L x W + L x H + W x H) = 2 { (8)(6) + (8)(12) + (6)(12) } = 2(48 + 96 + 72) = 2(216) = 432. Choice D is correct.

14. France: 10 million wearers x (0.29) = 2,900,000 between 19 and 30
    India: 20 million wearers x (0.19) = 3,800,000 between 19 and 30

Total number of people in both nations between 19 and 30 who wear contact lenses = 6.7 million. Choice C is correct.

15.   5 million (0.01) = 50,000 under age 10.   5 million (0.15) = 750,000 over age 51. 750,000 + 50,000 = 800,000 people can no longer wear them. Choice E is correct.

16. 8 million (0.05) = 90,000 users under age 10 x (0.4) = 36,000 wear blue lenses. Choice A is correct.

17. $(216 - 36)^2 / 81 = (180)^2 / 81 = 400$. Choice D is correct.

18. The expression simplifies to $c^2 + a^2 + bc$. Choice B is correct.

19. We can solve this using a proportion. $y/x = z/?$? = xz/y. Choice E is correct.

20. $(x - y)(x^2 + xy + y^2) = x^3 + x^2y + xy^2 - x^2y - xy^2 - y^3 = x^3 - y^3$. Choice E is correct.

QA30: Answer Key for Quantitative 30

1. To determine the median, we must first, arrange the numbers in ascending order: 234, 239, 243, 245, 324, 333, 343, 414, 433. The middle number, 324, is the median. Choice D is correct.

2. Volume = (2/3)(2/3)(2/3) = 8/27 = 0.2963 cubic feet x 36 lb/cubic feet = 10.67 lb. Choice A is correct.

3. $(a - 12)(a - 11) = a^2 - 23a + 132 = 0$. Choice D is correct.

4. $g^2 - 7g - 18 = 0$, $(g + 2)(g - 9) = 0$. g = 9 or –2. Choice B is correct.

5. To be a function, a relation must not repeat any of the first elements of its ordered pairs. The only answer choice that meets this requirement is Choice D.

6. If Susan paid $100 for her condo, then she sold it to Nathan for $60, which is 40% less. Nathan sold the condo to Janice for 20% more than what HE paid for it, which was $60. Nathan therefore sold the condo for $60 + (0.2)($60) = $72. The question asked us to determine what percentage of Susan's original price Janet paid for the condo. In this case, the correct answer is 72/100, or 72%, which is answer choice D.

7. $c(c^{a+b})/c^a = (c^1)(c^{a+b})(c^{-a}) = c^{1+b}$. Choice C is correct.

8. For the equation to equal zero, one of the terms in the numerator must = 0. Here, the numerator reduces to (x –8)(x-2). Hence, the correct answer is Choice B, which is -2, -8.

9. First, we must draw a table with the information we know.

Solution	Quantity (oz)	Percent Acid	Amount Acid (oz)
Original	10	15	10(0.15) = 1.5
Added	5	100	5(1.0) = 5
Final	15		1.5 + 5 = 6.5

In this case, the tabulated data tells us the entire story. The final 15-ounce solution contains 6.5 ounces of acid. 6.5/15 = 43.3% acid. Choice C is correct.

10. The surface area of the cube - 726 square feet - is composed of 6 equal sides. Thus, $726 = 6x^2$, where x= a side of the cube. $x^2 = 121$, or x = 11. The volume of the cube is $(11)^3 = 1,331$ cubic feet. Choice B is correct.

11. At the end of year one, the new price would be ($365,000)(1.06) = $386,900.
At the end of year two, the new price would be ($386,900)(1.08) = $417,852.
At the end of year three, the new price would be ($417,852)(1.04) = $434,566.08. Choice E is correct.

12. T solve, simply try each answer choice and see which one fits. The smallest answer that meets the criteria is 112, which leaves a remainder of 4 when divided by 6. Choice D is correct.

13. 28 + 48 + 36 + 26 + 30 + 28 = 196. 48/196 = 1/4. Choice E is correct.

14. Choice B is correct. The two integers are 18 and 36.

15. Convert to decimals and arrange in ascending order: 1/4, 2/7, 1/3, 3/8, 2/5. Choice C is correct.

16. To solve, we can use the following equation: 90 = (x + 96 + 81 + 79 + 87 + 100) / 6. When we solve for x, it is 97, which is Choice C.

17. For any given toss, the probability of getting heads is ½. For three tosses, we just multiply the three probabilities: ½ x ½ x ½ = 1/8. Choice C is correct.

18. 6 x 6 x 6 = 216. 6 x 6 x 6 x 6 = 1296. Hence, 3 is the largest integer value of x. Choice C is correct.

19. $3x^2 - 2xy + y^2 = 3(3)(3) - 2(3)(4) + (4)(4) = 27 - 24 + 16 = 19$. Choice A is correct.

20. $(x + 5)(x - 4) = x^2 + x - 20 = 0$, so Choice E is correct.

WA1: Answer Key for Writing Section 1

Improve Sentence

1. This sentence is awkward because of the compound verb structure, which includes two different tenses. Additionally, the subject and verb are separated by a long modifying phrase. The correct answer is D, which fully states each phrase and includes the correct tense for each verb (never have *been* allowed and never will *be* allowed).

2. Choice D is correct. The other answer choices introduce new errors (or additional information that was not in the original sentence).

3. In choosing between *I and we*, students should use the same pronoun they would use if Cara was not mentioned in the sentence. The correct pronoun is *me*, which is answer choice B.

4. Choice D is correct. The word *each* is singular, which requires the singular pronoun *she*.

5. The original sentence contains an error in parallelism. The menu items must all be presented consistently in the sentence. Hence, answer choice C is correct.

6. Choice D is correct. The sentence contains a misplaced modifier. It is also written in the passive voice. Only choice D corrects both mistakes without making an additional one.

7. This is not a sentence because it lacks a verb. Answers C, D and E correct the problem, but Choice D does it best.

8. Choice D is correct. The correct combinations of pronoun and verb are *immigrate into* and *emigrate from*. Only Choice D uses the correct combination.

9. Choice C is correct, because is converts both passive verbs to active form, without changing the meaning of the sentence.

10. Choice B is correct. The original sentence uses the word *elude* instead of *allude*. *Elude* means to avoid, while *allude* means to refer.

11. Choice E is correct. The original sentence uses *farther* instead of *further*. *Farther* refers to distance, while *further* refers to degree.

12. Although this sentence contains many potential idiomatic traps, the error is actually in the subject-verb agreement. The word *agenda* is singular; the verb should therefore be *was presented*, not *were presented*. Choice E is correct.

13. Choice D is correct. It is grammatically incorrect to use the expression "the reason why is because." Hence, only answer choices B, D and E are viable possibilities. Of these, B and D contain the error *compared with*, instead of *compared to*. Hence, choice D is correct.

14. The correct choice is A, which uses the correct verb form, *had lain*. This sentence uses the verb *lay* in a hypothetical "if" clause, which requires the unusual form *had lain*.

Identify Error in Sentence

15. In this question, the absence of commas obscures the singular nature of the subject, which is *inflation*. The correct answer choice is B. Here is a possible revision: *Inflation, together with rising employee wages and spiraling health care costs, is crippling America's small businesses in an unprecedented manner.*

16. Clause B contains an error in subject/verb agreement. The plural subject *advancements* requires the plural verb *have been*.

17. The way the sentence is currently written, we don't know if *it* refers to IBM or Cisco Systems. Answer choice C is a classic example of a pronoun with an ambiguous reference. The sentence should be re-written to clarify its meaning: *After agreeing to expand its list of approved vendors, IBM entered into a strategic alliance with Cisco Systems.*

273

18. Answer choice C is correct. The correct wording of the sentence should be: *Bethany offered the rich dessert to whoever finished the tuna casserole.*

19. Choice D contains an error in parallelism. It should read *to that of a prescription drug.*

20. This is not a complete sentence. The error is clause C, which should be *perform,* rather than *performing.*

21. The error is C, which should be *waited for.*

22. Clause D should be re-written to eliminate the passive voice. *The National Weather Channel reported widespread damage from Hurricane Rita, which arrived three weeks after Hurricane Katrina.*

23. In clause B, the word *liable* is incorrect. It should be replaced by *likely.*

24. In clause D, the word *indefinite* should be used, instead of *indecisive.*

25. Clause D should be *equally among,* not *equally between.*

26. Choice B contains an idiomatic error. The correct phrase is *higher than that.*

27. Choice B contains an idiomatic error. The correct phrase is *agree with,* not *agree about.*

28. The correct answer choice is C. The correct wording is: *Although Jane tries to forget, she remembers the accident as if it occurred yesterday*

29. In this sentence, the word *frequently* (answer choice C) is positioned in a manner that confuses the meaning of the sentence. Are the twins supposed to take their vitamins "frequently?" Or does "frequently" refer to how often Mrs. Davis reminds them? To clarify, the sentence must be re-written in one of the following ways: **Either:** Mrs. Davis frequently told her twins to take their vitamins. **Or:** Mrs. Davis told her twins to take their vitamins frequently.

Improve Paragraph

30. The sentence contains two verbs in the passive voice, which should be re-written in the active form. Answer choice E is correct.

31. In this question, the writers offer several ways to eliminate sentence two by combining it with other sentences. The BEST option is answer choice E, which blends it seamlessly into sentence three.

32. Choice C is correct, because it adds a verb to the sentence and articulates the concept in a concise way.

33. In this case, both sentences are grammatically correct, but there is no logical connection between the two. Upon further inspection, we see that we cannot eliminate either sentence, because each conveys critical information that is not presented elsewhere in the passage. Thus, we can eliminate answer choices A and E. If we reverse the order of the sentences, we improve the flow somewhat, but we are still left with an awkward transition between sentences 5 and 6. Thus, our task boils down to evaluating choices C and D, which offer two potential revisions. Of the two, Choice C is preferable. It provides a logical transition between the two sentences without any odd or awkward phrases. Choice C also does not omit any key information from the original passage.

34. In this question, the correct answer must replace the passive phrase *was accepted into* with the active form of the verb. Only answer choices B and E offer that correction. Choice B, unfortunately, adds a new error by including the odd (and incorrect) phrase *had not been unaccustomed.* This leaves us with answer choice E as the best revision (of the five options that were presented to us).

35. This is an acceptable sentence that can only be **improved** by answer choice D. The other choices, although reasonable, are not as specific or on-point. Choice B overstates the tone of the conclusion, while choice E deletes the details about the canine breeding cycle.

274

WA2: Answer Key for Writing Section 2

Improve Sentence

1. This example is notable for two reasons. First, it contains a prepositional phrase that makes the singular subject *prison* appear to be plural. Because of this trick, many students do not see that the sentence is correct as originally written (A). By simply adding commas or parentheses, the difference is significantly easier to discern: *Prison, as well as restitution, was the thief's dismal fate. Prison (as well as restitution) was the thief's dismal fate.*

2. Although this sentence includes two singular names, the subject is singular because they are joined by *neither* and *nor*. Hence, the correct answer is C, which uses the singular verb *was*.

3. Prepositional phrases require objects, rather than subjects. Hence, the correct pronoun is *her*, not *she*. Answer choice B is correct. Note that the writers also tried to confuse students by using the word *accept* in two of the answer choices.

4. In this case, the writers use pronouns inconsistently in the original sentence (*one, you*). The correct answer must use one or the other, but not both. The best choice is D.

5. The sentence is correct as written.   Choice A is correct.

6. There are two errors in this sentence. First, the verb is in the passive voice. Second, the modifier *in good condition* should be closer to the word it modifies, which is *stove*. The best correction is D.

7. This is not a sentence because is lacks a verb. Choice C is the best correction.

8. Choice C is correct. The original sentence contains an incorrect verb/preposition combination (it should read *conform to*, rather than *conform with*).

9. Choice D is correct. The correct phrase is *more than*, not *more then*. Choice D also replaces a passive verb (*was financed*) with the active form (*financed*).

10. *Effect* is a noun that means *a result*, while *affect* is a verb that means *to influence*. The correct answer is D.

11. The subject of the sentence (*stress*) is singular and requires a singular verb (*is*). The correct answer choice is D.

12. Choice D is correct.

13. Choice B is correct. The entrepreneur is a person; hence, the correct descriptor is *who*, not *that*.

14. The sentence is correct as originally written. A

Identify Error in Sentence

15. The subject of the sentence is *inner city students*, not *there*. Consequently, the mistake is answer choice C because the verb "are" is unnecessary. The correct version of this sentence is:
Despite the influx of Federal money into education, many inner city students do not receive a good education.

16. In this case, we have plural subjects (teachers, counselors) joined by *neither* and *nor*. Hence, the verb should be plural. The error is C, which should be *have finished*.

17. The error is in clause B, which shifts the pronoun from *one* to *you*. Whichever one is chosen should be used consistently.

18. Clause B contains an error in pronoun usage. The correct phrase is *few of whom*.

19. The phrase in Clause D includes an error in parallelism. It should be *how to relieve pain*.

275

20. In this sentence, the phrase *by practicing every weekend*, modifies the wrong noun (the student is practicing, not her performance). Answer choice D is correct. The appropriate revision would be: *By practicing every weekend, including nights when several parties were held, she improved her performance dramatically.*

21. The error is D, because it is unclear who was wearing the string bikini (Diane or her son). The sentence should be re-written*: Diane wore only a string bikini and a lot of lotion when she went to the beach with her son.*

22. Clause C should be re-written to eliminate the passive voice. A possible correction: *When they least expected, scientists found a drug to mitigate the spread of cancer.*

23. The error is clause C, which should be *cannot elude*, rather than *cannot allude.*

24. Choice D is correct. The correct word is *fewer*.

25. Clause D has an idiomatic mistake. The correct phrase is *capable of killing.*

26. Clause B uses the wrong preposition. The correct phrase is *from the American Red Cross.*

27. In this question, the correct answer choice is D. Jason's stamina and muscle tone are like *those of a* seasoned athlete.

Improve Paragraph

28. Choice E is correct. Choice D, although tempting, attributes religion and discipline issues to the same set of parents, which is not necessarily the case. It is a subtle point, but a possible mistake that Choice E avoids.

29. Choice D offers the best revision.

30. Choice A is correct. The first paragraph offers the arguments in favor of home schooling.

31. Choice C is correct. The sentence introduces the arguments against home schooling.

32. Choice C is best. The phrase *On the other hand*, alerts the reader that the second paragraph will present the argument against home schooling. Further, the word *socialization* needs to be put into its proper context the first time it is used. Choice C makes both of these changes.

33. Choice C is best. It puts the comment into the proper context, by noting that it is based on the evidence available to date. The author does not reveal how old the studies are, which prohibits us from choosing Choice E.

34. Choice A is correct. The author is objective and gives equal weight to each side of the argument.

35. Choice C is correct. In sentence 12, the author clearly states his conclusion: parents who home school do so because they feel it is in the best interests of their children.

WA3: Answer Key for Writing Section 3

Improve Sentence

1. The full version of the sentence is *Either Mary is lying or he is lying.* Both subjects require the verb *is.* Hence, the correct answer choice is B.

2. The word *school* is singular and requires the singular verb *was.* The only answer choice that makes this correction without creating additional errors is C.

3. In this sentence, the word *whoever* (which is a subject) is incorrectly used as an object of the preposition *to.* The word *whomever* should be used instead. Answer choice B is correct.

4. In this sentence, we have a pronoun *(him)* modifying a gerund *(joining).* The sentence is incorrect in its original form, because the pronoun should be in the possessive case (*his,* not *him*) to properly modify the noun. *Mr. Davis has no objection to his joining the class.* The correct answer choice is E.

5. In this question, David's three activities after the SAT must be presented in a consistent manner. The proper combination of verbs is *walk* home, *lie* down and *then call.* Answer choice E is correct. The writers added an additional level of difficulty by including the verb *lie,* which is often used incorrectly as *lay.* To answer this question correctly, students needed to catch the error in parallelism **and** avoid the incorrect verb trap.

6. This sentence has a misplaced modifier; it also omits the subject of the sentence. The correct answer is C, which solves both problems.

7. Choice E is correct. The correct phrase is *provoked by,* not *provoked from.*

8. The expression *being that* is always wrong. The correct answer is C, which substitutes the word *since.*

9. Choice D is correct. It eliminates the awkward (and incorrect) phrase *on account of;* it also clarifies the reason the IRS agents stormed the office.

10. Choice D is correct. The original sentence contains an incorrect word choice. *Each other* should be used when referring to two people, while *one another* should be used when referring to more than two people. Choices D and E make this correction, but Choice D does so succinctly.

11. Choice C is correct. It contains a strong, active verb; it places the adjective *astonishing* in front of the correct noun; finally, it retains the meaning of the original sentence.

12. In this sentence, the correct answer must include both forms of the verb *to take.* The only answer choice to do so is D, which is correct. The resulting sentence correctly presents both verb tenses: *Cathy has not taken and she will not take illegal drugs.*

13. The correct answer must match the verb tense in the second half of the sentence. Answer choice E is correct: *Because Gina had lain in bed for several months after her accident, she developed atrophy in her leg muscles.*

Identify Error in Sentence

14. Clause B contains an error in verb expression. There are several possible corrections, depending on whether or not the actress still admires Katharine Hepburn. If her admiration is current, the clause should read, *that she has always had.* If it is strictly in the past, then the clause should read, *that she used to have.*

15. Choice B is correct. The correct phrase is *had edited.*

16. The error is in clause B, which uses inconsistent pronouns. Instead of *their,* the word *one's* should be used (to match the previous pronoun in the sentence).

17. The error is in clause D, which should use *its eradication* instead of *their eradication.*

18. Clause D contains a misplaced modifier. A possible correction: *To gain support for her candidate, Diane wore her political t-shirt to the television debate, which millions of people watched.* This correction also eliminates a passive verb (which was not one of the four possible errors).

19. The error is in clause B, which uses the word *when* incorrectly. The correct proposition is *that*.

20. The error is B, which includes a passive verb tense. The sentence should be re-written as follows: *Because of an equipment malfunction in the massive auditorium, the occupants of rows six through twelve could not hear the chorus.*

21. Clause D contains the wrong word. It should state *fewer interactions with employees*.

22. Choice A is incorrect. Sentences should never begin with the phrase *due to*. Use *Because* instead.

23. Clause A should be *prospective buyers*, not *perspective buyers*.

24. Choice E is correct. The sentence is correct as written.

25. Clause D includes a common error in formal writing. In this situation, a gerund should be used rather than an infinitive: *Stephanie embarked on a weight loss program in an attempt to attract an eligible bachelor.*

26. Choice E is correct. This sentence contains no errors.

27. Clause D presents an illogical comparison. The correct phrase should be *than those from the local pet shop.*

Improve Paragraph

28. Choice D is correct. It combines the two sentences in a clear and efficient manner.

29. Choice E is the best revision.

30. Choice C is correct. The sentence explains the legal loophole that allows Computer Systems to claim its products are made in the USA, when the components themselves are not.

31. Choice E is correct. The author is referring the company's deceptive claims that their products are made in the USA.

32. Choice B is the most eloquent revision.

33. Choice D is best.

34. Choice D is correct. The author reveals his anger by using words such as *exploit, not ethical, deceptive* and *beware*.

35. Choice C is correct. The passage is written in simple language that is aimed at the general consumer. The first and final sentences also clearly indicate the author's intended audience.

Improve Sentence

1.   The word *quantity* is singular and requires the singular verb *was*. The only answer choice that makes this correction without creating additional errors is B.

2. The verb tense should be the past perfect tense, which indicates that an action or event was completed before another action or event began. Choice E is correct.

3. Choice E is correct. The original sentence is an overwritten (and somewhat pompous) version of a very simple concept.

4. Choice A is correct. The original sentence contains no errors.

5. Choice E is correct. In the original sentence, the two concepts are not presented in a parallel manner. In Choice E, it is clear that the sentence is comparing the *quality of care* in the two locations.

6. Choice D is correct. The original sentence contains a misplaced modifier. Although Choice C also corrects the mistake, it changes the meaning of the sentence.

7. This is not a complete sentence because it lacks a verb. The best revision is Choice C, which uses an active verb.

8. This question is tricky because it is subtle. The correct answer is Choice E, which corrects the passive verb by separating the two phrases by a semi colon. The other choices that correct the verb unfortunately add new errors.

9. The correct answer is choice C, which eliminates the incorrect opening (*in spite of*), without changing the meaning of the sentence or adding details that were not originally there.

10. Choice C is correct. It conveys the concept correctly and eloquently, without changing its meaning.

11. Choice D is correct. Choice E is tempting, but it introduces the word *compare*, which implies something more than the original sentence.

12. Choice E is correct. The word *at* is unnecessary, because *where* already indicates location.

13. In this sentence, the correct verb is *had studied*, which is answer choice C.

14. In this sentence, the word *guests* fails to denote the possessive form. The only two answer choices that make this correction are D and E. Choice D, unfortunately, creates a new error by using the word *premature* incorrectly. The correct answer choice is E.

Identify Error in Sentence

15. One common trick is the inclusion of extraneous phrase in the sentence, which makes it difficult to identify the subject and verb. In this sentence, the subject (remains) is plural, which requires the verb *suggest that*, rather than *suggests that*. The error in the sentence, therefore, is C.

16. The error is D, which should be *and goes to school at night*.

17. Clause C should read *as she*.

18. Choice E. The sentence is correct as written.

19. Clause C contains the passive voice; it is also a misplaced modifier. A possible correction: When the election committee announced the results, including those for the contentious Senate race in District 3, Senator Smith conceded defeat.

20. Clause B contains an extraneous word (*any*) that should be omitted from the sentence.

21. Clause D uses the wrong word to describe the extent of Juan's job. It should read *a number of problems* or *many problems*, not *a large amount of* problems.

22. Clause C should be *affected*, not *effected*.

23. Choice A is correct. The correct phrase is *After completing*.

24. Choice E is correct. This sentence contains no errors.

25. Clause D uses an infinitive instead of a gerund. The sentence should read: *Clara will stop at nothing in her efforts to eradicate discrimination in the workplace.*

26. This question employs a rare, contrary-to-fact conditional statement beginning with an "if" clause. The correct answer choice is B, because the verb must be in the past subjunctive form (*were*).

27. Clause C uses the wrong conjunction. The word *and* should be used instead of *while*.

Improve Paragraph

28. Choice B is correct. Although there are no mistakes in the first sentence, it benefits from the use of a stronger and more specific verb.

29. Choice D is correct. At first, Choice E seems tempting, because it presents several thoughts in one sentence. Unfortunately, it is long and awkward sentence that retains the vernacular expression "*go to town.*" Instead, we should split the material into two sentences (one for each sex), which gives the paragraph a better flow.

30. Choice B is correct. Choice A is too broad, while answer choices C, D, and E are incorrect for the first paragraph.

31. Choice C is correct. The second paragraph explains the relevance of the FDA study. The author opens with a question to drive this point home.

32. Choice D is best. By joining the three sentences, we get better flow. Choice D does so in the most accurate manner.

33. Of the five alternatives, Choice A is best. The other answer choices either omit information or contain errors of parallelism,

34. Choice B is best. It provides the most accurate information in a smooth and logical manner.

35. Choice B is best. The passage stresses the need to develop sweet snacks for teen girls and salty snacks for teen boys. Of the five alternatives, only Choice B captures this idea.

Improve Sentence

1. When two subjects that would normally command different verbs are joined by *or/nor,* the subject that is *closer to the verb* determines the person. In this case, the subject *you* is closer to the verb than *Sara.* Hence, the verb must agree with the subject *you.* But what about Sara? Here's where it's important to remember the directions at the beginning of this section of the SAT. The writers have asked you to select the BEST way to correct this awkward sentence, which is to place the correct verb next to each singular subject: *Either Sara is guilty or you are guilty.* The correct answer is C.

2. Choice A is correct. The sentence is correct as originally written.

3. In this sentence, the pronoun *they* (which is plural) refers to the word *husband* (which is singular). To correct this sentence, the subject and pronoun must match in number. Hence, the correct answer choice is C, which uses the singular pronoun *he.*

4. The word *everyone* is always singular, so it requires a singular pronoun in this sentence. Answer choices D and E are the only ones that use *his* instead of *theirs.* Choice E, however, changes the meaning of the sentence by changing the word *will* to *should.* Therefore, the correct answer choice is D.

5. Choice E is correct. This sentence has a misplaced modifier that confuses its meaning. Unfortunately, the answer choices that move the modifier closer to its subject are even more confusing than the original sentence. The best answer is therefore choice E, which lengthens the sentence, but clarifies its meaning.

6. This is not a sentence because it lacks a subject in its main clause. Choice C is the best correction.

7. In this question, the phrase *he was sold* includes a passive verb, which should be expresses as an active verb. Choice D is correct.

8. Choice E is correct. *Disinterested* means objective or unbiased, while *uninterested* means not caring about something or someone.

9. Choice C is correct. The original sentence makes a common error by using the word *if* instead of *whether.* (*Whether* introduces a choice, while *if* introduces a condition.)

10. Choice C is correct. The original sentence contains the erroneous expression *different than,* which should be *different from.*

11. Choice E is correct. The phrase *nowhere near* is cumbersome; instead, be definitive by stating *not enough.*

12. The correct way to modify the verb is by using the adverb *quietly.* Answer choice C is correct.

Identify Error in Sentence

13. Clause C includes the wrong verb, which should be *have* (rather than *has*).

14. Choice E is correct; the sentence is correct as written.

15. Clause D makes a faulty comparison. The underlined portion should read *should be similar to that in.*

16. Clause A is incorrect. It should read *Who is to* or *Who should.*

17. In formal writing, the final phrase (answer choice D) contains an error in parallelism. Although the test writers simply require students to identify the error, by fixing it, we can more easily see the original mistake: *After the science fair, Mrs. Chaney praised Alison for her appearance, choice of topic and organization.*

18. Clause D contains a misplaced modifier. As currently written, it is unclear whether the room or the desk clerk reeked of cigarette smoke. The sentence should be re-written to place the modifier closer to the noun that it modifies: *Although I understand that not all hotels can offer smoke-free rooms, I do not understand why a desk clerk assigned me a room that reeked of cigarette smoke.*

19. This is not a complete sentence. To rectify, clause C should be changed to *hedged.*

20. The error is in clause D, which should be *provoked by*, rather than *provoked from.*

21. The error is clause C, which is an awkward comparison. Instead, the sentence should read *Using a typewriter in the computer age is similar to using a slide rule instead of a calculator.*

22. Clause C should be *to effect*, not *to affect.*

23. Choice D is correct. The correct phrase is *was hardly.*

24. In this sentence, choice A is correct. The original sentence uses the wrong verb (lie vs. lay) and has conjugated it incorrectly. The correct revision is: *If Grace had laid her pursue on the table, it might not have been stolen in the robbery.*

25. Clause A contains the incorrect verb tense. The sentence employs a contrary-to-fact conditional statement that begins with the word "if." Hence, it requires the past subjunctive form of the verb, "were to observe."

Improve Paragraph

26. Choice E is best. By combining the three sentences, the information is presented in a smooth and logical manner.

27. Choice E is best. This change replaces two ambiguous words *(this* and *things)* with more specific details.

28. Choice D is correct. By adding the word *process*, we create a simple yet effective sentence to end the paragraph.

29. Choice A is best. The first paragraph defines osteoporosis and explains its cause.

30. Choice D is correct. The items listed in paragraph two prevent the loss of bone density. This term should be stated explicitly in the first sentence of the paragraph.

31. Choice E is correct.

32. Choice D is correct. The word *second* is necessary to continue the "list" that the author began in the beginning of the paragraph. This revision also offers the most concise explanation for the exercise requirement. Choice C omits the phrase *each week*, while Choice E omits the key word *aerobic.*

33. Choice D is correct. Choice E changes *should consider* to *must*, which is not the author's intention. Choices B and C, although grammatically correct, are more awkward than Choice D.

34. Choice B is correct. It summarizes all points in a smooth and concise manner.

35. Choice C is correct. The second paragraph offers three ways to prevent osteoporosis or minimize its effects.

WA6: Answer Key for Writing Section 6

Improve Sentence

1. Choice C is correct. He singular subject *use* requires a singular verb *makes*. The other answer choices that make this correction also introduce other errors.

2. Choice C is correct. The sentence includes two phrases with different verb tenses; hence, each must be stated in full: *People convicted for fraud never have been honest and will never be honest.*

3. Choice C is correct. In this sentence, the pronoun is the subject of the gerund *joining*. As such, it must be in the possessive case, *his*.

4. Choice C is correct. This sentence contains two ambiguous pronouns (*her* and *she*). The correct answer choice must clarify to whom each refers without changing the meaning of the sentence. Of the possibilities, Choice C is the only option that fixes the error without altering the original sentence.

5. Choice B is correct. The original sentence contains an error in parallelism. The word *swimming* should be used in both parts of the sentence. Although Choice C uses *to swim* in both parts of the sentence, it introduces a new error.

6. In sentences with modifiers, try to determine the noun that is being modified. In this case, the implied noun is *we*, **not** *our plans*. Hence, the correct answer choice must use *we* as a noun. This narrows our answer choices to C, D, and E. Of the three, answer choice C is best.

7. The correct answer is Choice E, which eliminates the passive verb and replaces *formerly* with *formally*.

8. This sentence contains a passive verb. The correct answer, Choice D, corrects the mistake and uses the correct subject (*the audience*). The other choices either fail to correct the verb error or use an incorrect subject.

9. Choice D is correct. Because there are three candidates, the correct word is *among*, not *between*. Further, the candidates themselves are not equal; their qualifications are. Choice C makes these corrections.

10. Choice E is correct. The expression *kind of grades* is incorrect; it should be replaced by *similar*.

11. Choice E is correct. The original sentence contains two errors. First, there is a misplaced modifier (Clara was paid little money, not her hands). Second, the word *inflicted* in used instead of *afflicted*. The correct answer choice must correct both mistakes. Only Choice E corrects the modifier AND uses the correct phrase *afflicted with*.

12. Choice D is correct. The original sentence uses the word respectfully instead of respectively. Only Choices D and E correct this mistake. Choice E, unfortunately, changes the meaning of the sentence.

13. Choice C is correct. When three or more people are being compared, the correct term is *widest*, not *wider*.

14. The correct choice is A, which is the best option of all five choices. Choice D is tempting, but it omits the words "for covering," which are essential in this sentence.

15. The error in the sentence is the inconsistency between *to snap back* and *attempting to reconcile with him*. Answer choices B and E shorten the sentence quite nicely, but they do not correct this inconsistency. The only answer choice that makes the correction is C, which is the correct answer. Although the sentence is long-winded, it is grammatically correct.

16. Answer choice D is correct, because it contains the correct verb tense in both parts of the sentence.

17. In its original form, this statement was not a complete sentence, because it lacked a verb. Although both C and E add a verb, answer choice C adds an error in the latter part of the sentence. The best answer to the question is choice E.

18. The error in this sentence is that the second clause is not joined logically to the first. The best answer choice will subjugate one clause in favor of the other in a grammatically correct manner. Of the five answer choices, E is the best.

Identify Error in Sentence

19. The error is C, which should be *came home*.

20. Clause C has an error in subject / verb agreement. The correct phrase is *was a graduate*.

21. Clause B has an error in subject-verb agreement. The verb should be *are* to reflect that there are two items on the agenda.

22. Clause A should read *across from Jane's house*.

23. Choice D is correct. The statement should read: Rachel enjoyed modern dance for its gracefulness, musicality and storytelling.

24. The error is C, which suggests that the museum carries the passengers, rather than the bus. The sentence should be re-written to place the modifier closer to the word that it modifies: *We took a bus that carried more than two thousand passengers to the history museum.*

25. This is not a complete sentence. The error is in clause A, which should be "*He lived.*"

26. The error is D, which should be *in handling*.

27. This sentence contains a passive verb in clause C, which should be re-written in the active voice: *To address the needs of Hurricane Katrina victims, the American Red Cross established a fund in all fifty states for victims to buy food, clothing and essential medical supplies.*

28. The error is in clause D, which includes the incorrect spelling of the word *hostel*.

29. The error is clause C, which should be *had already*, not *had all ready*.

30. Clause A should be *Because*, not *Being that*.

31. Choice A should read *could have gone*, not *could of gone*.

32. Choice B is correct. The subject is singular and therefore requires the singular verb "*is scheduling.*"

33. The error is A. The word *irregardless* is not standard English; it should be replaced by *regardless*.

34. Choice E. The sentence is correct as written.

35. Clause B makes an error in comparison. The word *unique* implies one of a kind. Hence, there is no need to add the word *most*.

Improve Sentence

1. Choice B is correct. The verb in the second clause should be had waited.

2. Choice D is correct. The only error in this sentence is the verb *sunk*, which should be *sank*.

3. As written, there is a pronoun error; the sentence also uses *between,* rather than *among.* The best solution is choice E, which eliminates the mistake and uses the active voice.

4. The sentence is correct as written (Choice A). Whoever is the correct pronoun, because it is the subject of the subordinate clause.

5. Choice E is correct. The words *quickness* and *eloquently* are not parallel in the original sentence. Choices B and E correct this mistake, but Choice B is not as concise.

6. Choice A is correct. This question is tricky because the statement is so vague. Although answer choices D and E provide more information, we do not know (as readers) if the information is accurate. We only know that Bill had reservations about the party. We don't know if he actually attended it. Hence, the best answer choice is A, the original sentence.

7. This question is as subtle as the SAT gets. The error in the sentence is clear, but several answer choices "could be" correct. Choices A and D can easily be discarded, because they have punctuation errors. Choice B, which sounds terrific, is incorrect because it presumes a cause and effect relationship by using the word *because.* Unfortunately, the sentence is taken out of context, which means that do don't know if there is a cause-and-effect relationship between the two clauses. Hence, we are left with choices C and E. Choice C is written in the passive voice, which makes E a better choice.

8. The initial phrase *it was reported* is in the passive voice, which Choices C – E correct. Of the three, choice D is the only version that also corrects the second passive verb *had been notified*.

9. Choice C is correct. Although the original sentence uses the word *among* incorrectly (rather than *between*), neither word is necessary in the sentence.

10. Choice E is correct. When comparing two people, the word comparing their speeds should be *slower*, not *slowest*. Choice E makes this correction in the most concise and straightforward way, without omitting key information.

11. Choice B is correct. The word *beside* means "next to," while *besides* means "in addition to."

12. Choice D is correct. The correct word is *alluded*, not *eluded*. Choices D and E both make this correction, but Choice E is too wordy and awkward (particularly the word *problematical)*.

13. Choice C is correct. The original sentence has two errors. First, the phrase *and less satisfaction* is not correct. Second, *buying* and *to buy* are not parallel. Choice C corrects both errors without changing the original meaning of the sentence.

14. The sentence is projecting into the future; it is correct as originally written. A

15. This sentence, as originally written, contains an error in subject/verb agreement. Because the word *phenomena* is plural, it requires the plural verb *were*, rather than *was.* The answer choices offer students a choice of subject and verb combinations, but they agree in number only in choices D and E.

Interestingly, the writers have further confused the issue by including answer choices with the word *imminent* in place of *eminent* (*eminent*, which means accomplished, is correct). Therefore, the correct answer choice is E, which offers the correct agreement between subject and verb and the correct adjective (eminent).

16. In this sentence, the word *whomever* is used correctly. Choice A is correct.

17. This sentence is presenting a hypothetical situation. The correct verb is *were to see*, which is Choice B.

18.   In choosing between *I and we*, students should use the same pronoun they would use if the cheerleaders were not mentioned in the sentence.   The correct pronoun is *me*; the sentence is correct as written, which is Choice A.

Identify Error in Sentence

19. Choice E, no error.

20. The error is A, which should be *what will happen*.

21. The error is B, which should be *insist that*.

22. The error is C, which should be *he will most likely*.

23. The error is in clause D, which uses the incorrect verb. The word culture is singular, which requires the singular verb *is*.

24. Clause B includes the wrong pronoun. It should be *my sister and me*.

25. Choice E is correct. The sentence is correct as written.

26. This is not a complete sentence because it lacks a verb. To rectify, clause A should be changed as follows: *The eminent director's childhood in Canada was the inspiration for his many films about rural challenges.*

27. In this case, the error is the idiomatic mistake "agreed with," which should be "agreed to." Answer choice B is correct.   This question is tricky because the phrase "agreed with" is not *always* wrong. In this context, however, the correct expression must capture the union's response to the contract terms. They did not *agree with* them; they *agreed to adhere to them*. The distinction is subtle, but valid.

28. The error is C, which is written in the passive voice. The sentence should be re-written to identify who made the decision: *After careful deliberation among all parties, including a heated discussion about the true meaning of community, the committee decided to proceed with the development.*

29. In clause C, the correct word is *rise*, not *raise*.

30. The error is in clause C, which uses the verb *complimented*, rather than *complemented*.

31. Choice D should read *different from what*, not *different than what*.

32. The mistake is in clause A, which should read "*If I were she.*" Why? Because the first clause is not fact, which means that we must use the subjunctive form of the verb (If *I were*, not If *I was*). Further, the phrase "to be" requires that the pronoun be a subject, not an object (*she*, not *her)*.

33. The error in this sentence is C, which includes the double negative *couldn't hardly*. The correct version of the phrase is *could hardly*.

34. Clause A is incorrect. There are several possible revisions, but the easiest one is simply to replace the phrase with *Although Jenny wanted.*

25. Clause C uses an infinitive instead of a gerund. The sentence should read: *The models will double their workouts in their efforts to slim down before the show.*

Chapter 4: Final Strategies for Individual Success

As you work through the 1,001 sample questions for the SAT, you may become overwhelmed by the material on the test. Don't panic. Your next step is actually the most critical one: developing a specific plan to master those strategies for the day of the test.

From our experience, no two students have the same strengths or needs; subject areas that are easy for one student can be incredibly difficult for another. To whatever extent possible, you should use this publication to assess your needs. Then, develop a plan to address them.

1. Additional Preparation. If you need additional preparation for the test, please refer to our other publications. *Guerrilla Tactics for the SAT: Secrets and Strategies the Test Writers Don't Want You to Know* presents the underlying math and grammar concepts on the exam, along with the tricky ways the test writers will try to confuse you. For those who are struggling with the quantitative section, *Math Word Problems for the SAT: When Plugging Numbers into Formulas Just Isn't Enough* offers a complete review of the thirty types of word problems you are likely to see. Learn how to answer these questions quickly and accurately on the day of the test. Finally, for students who are comfortable with the concepts on the SAT and **really** want to challenge themselves before the big day, we are delighted to offer *The Toughest SAT Practice Test We've Ever Seen*. Use this publication – and complete the mock exam - AFTER you have completed your preparation program. See how your performance compares to those of other highly competitive students.

2. Regular Practice. As you prepare for the test, set realistic (but achievable) goals for your performance. Depending on the amount of time you have to prepare, you might commit to the following:

> learning 20 new words per day
> reviewing 3 math concepts per day
> reviewing 3 grammar topics per day

Since no two students are alike, no two study plans will be identical, either. The important thing is to develop (and stick to) a plan that works best for YOU.

3. Put (and keep) the SAT into Perspective. Because of its importance in the college admissions process, the SAT inspires a sense of dread in many students. As a result, some of them, regardless of their intelligence, GPA or study plan, will psyche themselves out on the day of the exam. To whatever extent possible, try to avoid this "all or nothing" mentality.

I know what you're thinking; it is easier said than done. How in the world can you stay calm when so much is at stake? Well, first, it helps to keep the SAT in perspective. Yes, it is an important exam; many colleges base their decision at least partially on a candidate's SAT scores. But here's the FULL context of the test:

It is highly predictable in format and content, which makes it extremely easy to prepare for. By reading this publication, you have taken an important step toward developing a competitive edge

Whenever you start to feel overwhelmed, take a step back and put your concerns into the proper context. Then, channel that energy into something constructive, like preparing for the exam!

4. Plan for the Future. After the SAT, if you are not satisfied with your scores, don't feel defeated or depressed. Remember, the SAT is only ONE piece of information that colleges use in the admissions process. An increasing number of colleges no longer require SAT scores; other universities request them, but do not use them to screen or rank applicants. Depending on where you choose to apply (and the strength of your overall application), a disappointing SAT score may not be a deal-breaker.

From our experience, the SAT does not define the intrinsic personal strengths that are essential to succeed, such as integrity, motivation and passion. Over the years, we have seen a number of students who earned top SAT scores fail in other aspects of life, because of deficiencies that were not measured by the exam. Just as often, we have seen students who earned average SAT scores build successful and satisfying careers in fields they were passionate about.

No doubt about it - your SAT score may influence your ability to get into a select group of U.S. colleges and universities. It will **not**, however, define who you are, what you will accomplish, and the contribution you will eventually make to society. By all means, do your best on the test; you should definitely put your best foot forward in the entire application process. But don't fall into the trap of thinking that your SAT score defines you. You are more – *much more* – than the results of a one-day test.

Good luck with your preparation!

www.ingramcontent.com/pod-product-compliance
Lightning Source LLC
Chambersburg PA
CBHW080526090426
42733CB00015B/2505